Peaceful  D0000162

Peaceful Kids

Peaceful Parents, Peaceful Kids

Practical Ways to Create a Calm and Happy Home

Naomi Drew

KENSINGTON BOOKS
http://www.kensingtonbooks.com

The Ladder of Peacemaking reprinted from *Learning the Skills of Peacemaking* by Naomi Drew, 1986, B.L. Winch & Associates/Jalmar Press. Used with permission from B.L. Winch & Associates/Jalmar Press.

KENSINGTON BOOKS are published by

Kensington Publishing Corp.
850 Third Avenue
New York, NY 10022

First Kensington Paperback Printing: October, 2000
10 9 8 7 6 5 4 3 2 1

ISBN 1-57566-608-1

Printed in the United States of America

This book is dedicated to children everywhere because they are our hopes, our dreams, our future.

ACKNOWLEDGMENTS

To my wonderful husband, Mel, without whose love and support I could not have written this book.

To my beloved sons, Michael and Tim, whose lives inspire me in countless ways.

To my parents, for the gift of creativity and the ability to see beyond boundaries.

To my friend and professional colleague, Robin Levinson, who gave me the initial impetus for writing this book.

To my agent, Gareth Esersky, who believed in *Peaceful Parents, Peaceful Kids* from the start.

To my editor, Tracy Bernstein at Kensington, whose faith in this book has meant so much to me.

To my colleague and friend, Eileen Zweig, who read every page of this manuscript and gave me invaluable feedback.

To family therapist and friend, Anita Arnold, for her generous and encouraging comments.

To my sister, Joan, who first came up with the idea of putting a vision in your pocket.

To Barbara Lerman Golumb, for the wonderful Good Deeds Calendar for kids.

To Rita Varley, librarian of the Philadelphia Yearly meeting, who provided me with comprehensive resource lists.

To all of the people I interviewed for this book whose stories appear on its pages.

To the guiding spirit within us all that sometimes works in strange and unexpected ways.

CONTENTS

Introduction

The fact is, there is no foundation, no secure ground,
upon which people may stand today if it isn't the
family.

—Dr. Morrie Schwartz

Parenting isn't an easy job. We love our children more than we can say, but we're not sure how to help them grow into happy, caring people with a healthy sense of self. We are bombarded with so much information we don't know where to turn. Different books we read give us contradictory information, and when we turn on the TV, we hear something else. Yet all we're looking for is a balanced, common-sense approach to parenting that helps us live in peace with our children and prepares them to live in peace with others. As one parent said to me the other day, "Some kids turn out beautifully; others can break your heart. I wish there was a compass to guide us in the right direction."

The good news is we *can* move in the direction of raising happy, cooperative, respectful children. And there *are* proven, practical, concrete strategies to help us do this. Let's look at the following two scenarios to see how understanding what to do can spell the difference between peace and disaster.

The Supermarket—Scenario 1

As usual, Marge is in a hurry as she stops off at the supermarket to pick up a few things. She remembers that Dr. Carlson, the family dentist, has made a strong recommendation that 5-year-old Steven no longer eat sugary cereals. She'd mentioned this to Steven after his appointment with Dr. Carlson last week, and she's hoping he won't put up too much of a fuss when she picks up a different cereal than he's used to. Marge hates the power struggles that often go on between them and she hopes they're just part of a "stage." Gritting her teeth, she grabs a shopping cart and walks with Steven toward the cereal aisle.

Within moments Steven says, "Mommy, I want Frosted Flakes."

"No sugary cereals, Steven," says Marge. "You know what Dr. Carlson said. Sugary cereals are bad for your teeth. Remember? You don't want to get cavities, do you?"

"But I want Frosted Flakes, Mommy," Steven replies, a demanding edge in his voice.

Fearing a power struggle, but wanting to stand firm, Marge tries reasoning with Steven. "You don't want to have to get a filling, do you? Why don't we see if there's another kind of cereal we can find?"

"I don't want any other cereal. I want Frosted Flakes!" Steven demands.

"Don't use that tone of voice with me, Steven. I said no! We're not getting Frosted Flakes today!" retorts Marge sharply.

"But I WANT FROSTED FLAKES!" demands Steven, even louder now.

"I said no! Do you understand? N-O!" Marge retorts angrily, spelling the word for emphasis. This irks Steven further.

"But Jason Landry eats Frosted Flakes and Cookie Crisp. He doesn't have any cavities. You're just saying no because you're mean, and so is Dr. Carlson!" shouts Steven, as his eyes fill with tears.

"That's it!" barks Marge, her face flushing. "If you say one more word about Frosted Flakes, you're going to lose TV for a week! Do you understand?"

Now Steven goes into full-scale wailing. Marge's pulse starts racing and her mouth gets dry. Not another scene, *she thinks despairingly. She looks around and sees the store manager watching her out of the corner of his eye. Feeling desperate, Marge grits her teeth, grabs a box of Frosted Flakes from the shelf, and quickly throws it in the cart.*

"There, are you happy now?" she snaps at Steven, resentfully.

Steven immediately stops crying, takes the box of Frosted Flakes out of the cart and holds it close. "Thanks, Mommy," he says, looking up at Marge with a smile.

"Yeah, great, you're welcome," she says with an edge. Marge feels defeated and resentful. There must be a better way to handle situations like this, *she thinks to herself in frustration as she and Steven proceed toward the checkout counter.*

How many times have you felt like Marge, wanting to do what's best for your child, but having your good intentions thwarted when your child resists? Have you ever thrown up your hands in frustration and said, "There's got to be a better way"? Fear not—there is; that's what this book is about.

Read on to see how this scenario could have been altered through planning, communication, problem solving, and sticking to one's standards—all critical elements of peaceful parenting.

The Supermarket—Scenario 2

Kate and her husband Jeff have been working hard to create a more peaceful family. They have started the practice of family meetings where they involve their 5-year-old daughter, Wendy, in some decision making. Concurrently, they've set clear standards for positive behavior, letting Wendy know what is expected, consistently sticking by the standards they've set, and acknowledging any positive behaviors they catch Wendy in the act of.

As a result, Wendy, who has always been strong willed, is becoming more cooperative and less apt to engage in power struggles. Wendy has begun to understand that nagging and fussing don't work with her mom and dad.

Kate and Jeff have recently agreed to eliminate sugary cereals from their family's diet. Wanting to prepare Wendy for this before their next shopping trip, they talk about it during a family meeting. When Wendy balks at the news, they hear her out but give the clear message that this particular decision is not hers to make. Letting Wendy know they expect her cooperation, they ask for her "help" in finding new and healthier cereals.

Wendy is thus prepared when Kate takes her to the supermarket the next day. When they get to the cereal aisle, however, Wendy reaches up for the Frosted Flakes, hugs the box, and says, "Mommy, I know what we talked about, but I really want Frosted Flakes. I promise I'll brush my teeth every time I eat them. OK?"

Hearing what Wendy says, and wanting to validate her feelings without giving in to them, Kate says, "I understand how you feel, Wendy. You really love Frosted Flakes and you'd love to keep eating them. You're hoping I'll change my mind, aren't you?"

"Will you, Mommy, please?" asks Wendy. "I promise I won't eat anything else with sugar if you just let me have Frosted Flakes."

"I'd love to let you have them if they were good for you, Wendy, but they're not, and we agreed as a family that we're all going to try to cut back on sugar, including sugary cereals. I'm sorry you're dis-

appointed, but this is the decision your dad and I have made," Kate says gently but firmly, looking directly into Wendy's eyes.

Kate has made sure not to come to the market when they're in a big hurry, so it's easier for her to remain patient. "Take a look at these," she says, holding up two boxes of cereal. "This one has raisins and this one has dates, so they'll both have some sweetness. And here's one more," Kate adds, showing Wendy another box of cereal containing blueberries. "Which would you like to buy today?"

"I want these," says Wendy, holding on to the Frosted Flakes.

Here's where Kate realizes she needs to let Wendy know her limits. "Sorry, Wendy," she says, continuing to be firm but gentle. "No is no, and that's that. You can either pick out another cereal now, or else I'll have to do it. The choice is yours." Here Kate is giving Wendy a choice, but it is clearly within the boundaries she, as the mother, has set.

Wendy considers her options. She realizes that nagging doesn't work because she's tried it before. Each time, her parents have been consistent in not giving in to it. Wendy thinks for another moment, puts down the Frosted Flakes, and says, "OK, Mommy, how about if we try these two?" She gestures toward the cereals with the raisins and blueberries.

"Good choices, Wendy," says Kate, giving her daughter a big hug. "I'm very proud of you for cooperating. Wait till Daddy sees the new cereals you picked. I bet he'll want to try them both." Wendy beams up at her mother, proud of her good choices in both cereal and behavior.

Scenarios like this one are not only possible, they are probable when you have at your disposal the skills of peacemaking. Kate and Jeff have been using these skills to help them raise a more peaceful child and create more peace in their home. They use as their compass the following Seventeen Keys to Peaceful Parenting:

The Seventeen Keys
To Peaceful Parenting

Key #1:   *Peace begins with me.*

Key #2:   *I have made my home a place of kind words.*

Key #3:   *I catch my children in the act of positive behaviors and praise them immediately, specifically, and sincerely.*

Key #4: *I spend at least 15 to 20 minutes a day with each child, listening, interacting, and giving my full attention.*

Key #5: *I am clear on the standards of behavior I expect of my children. I honor those standards and expect my children to do the same.*

Key #6: *I provide my children with empty spaces of time during which they can just "be kids."*

Key #7: *I hold regularly scheduled family meetings where my children have a voice in the workings of our family.*

Key #8: *I have set a foundation for peacefulness in our home by creating with my children "Guidelines for a Peaceful Family."*

Key #9: *I always remember that I am the parent and deserve to be listened to.*

Key #10: *I have fair, reasonable consequences for negative behaviors which I only use when necessary.*

Key #11: *I listen with all my heart to what my children have to say, and teach them to be good listeners for others.*

Key #12: *I teach my children how to handle anger in nondestructive ways and I model this consistently.*

Key #13: *I resolve conflicts peacefully and teach my children to do the same.*

Key #14: *I find ways to help my children succeed.*

Key #15: *All my actions are guided by love, compassion, fairness, respect, and integrity. I nurture these attributes in my children.*

Key #16: *I live my commitment to peaceful parenting; my commitment guides all my actions.*

Key #17: *I remember daily that we each have an impact on the world around us and I teach this to my children.*

These keys are woven into every chapter you are about to read. As you do, you will discover how to integrate them into your life and the lives of your children. Like Kate and Jeff, you will learn the secrets to becoming a peaceful parent and raising peaceful kids.

By reading each chapter carefully, doing the recommended exercises, and modeling what you learn, you'll help yourself feel more grounded in the principles of peaceful parenting. When this happens, you'll be well-equipped to help your children:

- be better listeners
- talk out differences instead of fighting
- reduce the frequency of future conflicts
- calm themselves when angry
- avoid explosive outbursts
- develop greater empathy, self-esteem, and conscience
- accept differences in others
- become more responsible human beings

Philosopher Norman Cousins said, "The starting point for a new reality is now." By providing yourself and your children with new skills, you will help shape a more peaceful reality in your home and in your lives. How do I know this? Because I've lived these skills and concepts myself as a parent, teacher, workshop leader, and author, and have witnessed their results over the past twenty-five years.

My first book, *Learning the Skills of Peacemaking*, was one of the first to introduce peacemaking to the public schools. When I wrote it, I had no idea how it would be received. To my amazement, educators around the country started embracing it and sharing it with their colleagues. Teachers and administrators were excited, saying it met a need no other book had met before. *Learning the Skills of Peacemaking* was soon translated into Russian, Hungarian, Romanian, and Portuguese, bringing the same strategies you are about to learn to adults and children in different parts of the world.

"When are you going to write a book like this for parents?" became the question most repeatedly asked by parents whose children were learning peacemaking in school. At the same time, teachers began noting changes in their students, along with improvements in their relationships with loved ones at home. As one teacher said, "When I first learned about peacemaking, I figured it would just be for my students. But everything I was teaching in school made so much sense, I decided to try it at home, too. Now I have more time to teach because my students are getting along better, and at home my children are having fewer conflicts!"

Parents whose children were learning peacemaking in school were excited about the differences they began seeing at home, too. A mother of three girls commented, "My girls used to bicker with each other constantly.

Now they know how to cool off when they're angry and work out their disagreements in a much more civil way. I wish I had some way of learning how to use these skills myself."

Over and over, people who had been touched in one way or another by *Learning the Skills of Peacemaking* kept asking for something like it they could use at home. Finally I knew I had to write this book.

Peace Starts With Each Individual

This is the most important underlying idea in *Peaceful Parents, Peaceful Kids*. The days of close-knit extended families have passed, and most children are raised by parents who both work, or by single parents. Our lives are so filled with constant, pressured activity that there's little time for rest, reflection, and relaxed interaction. The nature and texture of family life have altered profoundly, hindering our sense of peace and connectedness. But there are things we can and must do to increase our sense of peacefulness, and the effects of our own example can be profound.

When we take steps in our daily lives to get along with others, work out conflicts, listen when people speak, communicate respectfully, let go of anger, and respect differences, we affect the world in a positive way. Starting gradually, with ourselves and the people we are close to, our relationships begin to improve, causing a ripple effect. Before long, we see that by living the skills of peacemaking, we make a positive difference in our own lives and the lives of every person we touch.

This brings us to another important theme.

We Are All Interconnected

Our molecules interchange continuously. We breathe the same air, travel the same roads, experience similar challenges, think similar thoughts, and want much the same things for our children. This goes beyond the boundaries of our own country. In our global society, where we read the same headlines and view the same images transmitted by satellite or computer, we are far more connected to each other than we realize. Take a look at the global money market: The Nikkei goes down in Japan, and the American stock market falters. A rain forest is felled in Brazil, and the air that we breathe is compromised.

On a more personal level, we live side by side with others. One of the great challenges of our times is to discover ways we can coexist peacefully, sharing the same resources and setting the groundwork for a livable future for our children.

We are, in fact, interconnected, and are thus faced with the question of how to make our connections work.

If all schools and families began teaching and living the skills of peace-making, we would have the potential to change the texture of human relationships and the world at large. Try to imagine for a moment your family being one of many to do this. Think about respect, acceptance, responsibility, care for others, and nonviolence being nurtured by larger and larger numbers of families. Imagine this starting right in your own home.

Think of your family as one link on an interconnected chain that spans all of humanity. As you teach and model the skills of peacemaking, you will affect your children's lives well into the future. The attitudes you convey, the actions you take, and the decisions you make create the quality of your family's link in the larger chain of humanity, multiplied over time. That's how much power you have as a parent; that's the difference you make from the moment your child is born. What you teach today will touch your children and the world around them for the rest of their lives and into the coming generations.

CHAPTER 1

Becoming a More Peaceful Parent: Getting Started

I have a need of silence and of stars.
Too much is said too loudly. I am dazed.
The silken sound of whirled infinity
Is lost in voices shouting to be heard.
—William Alexander Percy

Peaceful Parenting Key#1:
Peace begins with me.
~

The Challenge of Peaceful Parenting in a Stressful World

How do we manage to feel peaceful in a topsy-turvy world? How can we raise peaceful children when we don't feel peaceful ourselves? In this chapter, you will discover a variety of strategies to help you become more peaceful in the face of all the "topsy-turviness" of life. But first let's look at where all this "topsy-turviness" comes from.

Stress Overload

Stress. Just the sound of the word makes my heart pound a little faster. How about you? Are you stressed? Do you find yourself living a treadmill life, where rushing is the norm and there seems to be not enough hours in the day? Is so much of your time usurped by responsibilities, obligations, and schedules that there seems to be little time left for your children? Do you find yourself hurrying from task to task trying to accommodate your children's needs as best you can, while haunted by the sense that what you're giving isn't enough? Are you like so many parents who look around at the state of children today, aware of so many incidences of youth crime, violence, drugs, and suicide, and worry that you might not be able to prevent your children from being affected? If you feel this way, you are not alone.

Stress overload is one of the chief blocks to living a peaceful life. Where does all this stress come from? Tufts University psychologist Dr. David Elkind believes a key source of stress is the mind-boggling rate of change we are forced to live with every day. Along with this he sees three other sources:

Fear resulting from living in an increasingly violent society.

A sense of disconnectedness caused by divorce, separation, and living far away from one's extended family.

Professional insecurity rooted in the growing realization that most of us can be replaced or "down-sized" at any given moment.

To this list I would like to add three other stress factors common to so many of us:

Guilt from the feeling that we never seem to have enough time for our kids.

The drive toward materialism that creeps insidiously into our lives and pushes us toward acquiring more, larger, and better things, while causing us to relinquish the time and simplicity we need to feel peaceful.

Spiritual emptiness emerging from a vague sense that something important in our lives is missing that we can't quite define.

Caught in a tangled web of stress and hustle, we forget that our children absorb the stress we experience, and their lives become more stressful as a result.

Ironically, it was once predicted that this time in history would be one of freedom and leisure. At the start of the 20th century, when the industrial revolution was taking hold, many believed its advent would insure those of us who live today more relaxed lives, unencumbered by the demands experienced in a preindustrialized society. Technology would free people from menial tasks, enabling us to work less and have more free time. Yet just the opposite has happened: as technology has developed, our lives have become busier, more complex, and filled with greater pressures. This is all taking its toll on our children.

Shifting Circumstances

Gone are the days of two-parent families with stay-at-home moms. According to a University of Chicago poll released in 1999, only 26% of American households are made up of married couples with children, and only 51% of America's children live with both parents. More and more children are either coming home to empty houses, being watched by baby-sitters, or attending after-school programs. Children as young as 5 are spending as many as 10 hours a day at school.

Larger numbers of children are left unattended during the hours after school, and some are spending this time engaged in inappropriate or illegal behaviors. Did you know that most of the crimes committed by young people take place between the hours of 3:00 P.M and 6:00 P.M.?

Materially, our priorities have shifted dramatically, too. How many families need to have the latest electronic gadget as soon as it comes out? Even the poorest among us are surrounded by a wide range of material objects: multiple TVs per household, VCRs, stereos, roller blades, computerized toys, name-brand sneakers—the list goes on.

Contrast this to the world we lived in growing up. When I was a child, most of the families in our middle-class neighborhood had one car, which was kept for years, one TV (if we were lucky), one record player, a couple of radios, and simple toys like balls, trucks, dolls, board games, jump ropes, and bikes. Was this true for you as well?

Life has changed so much since we were children. Some of these changes, unfortunately, have not been for the better.

Children Under Stress

Many of the changes we've just talked about have led to stress in children. They feel the pressure of time bearing down on their young shoulders, time that has to be filled with "meaningful" activities from dawn to dusk. They feel pressure to acquire the newest toys, gadgets, and clothing so they can keep up with their peers. And they worry about circumstances in the world around them: murders, kidnapping, the environment, war, and now, sadly, if they might be hurt or killed while they are in school. Listen to the words of some young children:

"So many people die from shootings. I have nightmares that someone might come to my school and kill everyone."—Steven, age 9

"I worry that kidnappers will come into my room at night."—Kai, age 7

"I'm scared because people are in danger, just like animals."—Lee, age 6

Greater numbers of children are under stress than ever before. Stress leads to conflict, and conflict leads to violence. For the first time ever, our youth violence rate has risen beyond the rate of adult violence.

Dr. Georgia Witkin, director of the Stress Program at Mount Sinai School of Medicine in New York, lists ten major stress symptoms that are often seen in children, even as young as three years old:

- tantrums in preschool, disorderly conduct in older children
- behavioral regression (baby-like behavior)
- moodiness and irritability
- social withdrawal, sulking
- picking on siblings, fighting
- refusing to go to school or day care
- distracted concentration
- excessive whining or crying
- frequent daydreaming
- restlessness

What this all points to is the need to lower the volume of stress in our lives and in the lives of our children. After all, a peaceful family needs to start with us, the parents. Who else can our children look to to find out how to do it? Let me share with you how I learned this lesson myself and then brought it home to my children.

Bringing Peacemaking to My Own Family

When my boys were young, I well remember the constant feeling of rushing to stay one step ahead of the laundry, grocery shopping, professional obligations, and the care of our home. As a single parent, my responsibilities felt overwhelming, and the frustration of having so many created tension that affected all of us. No matter how much I did, there was always more to do, as though all my tasks multiplied in the act of completing them. I often felt irritable, and I would find myself snapping at my boys and taking my frustration out on them. Then I'd notice them taking their frustrations out on each other. It was a pattern I wanted to stop, but wasn't sure how, so I started searching for answers.

What I realized first was this: **We can't have a peaceful family unless**

we feel peaceful first. If I wanted to raise peaceful children, then I had to find a way to nurture peace within myself. But how? I knew I couldn't completely restructure my life. I needed both to work and raise my children. Much as I wanted to, I couldn't make the day any longer than twenty-four hours. It became clear that I would have to make some changes.

Let me share with you my five most important discoveries, things that enabled me to live more peacefully within the framework of my own life, things that I have since shared as I've worked with parents and children for the past two decades. It is my hope that incorporating the following five elements into your life will put you on the road to more peaceful parenting, as it did for me.

1. Your Keys to Calmness: Abdominal Breathing/Envisioning

The following exercise will become the bedrock of your increasingly peaceful life.

> Sit comfortably in a quiet spot and close your eyes. Breathe in deeply through your nose and out through your mouth several times. Clear your mind of the day's activities, allowing any passing thoughts to drift away.
>
> Next, bring into your consciousness a picture of the place you'd most like to be right now. Is it a sparkling white beach, a cool mountain top surrounded by blue sky, or a tropical island? Maybe it's the home you lived in as a child, or your own backyard. Choose the place that makes you feel most relaxed, and picture it as you continue breathing in through your nose and out through your mouth.
>
> As you breathe, imagine the breath going into your stomach, enabling the abdominal muscles to expand. Pretend your stomach is a large beach ball that you can inflate by the simple act of breathing. When you breathe out, allow the breath to leave slowly, evenly, calmly.
>
> For a few moments continue breathing deeply and picturing your peaceful place. If any unwanted thoughts come into your mind, let them pass, and redirect your consciousness back to the place you have been envisioning. Keep expanding your abdomen as you breathe, letting a newly accessed sense of calmness permeate your body. Allow the movement of your breath to soothe you and to soften any areas of tension. After five minutes, open your eyes.

Exercise:

> *Record in as distinct detail as possible what your peaceful place looks like. You can draw, write, or tape a picture of this spot onto the page you are using. When you need a way to calm down, come back to this page, and your peaceful place will await you.*
>
> *All you ever have to do is close your eyes to be back there again. This is your oasis, one that's available any time, any place.*

Practice this exercise each day for a few minutes, if possible. If you're really pressed for time, try doing the breathing in the car as you drive. As soon as you get to work, try sitting down at your desk, closing your eyes for a few moments, and taking a few more deep breaths. I know how hard it is to build in new routines when you already have so much on your plate, but trust me, this one works and it doesn't take much time.

Sometimes I do this at the end of my workday when I first get into the car. Instead of turning on the radio (or even the ignition, for that matter) I'll sit for a few moments in glorious silence, breathing deeply. I'll either close my eyes and picture my peaceful spot (the coast of Maine in the early morning sun), or I'll look up at the sky. One thing we can depend on in life is that the sky is always there for us to look at. If we're open, just the sight of it can be our touchstone to a more peaceful place.

Another way to use this technique is when we find ourselves reacting negatively to our children. The next time your child says or does something that upsets you, before reacting, go into another room—if you can—shut the door, and breathe deeply. Remember to expand your abdomen as you inhale; by doing so you will enable yourself to breathe very deeply.

Close your eyes as you breathe and bring into your consciousness your peaceful place. Encourage yourself to let go of the upsetting feelings, no matter how intense they may seem at the moment. Remember that by doing this, you will prevent yourself from making the original problem worse. Focus on your breathing and envisioning and try your best to relax the parts of your body that feel tense.

Even if you take just a few moments to do this, you will begin to notice a definable difference in your reactions. If you're like most people, you'll notice your pulse rate slowing and areas of tension relaxing. At the same time, your thoughts will become less negative, less reactive, less aggressive. Instead of thinking, "I'm gonna pulverize him!" you might start realizing what your child did wasn't worth getting quite this upset about. As your perspective shifts, you will gain the freedom to *choose* your actions rather than simply *react*.

This is a life-changing step—to be able to choose your reactions. This is precisely what we want our children to be able to do. When we have the ability to choose our reactions, we are no longer at the mercy of them. Think of the implications of this when it comes to handling anger. By modeling this, you will gain greater mastery over your own negative responses, and will set a positive example for your child. More on this in Chapter 7.

Abdominal breathing can be used to quell a variety of negative feelings. The next time you feel tense, fearful, or overwhelmed, take a few slow, deep abdominal breaths. By doing this, you feed your brain the oxygen it needs to think clearly and help you distance yourself from "automatic" reactions, those that come to us instantaneously, often rooted in our own childhoods.

As you breathe deeply, your body and mind begin to calm and you gain a greater degree of control over your emotional impulses. As Nobel Prize nominee author Thich Naht Hanh says, ". . . when we breathe consciously, we recover ourselves completely and encounter life in the present moment." *Abdominal breathing is essential for becoming a peaceful parent, so be sure to practice it daily.*

2. Defining Your Most Important Priorities

Another crucial key to becoming a more peaceful parent is to know clearly what your top priorities are. What do you believe are the most important things you can do for and with your children in the time you have with them?

Take some time to reflect upon this question: What memories do you want to create for your children? I'm not only talking about memories of special occasions, though they're important, too. I'm talking about the small, undefined snatches of time, those we don't usually pay much attention to, the spaces between moments which usually pass by unnoticed. These are far more important than we realize; they not only create the texture of our lives, they create the texture of the lives our children will remember as they grow up.

When I became a single mom, I took a long, hard look at my priorities. Aware that the amount of time I had to spend with my boys was finite, I knew I needed to examine what was most important to me in raising them. More than anything, I wanted my boys to feel loved, accepted, valued, and happy. I wanted them to remember our home as a nurturing place where they felt safe, calm, and relaxed.

It became clear almost immediately that showing my children love and affection, listening to them with an open heart, being physically and emotionally available to them, and creating a peaceful atmosphere in our home were the most important things I could do for my boys in our time together. These were my priorities. I strived to keep them in the forefront of my mind and allowed them to inform all of the decisions I made.

Over time, I started to notice that if I did something that was out of synch with my priorities, it didn't feel right to me on a gut level. As my inner voice began guiding me more and more, I began to realize I was actually happier when I lived congruently with what was most important to me—not what others expected, not what the neighbors were doing, but what was most important to me.

For example, when my boys were seven and ten, I left teaching so I could write my first book, lead workshops, and run a peace resource organization. I did this for two years, and although the work was exciting and made a contribution to "the larger world," it was an enormous commitment, subtracting from the already limited time I had with my children. Before long it hit me hard that I would never get this time back and that being with my boys was far more important than anything else I could do in this life. Spending so much time on my work started making me unhappy because it wasn't in harmony with my highest priorities.

This realization prompted me to return to teaching, a move I never regretted. My sons were more important to me than anything I could accomplish outside of their lives, and giving them the time they needed wasn't a sacrifice, it was something that made me feel happy.

When I started living congruently with my highest priorities, I experienced a deeper sense of peacefulness and freedom. The dissonance I'd experience when I was out of synch with what I valued most led me to the changes I needed to make. There were times I would look at colleagues still in the field I had left, and I would experience a twinge, like a child looking at the flashiest toy in the window of a toy store, thinking, "I want that."

In those moments I needed to remind myself of what was most important to me. Looking at how beautifully my sons have turned out, I know I made the right decision, and of everything I have ever achieved in this world, I consider them my greatest accomplishment.

Exercise:

Picture yourself twenty years from now. What do you want to be able to say about yourself as a parent? What do you want your children to be able to say about you, about their childhood, about themselves? Write about this.

Based on what you just wrote, consider this question: What are your highest priorities for the time you spend with your children? Write them down. Then write about ways you can bring your priorities to life.

Ask yourself if the life you are living now is congruent with your highest priorities. If the answer is no, ask yourself what you might want to change. Let's take a look at how some other parents handled this question:

Theresa and Alan, parents of 6-year-old Dereck and 4-year-old Tiffany, thought about this long and hard. They both basically agreed on what they wanted for their children: "To believe in themselves and to be independent and confident. We want them to know we believe in them and to remember their childhood as one where they felt supported in taking risks."

As Theresa and Alan reflected upon these priorities, they began listing the things they would need to do to make their priorities a reality. Here's what they came up with:

– We will accept Dereck and Tiffany as they are and encourage their independence as long as they are safe and considerate of others.
– We will keep our judgments in check and try to be as supportive as possible.
– We will celebrate their uniqueness, trying never to compare them with other children.
– We will praise their accomplishments.

After taking the time to talk about these priorities, Theresa and Alan decided they would each spend at least 15 minutes a night simply listening individually to each child.

For Alan, this was particularly significant. He'd always wanted to pay more attention to his kids, but exhaustion and stress at the end of his long work days had prevented him from doing so. Most nights prior to this, he would arrive home at 7:30, eat dinner, then fall into a chair and read the newspaper until he started dozing off to sleep. Alan's only nightly contact with Dereck and Tiffany were the big hugs he gave them when he walked in the door and the bits of conversation they tried to interject as he ate dinner, long after they had been fed.

Theresa, on the other hand, had been feeling frustrated because she never seemed to have enough time to enjoy her children at the end of a busy day. She was too overwhelmed by the nattering voice in her head that told her if she slowed down for a minute, everything would fall apart, so she kept herself in overdrive.

Theresa and Alan decided to change their routine. Theresa would cuddle up with one child on the sofa at night and either read or talk together while Alan gave the other child a bath. It was then that Alan started listening with an open heart, taking note of any small accomplishments and making a special point of offering praise and encouragement for risks they took.

For example, Tiffany had always been terrified of the monkey bars on the playground at her nursery school. She would often talk about how her best friend, Celia, could climb to the top, while she'd stay down on the ground crying from fear and frustration. Alan encouraged her to ask her teacher to help her up one rung each day until she felt confident to do it alone.

Within two weeks, Tiffany made it to the top of the monkey bars, and that night when she told Alan about her accomplishment, he clapped and told her how proud he was. The next time Tiffany was afraid to try something new, remembering this helped her summon up her courage.

Alan and Theresa both feel happier now that they've balanced their commitment to their priorities. The nagging feeling that Alan was missing his children's lives has lessened, and as tired as he is at the end of the day, he becomes energized by the growing bond he is forming with his children.

3. Downsize and Simplify

Sometimes the only key to bringing peace to our families is by making significant changes in our lifestyles. Take a look at the following scenario to see the decision one family made:

Karen, the mother of two small children, is a successful freelance writer who works out of her suburban home. Although her professional career was growing in leaps and bounds, she was becoming increasingly more irritable trying to juggle her energies between work and her children's needs. Karen's husband had a demanding job as a financial planner and worked late each night, so Karen was trying to do it all.

As her pressure mounted, her children became more agitated and aggressive. The tension would grow as the day went on, and by the time Karen's husband walked in the door, he'd be drawn into it, too. They knew something had to give.

Thus began the search for solutions—family counseling, parenting books, reward systems—but nothing seemed to work for long. Each solution was like a temporary Band-Aid that held things together for a short time. Then, boom, something would trigger the tension, and the whole family would be back where they started.

Then one summer day, the children were playing out back in the care of a sitter while Karen worked in her upstairs office. She peeked out the window to see how they were doing and caught sight of Katie pretending to be Dorothy in The Wizard of Oz. Karen watched as Katie skipped around the yard singing in the warm light of the sun, a basket on her arm. And as she watched, Karen was overwhelmed by a sense of the fleeting nature of her daughter's freedom and innocence.

The words that came into Karen's head are words she will remember for the rest of her life: "I should be out there with them. I'm missing it all."

Karen knew in that instant she needed to do whatever she could to make this possible, not just today, but every day. After thinking long and hard, Karen realized it was within her power to change things. She did not have to work as many hours as she did. Her work had become like a fast-moving train, and she needed to get off. She realized that living under a tight budget would be a worthy trade-off for getting back time with her children. Karen knew Katie's moments as Dorothy would swiftly disappear, and she didn't want to miss any more of them. As long as they could pay their bills, everything else could wait. Being with the children was more important. That night, Karen and her husband figured out ways they could juggle their finances to live primarily on his salary, with Karen working part-time.

This was a major turning point for Karen's family. Before long, Karen's sense of irritability lessened, her children became more relaxed, and her husband found himself walking into a much different home at the end of the day. The decision they made on the day of Karen's epiphany has guided her family into a far more harmonious life, one congruent with their highest priorities. Moreover, Karen feels a deeper sense of peace within herself.

Look at your own life. Is there a way you can simplify it—perhaps not as dramatically as Karen did, but in some way that would work for you? Is there anything you can eliminate or change? Sometimes it's just "one more thing" that throws us out of balance and increases the tension. When we eliminate that one thing, the balance returns. In Karen's case, it was her job. In your case it might be something much less drastic.

Sometimes we get so caught up in keeping up with our standard of living or acquiring new things that we forget what's most important: the quality and amount of time we spend with our children. Think about this as you complete the following exercise.

Exercise:

> What can you eliminate or change that hinders the quality of your life and your family's? Are there elements of your life that are not congruent with your highest priorities? Can you change any of these things even in small ways? Write about this.
>
> List concrete steps you can begin to take now to downsize and simplify your lives, leaving room for the things that are most important.

4. Program your mind for successful parenting

Leslie is the mother of two children, ages 4 and 7. In assessing her positive and negative parenting qualities during a workshop, she came up with a picture many of us share. On the positive side, Leslie knew she was warm, caring, and involved. On the negative side, however, she realized she could be impatient and critical. Leslie was proud of all her wonderful qualities, but at the same time, she felt guilty about her negative qualities and feared she might be undermining her children's self-esteem, just as her mother once did to her.

Like Leslie, we all have positive and negative traits as parents. We might be loving, good-humored, concerned, and reliable on one hand, yet controlling and short-tempered on the other. All of our traits make us the multifaceted people we are.

Exercise:

> What positive qualities do you see in yourself as a parent? List them, then acknowledge yourself for all the wonderful traits you possess.

Now reflect upon the negative qualities you see in yourself as a parent. Some people have no trouble listing their negative traits—they seem only too conscious of their shortcomings. For others, this is a little harder, but human nature encompasses the dark side as well as the light. To acknowledge our full humanity, we must be willing to accept all the different facets of ourselves, good and bad. Even our most heralded role models have dark sides.

As I write these words, I think about something I recently read about Helen Keller, one of my personal heroes. In my mind there are few people who have ever manifested brilliance, tenacity, and transcendence to the degree Helen Keller did, but according to her biographer, Dorothy Herrmann, Helen Keller could also be "petulant and spiteful." Reading about her dark side was somehow reassuring to me; it gave me permission to be human, too, human and imperfect.

When we can fully accept our dark side as well as our light, we can free ourselves to make choices that were previously unavailable. By accepting that our negative traits exist, we can take full responsibility for them, and enable ourselves to turn them around.

Exercise:

What are some of your negative traits as a parent? List them.

When Leslie realized that she had inherited her mother's impatience and criticalness, she decided she needed to break the cycle. Often, we pick up both positive and negative parenting traits from our own parents. How many of us have found ourselves sounding like one of our parents and then cringing at the thought? Without wanting to, we've absorbed some of the negatives we were raised with, yet we've been unaware we have the power to change them. *Positive goal statements can help us change the things we choose.*

In order for Leslie to become the kind of parent she truly wanted to be, she needed first to think about the qualities she wanted to change. She realized that, more than anything, she wanted to be patient and accepting, rather than impatient and critical, always nurturing her children's good feelings toward themselves. Based on this, Leslie created the following three goal statements:

- I am patient with my children.
- I see my children as whole and lovable exactly as they are.
- I continuously express acceptance and appreciation toward my children.

Even though these goals had not yet come to pass, Leslie wrote them in the present tense. By doing so, she encouraged her mind to put them into practice right away, not in the future. In addition, goal statements should be framed in a positive way, focusing on what we want to *achieve* rather than what we want to *avoid*. We can make our goal statements a reality by repeating them daily and envisioning them coming to life.

Before learning to do this, Leslie would berate herself each time she was impatient, often comparing herself to other mothers she believed to be more patient than she. Each time she did, she reinforced her own negative feelings, believing this aspect of her parenting was out of her control. After creating positive goal statements, however, Leslie began to feel a greater sense of control over her negative traits, and as she did she changed her behavior. Here's how it happened.

After Leslie wrote down her goal statements, she posted them on her bedroom mirror next to her list of Parent Priorities. Every night and every morning she would read them to herself, and on her way to work each day she would repeat them in the car. As she did so, she would picture herself responding to her children in a more patient, accepting manner.

By repeating her goal statements each day and picturing them manifesting, Leslie was engaging in mental rehearsal, the same way athletes do when preparing for a big event. The mental picture Leslie created day after day enabled her mind to start reprogramming itself. When she could clearly picture herself in the act of responding patiently toward her children, concurrent actions began to follow.

As Leslie grew more and more accustomed to this new picture of herself, she became less likely to give in to impatience or criticism. When she felt either one coming on, she would focus on her goal statement, "I am patient with my children," bringing a patient picture of herself into her mind. By doing this, she was able to detach from her usual automatic responses, thus avoiding the words and actions that had made her feel so guilty in the past.

Next, she could *choose* a new action. For example, when 7-year-old Josh spilled his milk at the dinner table, she was tempted to snap, "How could you be so careless? Why don't you pay more attention to what you're doing?"

This is exactly how Leslie would have responded in the past. Instead, she stopped, took a few slow, deep abdominal breaths, and silently repeated her goal statement: "I am patient with my children."

Now she was primed to choose her words, rather than allowing them to choose her. As she did, Leslie realized Josh felt worse about the spilled milk than she did. She noticed a look of fear and insecurity in his eyes, as if he were thinking the same negative words she might have otherwise directed at him.

When Leslie realized this, her eyes welled up with tears, and she hugged Josh. He looked at her in complete surprise as she said, "Come on, Josh, let's clean this up together. I know you didn't mean to do it."

Goal statements are very powerful. They can help us become the parents we really want to be. By continuously putting her goal statement into action, Leslie began to create a new image of herself as a parent. She still had to catch herself when her old impatience would arise, but as time went on this became easier and easier. More than ever, Leslie felt truly good about herself as a parent.

Exercise:

Positive goal statements help us determine the qualities we want to develop in ourselves. What qualities do you want to further develop or acquire as a parent? Formulate three or four statements of what you want to accomplish. Phrase them in the present tense, make them positive, and keep them simple. Like this: "I react to my children with kindness and respect."

My Positive Goal Statements:
1. 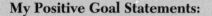 _____
2. _____
3. _____

Copy your goal statements onto note cards to hang in your room or in any space that is uniquely yours. Read and say these statements daily as often as you can. As you do, picture your goal statement coming to life. Start and end each day with the reading of these statements. Goal statements are very powerful. They can change your life.

Be Good To Yourself

Becoming a more peaceful parent means indulging yourself when you need it most. I promise you that by taking care of yourself and nurturing your own needs, you will be better able to nurture the needs of your family. This is one of the most essential elements of peaceful parenting.

Think of the source you give from as a well. If your well is dry, you have nothing left to give to the people in your life. The only way to replenish your well is by giving to yourself. This is not a selfish act; it's an act of self-preservation, and by taking care of ourselves, we give our children permission to do the same. When we are depleted, we have no source to draw from. Take a look at the following scenario, and see if it sounds familiar:

Dawn and Mark, parents of 5-year-old Jake, have demanding jobs where they often work late. Life is hectic, and every day starts while the sky is still dark.

It's 5:45 A.M. and the alarm clock buzzer awakens Dawn and Mark with a sudden jolt. They quickly rise, shower, start breakfast, and wake Jake. Remember the old TV game show "Beat the Clock" where, in order to win the game, the players had to perform a large array of tasks in a minuscule period of time? Well, this is how Dawn and Mark feel as they rush around getting themselves and Jake ready for the day. By the time they walk out the door at 7:45, they're ready for a break.

But the break never comes. Both Dawn and Mark drive to work in heavy traffic, then face a mountain of correspondence, phone calls, and meetings all day long. By 5:00, when Dawn leaves to pick up Jake from the sitter, there's usually still a ton of work on her desk. Often she's late, and when she finally arrives, Jake is moody and whining.

Today Dawn can't be late because Jake has gymnastics, so she stuffs her leftover work into her briefcase, careens out the door, and fights traffic all the way back to the sitter and then to gymnastics. By the time Dawn gets Jake home, it's 6:45 and he's hungry, irritable, and insisting on her attention.

Exhausted, Dawn ignores an overwhelming desire to flop in a chair and "crash." She doesn't allow herself to do so, thinking that if she lets herself sit down, she'll never get up.

Instead, she starts unloading the dishwasher and preparing dinner, all the while listening to Jake's complaints about gymnastics mingled with his demands for a cookie. Superimposed in Dawn's head like a neon sign is the list of things she still has to do before the night ends. Beneath all the shoulds is Dawn's need to just plain stop and give herself a break. But she believes the entire structure of her family's life would crumble if she did.

Mark won't be getting in until 8:00 or later, since it's his turn to work out tonight. So Dawn pushes through her feelings of exhaustion and finds herself being short-tempered with Jake as she feeds and bathes him. By the time Mark comes in and they sit down to eat, Dawn has a sense of free-floating irritability that she can't help but direct at Mark.

She knows the day is still not over. After dinner, she and Mark will be faced with the list that was floating through her head earlier: the kitchen to straighten, laundry to throw in, Jake's "S" homework from kindergarten, and lunches to prepare.

By 11:30, even though everything's not finished, Dawn and Mark fall into bed exhausted. The alarm is set for 5:45 and they both know they will have to repeat this same routine tomorrow and the next day and the next. Dawn feels trapped.

Does this scenario ring true for you? Are your days so full you can't help but completely ignore your own needs? This is endemic in our culture. We schedule and compress every ounce of time we have, and there's a palpable absence of empty spaces. No wonder we're tense. We believe, as Dawn did, that we're too boxed in to make any changes, but that's not necessarily true. Sometimes one small change can make a huge difference. Take a look at the next scenario to see a different approach:

Meg is a teacher and Tom runs his own business, commuting into the city each day and returning home late in the evening. As parents of 8-year-old Amy and 6-year-old Tara, Meg has the responsibility of taking the girls to all their after-school activities. With the demands of work, home, and childrearing, Meg, like Dawn, feels tense and anxious. Although she and Tom agreed they wanted to provide the girls with as many enrichment activities as they could, Meg is growing weary of all the chauffeuring.

Meg recently said, "I'd feel like a new person if I only had some time after work a few days a week to relax and unwind. But it never seems to happen."

"What's stopping you from doing it?" I asked.

"It's those damned piano lessons," she said. "If I didn't have to take the girls every Tuesday and Thursday, I'd at least have two days each week with a little time for myself after work."

"So why are you continuing with the lessons? Do the girls want them?"

"No, they don't like going either," answered Meg.

"Then why are you bothering? Like you said, if you had that time after work, you'd feel like a new person," I responded.

"But Tom and I believe all little girls should play the piano," Meg replied.

"Is it worth it?" I asked. "Also, how is this congruent with your most important priorities as parents?"

"We've always believed in enriching the girls' lives with music and dance, but the truth is, feeling peaceful is an even higher priority."

In that moment, Meg became clear that giving up the piano lessons would actually help her gain what she so desperately needed: some free time at the end of the day a few times a week. So she took the plunge and canceled the lessons, much to her girls' delight. Now every Tuesday and Thursday she can do what she wants most when she comes home from work—soak in the tub with a hot cup of tea while listening to quiet music. Meg calls this "my date with myself," and in this single change, she restored some desperately needed balance to her life.

Think of your own life. What can you subtract to restore greater balance? What can you add to be kinder to yourself? Remember, being kind to yourself is neither selfish nor frivolous; quite the contrary. Being kind to yourself feeds the well from which you give to others. Acts of kindness toward yourself are necessities that will enable you to be more loving, compassionate, and available to the people you care most about.

Exercise:

Close your eyes for a moment. Picture what you would do right now if you could completely nurture yourself. Is it a soothing bubble bath, a brisk walk around the block under the starry sky, or a few precious moments of reading? Perhaps it's the silence of a room where you can simply be alone. What images, thoughts, or insights came up for you? Write them down.

Now think of some simple things you can do to nurture yourself within the framework of your life. Here are some suggestions to get you started:

– massage your neck for one minute when you feel tense
– walk outside and touch the grass
– keep a special stone or shell with you at all times; hold it in your hand and picture its source when you feel the need to ground yourself
– keep a supply of special teas available for a quick break
– write in a journal
– call a friend
– put on your favorite music and sing along with it

What can you add to this list?

Now think about this: Is there a simple thing you can change that will enable you to take better care of yourself? Is there a way you can eliminate some of the constant white noise of activity that surrounds you? Keep your eyes closed and reflect on this question for a moment. It is often the simple things that define the quality of our lives, the moment-by-moment choices we make. What new choices can you make that will lead you to a more peaceful place inside yourself?

Post a list of things you're going to do to nurture yourself. Buy what you need and prepare "goodie bags" of nurturing things for yourself—one for home and one for work. Start now.

Concluding Thoughts

Tonight, after your child is asleep, go into his room and take a look at him. As you do, suspend all other thoughts and allow yourself to be in the presence of your child's magnificence. Take a mental picture of your child in this moment. Now tuck the picture away to look at as time goes on. Life has such an evanescent quality; if we don't seize simple moments like this one, they fade away, never to be ours again.

I remember the first time this realization hit me 21 years ago. My second child, Tim, was only 6 months old. As I sat on a clear January day nursing him at the kitchen table, it must have been Providence that moved me to shed all other thoughts and focus my attention solely on him just for that moment.

What I saw still takes my breath away: It was my child's absolute exquisiteness—his moist pink skin, his corn-silk hair, his golden eyelashes catching the morning sun, and his tiny fingers curled around my own. My son's essence of goodness and beauty were completely revealed to me in that moment as I held him in my arms.

This experience became available to me only because I took the time to fully *be* in my child's presence, unencumbered by extraneous thoughts.

Since then, I have only been able to retrieve brief snatches of that moment in dreams and times of reverie, always hungering afterward for continued recollections of my son's baby self. But memories are fleeting and only given to us when we are quiet enough to receive them.

Knowing this sometimes brings me to a deeper realization, one that catches in my chest with a sharp twist: I will never get those early years back. Never. Every minute of my children's growing up is behind me now, and I am left with the profound sense that once a moment has passed, it is gone forever. How grateful I am that I was guided to know this when my children were still young.

The most sacred task we will ever be given is to parent our children. Peace begins with us, and the actions we take today will create their quality of life and our own. We have the power to create within our homes peacefulness and nurturance, giving ourselves and our children a base of each to take out into the world.

Recap

Peaceful Parenting Key #1:
Peace begins with me.
~

Our first anchor on the journey to becoming a more peaceful parent is to take the following five steps:

- Learn how to calm yourself through the practice of abdominal breathing and envisioning.
- Define your most important priorities for the time you spend with your children, and live congruently with the priorities you have set.
- Create positive goal statements based on the qualities you most want to develop as a parent. Post them, review them daily, and say them in your mind, especially when you feel challenged.
- Downsize and simplify. Honestly assess your life. See what you can eliminate or change. Examine what gets in the way of balance, harmony, and peace in your family. Make a commitment to changing whatever you can that gets in the way of these attributes.
- Take care of yourself and do whatever is necessary to restore balance to your life. Discover what small things you can do each day to nurture yourself and feel relaxed. Sometimes very simple things can shift your mood. Find out what they are and incorporate these things into your life *every day.*

RESOURCES FOR PARENTS

Becker, Juliette. *Postcards for Peaceful Parenting* (audiobook). MindsEye Publishers, 1999. A clinical psychologist takes parents of young children on a journey where "mini vacations" relieve daily stress.

Breathnach, Sarah Ban. *Simple Abundance*. New York: Warner Books, 1995. A daybook of thoughts, quotes, and suggestions for a peaceful, harmonious life.

Carlson, Richard. *Don't Sweat the Small Stuff... And It's All Small Stuff*. New York: Hyperion, 1997. Tells us how to enjoy life more and contribute to the world we live in; helps people transcend stress and worry.

Covey, Steven R. *The 7 Habits of Highly Effective Families*. New York: Golden Books, 1997. How to build harmony in the home; communication, problem-solving, and goal-setting.

Elkind, Dr. David. *The Hurried Child*. Reading, Massachusetts: Addison-Wesley, 1981. Learn about the price of hurrying our children to grow up too fast in a hurrying world. Excellent.

Fay, Jim and Cline, Foster W. MD. *Parenting With Love and Logic: Teaching Children Responsibility*. Navpress, 1990. Tips for parenting without power struggles.

Flanigan, Beverly. *Forgiving Yourself: A Step-By-Step Guide to Making Peace With Your Mistakes and Getting on With Your Life*. New York: Macmillan, 1997. Letting go of guilt and forgiving oneself in order to heal relationships, gain inner peace, live more freely, and honor the self.

Hanh, Thich Nhat. *Peace Is Every Step*. New York: Bantam, 1991. A beautiful, easy to read book of practical ways we can make our lives more peaceful. Brilliant in its simplicity.

Peck, M. Scott. *The Road Less Travelled*. New York: Touchstone, 1978. A classic. Helps build a deeper understanding of self and others. Nurtures peacefulness in our relationships.

St. James, Elaine. *Inner Simplicity: 100 Ways to Regain Peace and Nourish Your Soul*. New York: Hyperion, 1995. Simplifying your life, nourishing the mind and spirit, the value of alone-time.

Vanzant, Iyanla. *Faith in the Valley: Lessons for Women on the Journey to Peace*. New York: Simon & Schuster, 1996. Tells the reader how to deal with low points in life and seek inner peace.

Websites

Family World Home Page—www.family.go.com—More than 40 parenting magazines offer articles and resources for parents.

Parents' Place—www.parentsplace.com—Articles, books, chat rooms, and other resources for parents.

Peacemakers—www.peacemaker.org—Books, games, posters, newsletter, a plethora of peace related resources. A rare find.

CHAPTER 2

Three Essentials
for Peaceful Parenting

*If we value our children's dignity, then we need to
model the methods that affirm their dignity.*
—Adele Farber and Elaine Mazlish

Peaceful Parenting Key #2:
I have made my home a place of kind words.
~

In the 25 years I have been working with parents and children, I have seen
that three essential elements tend to be present in peaceful homes. They are:

– Using kind words instead of put-downs, and speaking without blame
  when problems arise.
– Creating an atmosphere of affirmation, including catching one's children in the act of doing things right.
– Spending time each day paying attention to one's child and listening to
  what he has to say.

In this chapter, we'll be examining each of these three essentials and
ways you can integrate them into your home as much as possible.

Using Kind Words

Nothing undermines the peacefulness of our homes more than harsh
words. One of the most important steps we can take on the road to peace-

ful parenting is to make a hard and fast rule for ourselves, our children, and anyone else who lives with us: **No put-downs of any kind.**

Put-downs fuel stress, create animosity, and deplete self-esteem. They have no positive value, and therefore have no place in our homes.

Make your home a put-down free zone. In doing so, you will insulate against words that can ignite explosive situations. Think of put-downs as underground toxins that can easily seep out unless you take a firm stand against them. Begin by taking a stand with yourself, catching yourself whenever you're tempted to use a put-down, no matter how small. Otherwise you will pass the habit of put-downs on to your children. Take a look at the following example to see what I mean:

> *Corinne knew she had a habit of using put-downs, but was un-aware of the effect they had on her children. She'd grown up in a family where put-downs were constant, yet it never dawned on Corinne that she was carrying on this same pattern in her own home.*
>
> *Upset as she'd become when she'd hear her children calling each other names, Corinne didn't realize that they were actually following her example. This all began to change, however, on the day Corinne took her children to the local pool and had an eye-opening experience.*
>
> *"You're just a baby, a little stupid baby," Corinne's 8-year-old son Gabe shouted at his sister, splashing water in her face. "Baby, baby. Someone give the baby a bottle," he taunted as his sister's eyes filled with tears.*
>
> *"You big fat bully!" retorted 6-year-old Cara as she splashed water back in Gabe's face with a vengeance.*
>
> *"Cut it out or you'll both be out of that pool in a second!" yelled Corinne. "You're acting like a couple of brats!"*
>
> *As she shifted her gaze away from her two children, Corinne noticed the uncomfortable look of a mother sitting nearby. The woman's expression caught her off guard and triggered an uneasy feeling. Corrine stopped and thought for a moment about how her children had sounded. Then she thought about how **she** must have sounded as well. In that moment, it hit her—"We sound exactly like my family did growing up; my children are following in my footsteps!" Only then did Corinne realize her old way of communicating had to change.*

The habit of put-downs can be passed on through generations, as in Corinne's case. Leonard had the same experience. Leonard's grandfather used to call his father a lazy good-for-nothing. Leonard's father in turn called Leonard a lazy good-for-nothing. Now guess what Leonard calls his son (even though he hates himself for doing so). That's right—a lazy good-for-nothing!

Negative perceptions we have about ourselves are often rooted in the put-downs that were directed at us when we were young. "You're not as smart as your sister," or "You'll never amount to anything," or "You're so clumsy." Can you remember put-downs people directed at you growing up? They may have formed some of your most painful childhood memories, and you may have unknowingly internalized them. This is exactly what we *don't* want to have happen with our children.

We have the ability to break the pattern of put-downs regardless of past history or old habits. You can put-down proof your home by remembering four simple rules and teaching them to every member of your family:

- **Address the act, not the person.** "You're so disorganized, Terrence," makes it sound like disorganization is a personal character flaw of Terrence's—personal and permanent. The last thing we want to do is provide our children with negative images of themselves. Instead try something like, "Your desk needs to be organized, Terrence. Please take care of it."
- **Sarcasm counts as a put-down.** "Smart move, Jennifer," says her mom as Jennifer bumps into a table and knocks over a picture frame. Jennifer gets the message loud and clear: "You're a klutz!" Any type of sarcasm, including that which is couched in humor, is still a put-down. Avoid it completely and have your children do the same.
- **Avoid using put-downs against people who aren't with you.** "That Allison is such a jerk. Did you see the way she behaved at the party?" Comments like this will give your children the message that it's OK to use put-downs as long as the person you're talking about isn't around. Children are excellent mimics. Avoid giving them something negative to emulate.
- **Avoid using put-downs against yourself.** "I'm so stupid. I locked my keys in the car," says Dad. "I'm so stupid. I forgot my homework," says 10-year-old Clayton. Using put-downs against ourselves is just as damaging as using them against others and certainly a habit we don't want to pass on to our children. By honoring ourselves, we show our children that we have self-worth, and our children's self-worth is intrinsically connected to our own. Also, it's easier to honor other people when we honor ourselves.

Make your home a put-down free zone, and have your children be your partners in doing so. Hang a sign on your refrigerator, "This House is a Put-down Free Zone." Make this goal a family project, then watch for the positive results.

Learn to Use "I Messages" and Teach Your Children to Do the Same

In our quest to create an atmosphere where kind words are spoken, it's essential to learn how to use "I Messages"—simple declarative statements that express our feelings, thoughts, or observations, particularly when we're upset or angry. When we start from "I," we take ownership of our feelings and perceptions. "You" places blame on the other person and makes them the brunt of our feelings. "You" puts the other person on the defensive; "I" opens communication. Take a look at the following example:

Shelly's family is having dinner out with the relatives. Anthony reaches across the table to get the salt, almost knocking over his sister's glass. "You are so thoughtless, Anthony! You almost knocked that entire glass of water onto your sister's lap," admonishes Shelly angrily. Anthony lowers his head in embarrassment and wishes he could crawl under the table. Shelly suddenly begins to feel bad, realizing she's hurt her son's feelings. That wasn't her intention; the words just came out the wrong way.

Shelly thinks about another way she might have responded to her son: "Anthony, I want you to be more careful when you need something on the table. Please ask someone to pass the salt next time."

This would have communicated what needed to be said without demolishing Anthony. Shelly decides to catch herself next time she feels irritated or angry. More than anything, she wants to nurture good feelings between herself and her children. She knows the words she chooses are instrumental in doing so.

Albert Schweitzer once said, "Example is not the main thing in influencing others. It is the only thing." Our children learn by our example. Consequently, if we speak in "you messages," they will, too. Yet if we train ourselves to start from the "I," our children will learn to do the same. Our modeling is essential in setting the tone for a peaceful family. By avoiding put-downs and using "I messages" when we're angry, hurt, upset, concerned, or frightened, we take responsibility for the way we feel while pre-serving the dignity of the other person. Kind words can fully express what we need to say without being disrespectful.

Take a look at another scenario: Susie, age 5, runs into the street to get her ball. She doesn't check to see if a car is coming. Dan, her father, panics, runs out and grabs her, and says, "Haven't I told you a million times you have to look both ways? What's the matter with you?"

Susie's panic is now triggered, and she feels guilty to boot. Certainly Dan was frightened, but even in the face of fear, we can speak from the "I": "Susie, I *never* want you to run in the street like that again! What do you need to do every single time you step off the curb?"

In this scenario, Susie is aware that she did something wrong, but her bad feelings aren't compounded by guilt.

"I messages" help us maintain a healthy emotional balance in the family. They are authentic yet respectful ways of communicating what's on our minds. "I messages" should not be sugar-coated, but should express what we feel without hurting or blaming the other person. Take a look at a few examples:

- "I'm upset that you forgot my birthday. My feelings are hurt."
- "I'm so angry I could scream. I want you to pay for that broken win-dow out of your allowance. Ball playing is *not* allowed in the house!"
- "When I see the two of you fighting I feel *so* annoyed. The fighting has to stop, *now!*"
- "I need you to be honest with me. When you don't tell me the truth I feel like I can't believe anything you tell me."
- "I want you two to settle down right now. It's too noisy!"

All of the above "I messages" are honest and express authentic feelings, yet they don't lay guilt, blame, or a label on another person. As I said be-fore, "you messages" put people on the defensive. "I messages" open com-munication.

When you start using "I messages," your family may comment that you sound a little strange, as my son commented when I first started using them: "Mom, you sound weird when you talk that way. What are you doing?"

When he asked this question, I explained I was trying to find a way to not place blame or make him feel bad when I felt angry or upset about something. I told him it felt a little awkward to me, too, but this was a more respectful way of communicating, so I wanted to stick with it.

It was like learning a new language: first you have to translate everything from the old language in your mind before it can come out correctly. Each time I got angry, I would have to think the words first. "You're driving me crazy," would pop into my head, but before I let those words fall out of my mouth, I'd have to translate them into the new language: "I've asked you two to stop roughhousing, and I want it to stop now!"

In time, "I messages" became a fluid part of my working vocabulary. At some point, and I'm not sure how long this took, I actually started *thinking* in "I messages." That's when I knew I had mastered the new language.

Throughout this process, I would constantly reiterate to my boys when they were angry or upset, "Tell him (or me) what's on your mind, but start from 'I.'" Over and over, my boys would hear me starting from "I" and would be reminded themselves to do the same. Over time, the new language took hold in them also. In fact, I remember the most recent "I message" Michael, who is now in graduate school, gave me: "Mom, I'm really annoyed you called my new girlfriend by my old girlfriend's name!" How's that for a blunder?

Speak to your children in "I messages" even when they are preverbal, and when they learn to speak, rephrase things for them coming from the "I." For example, your 3-year-old says, "You're mean," when his big brother takes away his stuffed animal. Tell him to say, "I'm angry," instead. Keep reiterating, regardless of age, that your children "Start from 'I.'"

When you start using "I messages," try not to be deterred by the initial awkwardness. Just expect that it will be there for a while, as in any new skill you try to master. In those moments, remind yourself that the awkwardness will pass and that by using "I messages," you're taking a major step toward becoming a more peaceful parent and creating a more peaceful family.

Try the following exercise to help master the skill of giving "I messages." Read each scenario below and think about how you can turn "You messages" into "I messages." If you've never used "I messages" before, don't skip this exercise. It is designed to raise your comfort level.

Exercise:

Make sure your "I messages" are honest, direct, and authentic while being respectful toward the other person. Speak what's true for yourself in each situation, but make sure the person you're speaking to is left with their dignity intact.

Scenario: *Four-year-old Katie still sucks her thumb. It drives you crazy.*

"You message": *"You're acting like a little baby. Big girls don't suck their thumbs. Do you want everyone to think you're just a baby?"*

"I message": _____

_____

_____

Scenario: *Eleven-year-old Kyle has not raked the lawn, even though you asked him to do so an hour ago.*

"You message": *"You'd better march out there this minute and pick up that rake, young man. Do you hear me?"*

"I message": _____

_____

_____

Scenario: *Eight-year-old Jessica is playing with her food at the dinner table.*

"You message": *"Your manners are appalling, Jessica. Pick up that fork right now."*

"I message": _____

_____

_____

Scenario: *Your spouse has left his clothes on the floor after you've asked him repeatedly to hang them up.*

"You message": *"You're such a slob! I've asked you a million times to pick up your clothes!"*

"I message": _____

_____

_____

You'll be amazed at how relationships improve when you switch from "You messages" to "I messages." Each time you do so, you'll be teaching your children to do the same. In Chapter 8, we'll talk about specific ways to help your children practice this skill.

Peaceful Parenting Key #3:
I catch my children in the act of positive behaviors and praise them immediately, specifically, and sincerely.
~

Train Yourself to Catch Your Children in the Act of Doing Things *Right*

Catching our children in the act of doing things right is another of the most essential keys to peaceful parenting. By immediately acknowledging the positive, we hold up a mirror to our children that reflects back their goodness and competency. When we do this, we reinforce good behavior, cut down on negative behavior, and build our children's self-esteem.

Everyone likes to be appreciated. Think of yourself. Imagine your boss walking into your office and saying, "I'm so impressed with the job you're doing. I know how much you have to juggle just to get here every day, but you do it, and you're always here on time. On top of that, you're efficient, organized, and pleasant to be around. I really appreciate the qualities you bring to this office."

What would it be like if your boss acknowledged you like this on a regular basis? You'd probably love to go to work, not to mention how good you'd feel about yourself. In fact, you'd probably start performing better than ever. Think of all the good that could come out of your boss's acknowledgment.

The same holds true for children. The more we can catch them in the act of doing things right and acknowledge them for it, the more we reinforce all the good things they do: "Jamar, I'm so proud of the way you cleaned your room. You hung up all your clothes and put away all your things. Your room looks neat and organized, and you did it all by yourself. I'm so impressed! Wait till I tell your father what a beautiful job you did. He'll be just as proud as I am." You can bet Jamar will be quick to clean his room next time it's messy.

Coaching Yourself to Look for the Good

Take out two pieces of paper. On the first, list all of the negative behaviors you have observed in your child. On the second list all of the positive. If you have more than one child, start with the child you have the greatest difficulty with. As you list your child's positive behaviors, be as specific as you can and list **everything you can think of**, no matter how small.

Consider the list Janice started about her 6-year-old daughter Michelle:

<u>Michelle's Negative Behaviors:</u>

- – has difficulty getting along with her sister
- – won't share her toys with her sister
- – hits her sister
- – cries when she doesn't get her way
- – sulks
- – tells me she hates me when she's angry
- – throws tantrums

Janice was a little depressed when she first completed the list. So many things seemed wrong. But, with effort, she began the other list and was surprised to see all the good that was there.

<u>Michelle's Positive Behaviors:</u>

- – puts her clothes in the hamper
- – uses good manners at the dinner table
- – gives the dog water almost every day
- – puts the cap back on the toothpaste and puts the toothpaste away when she is finished with it
- – hangs up her towel
- – is quiet when she gets up in the morning on the weekends and lets us sleep
- – shares her toys with her friends
- – gives me lots of hugs and kisses
- – is a good reader
- – does well in school
- – does her homework independently
- – has a great laugh
- – can be a good listener
- – makes up with her sister when they have a disagreement
- – can play nicely with her sister from time to time
- – goes to bed when she is asked to
- – behaves well when we go shopping
- – shows her love in special ways

The trick with the list of positives is to add to it each week. Imagine yourself being a detective whose mind is honed to zero in on the subtlest details. Be vigilant in looking for even the smallest positive behaviors your child performs each day. Janice watched Michelle closely and tried to find new things that were favorable. It shocked her to realize how very many positive things Michelle did each day, things Janice had previously overlooked or taken for granted. It seems Janice was so frustrated by some of the negative things Michelle was doing that the negatives were completely permeating her perceptions.

Janice shared the second list with Michelle, but not the first. The list of negatives was just for Janice and her husband, Irv, and there was only one reason for making it: to help Michelle win. That's right, to help her win by giving her the support needed to overcome those negative behaviors.

Here's how this works: By looking at the list of negatives, Janice and her husband were clearly able to see the behaviors they most needed to catch Michelle **in the act of doing the opposite of**. So, for example, when Janice noticed Michelle sharing a cookie with her sister, she *immediately*, *specifically*, and *sincerely* praised Michelle for doing so, and gave her a big hug.

Helping Michelle "win" also included looking for patterns on the list of negatives. The most obvious to Janice was a pattern of jealousy toward Michelle's 3-year-old sister, Amanda. When Janice and Irv talked about this, they decided to come up with some things they could do to help Michelle feel more special. They agreed they would each spend more individual time with her, talking, listening, and cuddling. They also went to the library and took out several picture books on jealousy that they would read to Michelle and use as a vehicle to encourage her to talk about her feelings.

Along with these steps, Janice and Irv made a commitment to very deliberately catch Michelle in the act of every positive behavior they could observe. In doing so, they knew they would help build her self-esteem and reassure her of their love and approval while diminishing her negative behaviors.

Janice continued adding to the list of Michelle's positive behaviors daily, noting subtle changes as they occurred. For example, she wrote down, "didn't cry when we told her she couldn't have ice cream." Janice realized that even though this seemed small, it was actually a big step for Michelle. Each time Janice noted Michelle's positive behaviors, she would offer her praise and, later, record the behavior on her list.

As Janice continued expanding the list of Michelle's positives, she realized she and Irv had been entirely too focused on Michelle's negative behaviors. As a result, they had been out of touch with many of Michelle's good qualities. Janice recalled a conversation she'd had with her sister a few weeks earlier where she'd admitted, "Michelle is driving me crazy. She refuses to share her toys with Amanda and she cries whenever she doesn't get her way. I'm starting to think Michelle is just a difficult child."

After several weeks of listing Michelle's positive behaviors, sharing the list with Michelle, praising her every time she did something good, and employing the other strategies she and Irv had agreed upon, Janice noticed two big changes in Michelle and one big change in herself. Michelle started becoming less volatile and irritable, and she started getting along better with Amanda. Janice's change was of a different nature: She actually started seeing Michelle as an easier child than she had thought. As her frustration with Michelle lessened, Janice was able to appreciate Michelle more and handle her better. In time, Michelle's list of negative behaviors started to shrink and her list of positives expanded.

Janice and Irv used family meetings as another vehicle for helping Michelle "win." It was here that they worked on goal-setting and strategies to help her and Amanda get along.

For example, they discovered some of Michelle's tantrums came when Amanda would go in her room without asking and touch her things. The family decided to set a rule that both girls must ask permission before going into the other's room.

Michelle also believed Janice took Amanda's side too much. Janice realized that it was true. In her perception of Michelle as a difficult child, she tended to believe the bad things Amanda told her, and was quick to assign blame.

Janice promised Michelle she would try to be more objective when the girls had a problem, but at the same time she reminded Michelle that name-calling and hitting were not allowed under any circumstances. Clear discussions like this helped Michelle become more cooperative and willing to work on solutions.

Janice and Irv were vigilant in catching Michelle in the act of all positive behaviors. In doing so, they were setting Michelle up to win at home and to win in life.

The Process of Affirming

Catching your child in the act of positive behaviors and acknowledging them for it is also known as "affirming." For affirming to be effective, it needs to be *immediate, specific, sincere,* and *deserved.* Be careful never to give an insincere acknowledgment to your child as a means of control or manipulation. Insincere acknowledgments have a way of backfiring, as in the following example:

> *Claire was at her wit's end with her 8-year-old twins Jonathan and Jeremy. She found them to be wild, rambunctious, and difficult to control, and they frequently got her 2-year-old involved, which made things even worse. Though she tried to keep her temper at bay, somehow her disdain for the twins' behavior would leach out and make itself known in her facial expression and tone of voice. Although Claire wasn't aware of this, her twins could see her negative feelings in an instant.*
>
> *Claire thought she might have found a solution after attending a parenting workshop where she'd learned about affirming. The next day, Jonathan and Jeremy were sitting on the floor playing a video game. Before long, they started poking each other and getting silly, usually a prelude to their becoming out of control.*
>
> *Claire's tension began to mount, so she decided to do what was recommended in the workshop and look for one good thing they were doing to compliment them on. She swallowed her real feelings, plastered a smile on her face, and said through clenched teeth, "Boys, I like the way you're sitting. Now just try to stay that way." In moments, the boys started giggling, rolling around on the floor, and crashing into the furniture.*
>
> *I didn't think this would work with my two terrors. Maybe other people's kids, but not mine, Claire thought to herself.*

What Claire didn't realize is that affirming only works when it is sincere and deserved. Her first mistake was giving her boys an affirmation she didn't mean. What she really wanted to say was, "You guys had better not start disrupting this house like you always do. Just stay still and be quiet!"

Her second mistake was that the twins didn't *deserve* an affirmation. What they really needed was a warning like, "Guys, I'm noticing the two of you starting to get silly. If you can't sit quietly and play the video game the way you're supposed to, we'll have to turn it off." Or they might have needed to be given an alternative: "Guys, the two of you are starting to get silly. You can either turn the video game off or play it one at a time. Playing it together isn't working anymore. Which do you choose to do?"

Claire's third mistake was that she threw in a qualifier: "I like the way you're sitting. Now just try to stay that way." The second part of the affirmation invalidated the first. When we give an affirmation, it has to stand alone. If the boys had actually deserved to be affirmed, the qualifier would have ruined it.

Being Specific

"You cleaned up your toys so nicely, Jason. You're such a good boy," is vague and implies judgment of Jason's character. When we use affirmations like this one we give the message that our child's worth is somehow tied in to the praise. In Jason's mind he might be thinking, "And what about yesterday when I left my toys all over the place? Was I a bad boy then?"

A better affirmation might have been, "Jason, I like the way you cleaned up your toys. All of the blocks are back in the right box and the action figures are back on the shelf. Your floor is completely neat. Great job putting things away." Notice how this affirmation describes the behavior *in specific terms,* and includes no judgment of Jason.

Other Ways of Affirming

Next time you notice your child doing something positive, try affirming her in writing: "Dear Megan, I am so proud of the report you're handing in today. You worked very hard and you were completely organized. Your teacher is going to love it! Love, Dad." Finding a note like this packed in her lunchbox or left on the bed at the end of the day can give your child a tremendous boost, all while reinforcing positive behavior and building self-esteem.

Try leaving a Post-it note affirmation inside your child's notebook or reading book. What a great surprise to find words of acknowledgment at a time when you least expect it.

Affirmation can also be given when it's not tied to a behavior at all, simply as an act of love. "Dear Tim, You are so very special to me. You're a kind and generous person. I love you very much. Love, Mom." Kids never get too old to receive affirmations, and neither do adults. Try doing this with your spouse, too; he'll love it!

The more you affirm, the more you build trust, love, and self-esteem. Affirmations are the gentle pillow your child can rest his head on in the warmth of your peaceful home. Best of all, they're free.

Exercise:

What personal qualities can you affirm your child for? What are some of the affirmations you might say or write to your child?

Peaceful Parenting Key #4:
I spend at least 15 to 20 minutes a day with each child, listening, interacting, and giving my full attention.
~

Because life gets as busy as it does, it's absolutely critical that we take 15 to 20 minutes every single day simply to *be* with each child, giving them our full attention and listening with an open heart. Your partner can take one child and you can take another, as long as each child has 15 to 20 undistracted minutes with one parent each day.

Family therapist Marsha Weiss says this practice is vital in promoting good mental health and positive relations with our children. "Fifteen to 20 minutes is not a lot of time, but it can make a world of difference. I urge all parents to do this. This simple act will make a definable difference in your child's life."

I'm already hearing some of you say, "How can I find 15 to 20 *more* minutes in my day?"

If this question is coming up, it's time to take another look at your priorities and put 15 to 20 minutes a day for your child at the top of the list. What can you eliminate? Is there anything you *think* is important, but, on careful examination, really isn't?

After looking at this question, one mom I talked to stopped folding each entire load of laundry and would limit folding to the things that wrinkled too much if not folded right away. She gave every member of her family a laundry basket, filled it each week with the clothes she'd just washed, and let it go at that. If they didn't put them away, fine. No one in her family seemed to mind, and she discovered a little pocket of extra time in her life by doing this.

Of course, another option is to fold laundry with your child and have this as part of your special time together.

You can do any variety of activities during the 15 to 20 minutes you spend with your child, as long as you intently give your child *your fullest attention*. You can help with a homework assignment, read and talk together, set the table, get ready for bed, take a walk, or just plain talk. The thing to remember is to truly focus on your child and not allow interruptions. As Marsha Weiss says, "You will be amazed at the impact just 15 minutes can make. For some children, it is the only time they have to truly talk to their parents and be listened to. I recommend this to all my clients because it works."

Consider your life. Think of how you and your spouse can weave in 15 to 20 uninterrupted minutes a day per child. If you're a single parent, try alternating days for each of your children, or invite a relative over from time to time to give undivided attention to one of your children.

Exercise:

What can you change or rearrange so that you and your spouse or partner can each spend 15 minutes a day of uninterrupted time with each child? Write about this

Recap

Peaceful Parenting Key #2:
I have made my home a place of kind words.
~

Peaceful Parenting Key #3:
I catch my children in the act of positive behaviors and praise them immediately, specifically, and sincerely.
~

Peaceful Parenting Key #4:
I spend at least 15 to 20 minutes a day with each child, listening, interacting, and giving my full attention.
~

- Use and practice three essentials of peaceful parenting daily.
- "Kindness spoken here" can be your motto. Remember that put-downs have no place in your home, and make your home a "Put-down Free Zone." Also, learn how to give "I Messages" and teach your children to do the same. Avoid using "you messages," which put people on the defensive. When you have something to communicate, start from "I" and say what you have to say authentically and respectfully.
- Look for the positives in your child and make sure the praise you give is deserved. List your child's positive qualities and keep adding to the list each day.
- Find ways to arrange your time so you and your spouse or partner can spend at least 15 to 20 minutes a day of uninterrupted time with each child.

RESOURCES FOR PARENTS

Briggs, Dorothy. *Your Child's Self-Esteem.* New York: Doubleday, 1970. One of the best books I ever read as a parent; sensitive and practical. Don't miss it.

Chess, Stella and Thomas. *Know Your Child.* New York: Basic Books, 1987. Helps parents understand the roots of their children's different temperaments. Gives suggestions for dealing with different types of problems relating to each temperament.

Chopra, Deepak. *Seven Spiritual Laws for Parents.* New York: Random House, 1997. Find out seven key things you can do to enable your children to live their highest possibilities.

Clarke, Jean I. *Self-Esteem: A Family Affair.* San Francisco: Harper and Row, 1978. Self-esteem-building exercises within the family.

Gordon, Thomas. *P.E.T.—Parent Effectiveness Training.* New York: New American Library, 1975. Still a classic on communicating with your children and disciplining positively. Teaches how to give "I messages."

Horvath, Lisa K. *Parenting for a Peaceful Home: Challenges and Solutions for Almost Perfect Parenting.* Pittsburgh: Cathedral Publishing, 1997. Provides quick, how-to solutions for overcoming the tough challenges facing today's parents.

Lott, Lynn and Inter, Riki. *Chores Without Wars.* Rockland, CA: Prima Pub., 1997. Building cooperation among family members.

Witkin, Dr. Georgia. *Kidstress.* New York: Viking, 1999. What kids get stressed about and what you can do about it.

Youngs, Bettie B. *Stress and Your Child.* New York: Fawcett, 1995. How to handle stress in your children at home and in school; stress-management strategies.

Websites

The Family Education Network—www.familyeducation.com—Has information for parents and teachers of K-12 children. Includes 23 free newsletters. Endorsed by the National PTA.

Kidsource—www.kidsource.com—Parenting information and resources regarding education, health care and more.

Moms Online—www.momsonline.com—Contains helpful tips for parents, a newsletter, a chat room where parents can speak to each other via e-mail, plus more.

Our Kids—listserve@maelstrom.stjohns.edu—A support group for parents of children with special needs.

Parent Soup—www.parentsoup.com—Chat rooms for parents with a wide variety of resources.

RESOURCES FOR CHILDREN

Carlson, Nancy. *I Like Me*. New York: Puffin Books, 1996. Self-acceptance is the focus of this book. (Grades K–3)

Greenfield, Eloise. *She Come Bringing Me That Little Baby Girl*. New York: Lippincott, 1994. A little boy's jealousy over his new baby sister is quelled when he sees the importance of his new role in the family. (Grades K–2)

Hoffman, Mary. *Amazing Grace*. New York: Dial Books, 1991. Grace learns she can be anything she wants to be regardless of gender or color. (Grades K–3)

Hurwitz, Joanna. *The Down and Up Fall*. New York: Morrow, 1996. As she starts middle school, Bolivia is caught in a jealous triangle when friends Rory and Derek want to keep her to themselves. (Grades 3–6)

LeShan, Eda. *What Makes You So Special?* New York: Dial Books, 1992. A child's individuality and uniqueness are the focus of this nonfiction book designed to build self-acceptance. (Grades K–6)

Penn, Audrey. *The Kissing Hand*. Washington, DC: Child and Family Press, 1993. Adorable story of a little raccoon who learns he can take his mother's love wherever he goes. (Grades K–2)

Walsh, Ellen Stoll. *Brunus and the New Bear*. New York: Doubleday, 1979. Jealousy is the issue in this adorable book, in which Benjamin's bear becomes jealous of a new bear delivered to the house. (Grades K–2)

CHAPTER 3

Building a Foundation for Good Behavior: Standards and Limits

The ability to control impulse is the base of will and character.
—Daniel Goleman, *Emotional,* xii

Children need a clear definition of acceptable and unacceptable conduct. They feel more secure when they know the borders of permissible action.
—Dr. Haim Ginott, *Between,* 114

Peaceful Parenting Key #5:
I am clear on the standards of behavior I expect of my children. I honor those standards and expect my children to do the same.
~

The rhythms of a family are as complex and varied as those of a symphony. Parents are the conductors of the family symphony, setting the tone, defining the pace, and working to create unity. We strive to help each player perform to his or her fullest ability, both singularly and together. The standards we set are the behavioral principles that guide each member of the family symphony to play in harmony.

In our homes, the standards we define help our children understand what kind of behavior we expect of them so they can get along with each other, get along with us, and get along in the world. Harmony in the family is impossible to achieve without clear, concise, consistent standards.

When my boys were growing up, there were four main standards of behavior, each directly related to values I wanted to pass on to them:

– We treat each other with care and respect.
– We don't hurt each other physically or verbally.
– We listen to Mom and speak to her respectfully, whether or not we agree with what she has to say.
– We are honest.

I didn't want to set too many standards, because standards become less meaningful when there are too many. I didn't want to make a long list of "rules," because rules can only be used effectively when children have a part in defining them. What I wanted were some guiding behavioral principles that I believed in absolutely and felt compelled to have my boys live by. It was also clear to me that I had to honor my own standards if I had any intention of having my boys honor them.

We do our children a grave disservice by letting them get away with things they shouldn't. It serves neither us nor them if we "give in" when they do something wrong, harmful, or counter to our most important values. Children feel more secure when they know the boundaries of permissible action.

As difficult as it may be to honor our own standards when our child resists, it's essential for our own integrity and the integrity of our family that we do so. As long as our actions are rooted in love, compassion, respect, and fairness, our child will come to respect the standards and the limits we have set. In fact, over time our children become grateful for them.

Determining What Your Standards Are

What standards of behavior are important to you? Close your eyes and envision your family. Picture your kids on a bad day. How are they behaving? How are they talking to each other, to you? What are your reactions? What would you change if you could? Now make a mental list of some things you'd like to change about your children's behavior.

Now close your eyes again. This time turn around the scenario you just pictured. Envision your children behaving in a positive way. Picture your own responses. Now ask yourself this question: *"What standards of behavior can I define to help my children behave more positively?"* Below list three or four standards.

As you make your list, keep in mind that the standards you set are based on your key values, the ones you want your children to live by now and as they grow up.

Standards of Behavior:

1.
2.
3.
4.

When Jack and Maria decided to do this, here's what they came up with:

1. Our children treat each other kindly. There is to be no emotional or physical hurting of any kind.
2. Our children speak respectfully to us. No back talk.
3. Our children work out their problems with words, not fists.
4. Our children show care for the environment and the people in it.

Jack and Maria came up with these standards together. Jack didn't completely agree with the last one, but this was very important to Maria. She had seen too many of her children's friends showing a blatant disregard for the earth and she believed her children's behaviors should reflect a consciousness of the world they lived in.

Jack finally agreed to include this as one of the family standards. In doing so, he realized he would have to change some of his behaviors, like pouring oil down the sewer and not recycling old magazines. Jack and Maria agreed to have a family meeting where they would introduce the standards they had decided upon.

They also made a pact to stand behind each other 100%, and that if either of the children purposely disregarded a standard, they would talk to him immediately and follow up with some kind of relevant consequence.

Jack and Maria did two important things. They agreed to agree on their standards, and agreed that their standards would be non-negotiable. This meant their kids wouldn't be allowed to whine, nag, or talk their way out of behaviors that went against any standard. A standard was a standard, and that was that.

So the day 11-year-old Bradley punched 9-year-old James in the stomach for using his remote control car, Bradley was sent to his room and denied the use of the car for the next two days.

Later, Jack and Maria helped mediate the conflict (see Chapter 8 for mediation strategies), but their immediate task was not to give in to Brad's impassioned explanations as to why he was justified in punching his brother.

The great thing about standards is they just "are"; they render impossible the eventuality that excuses can justify bad behavior. Once the children realized this, life became easier in Jack and Maria's home.

You see, the root of many of our children's bad behaviors is our own inconsistency. When we are fair, consistent, and stick by our standards, our children become easier to handle.

Letting children purposely disregard standards erodes the foundation of a peaceful home. And when they try to do this (you can be sure they will), there are several effective things you can do:

1. Talk to your child immediately and address what happened.

Let your child know that what he did was wrong. Do this in a firm, matter-of-fact, but respectful way and use "I messages." Listen carefully to what's going on under the surface of your child's behavior and empathize where appropriate, but don't let the bad behavior go because your child has "a good excuse" for it. Next tell your child your expectation: "I expect the next time your brother takes something of yours without permission, you will use your words, not your fists, to deal with the problem."

2. Next, give a *fair, related* consequence or a firm reminder.

Tell your child a consequence will be given if the behavior happens again. In this situation, an immediate consequence would be appropriate, because Jack and Maria's most highly held standard was "We work out our problems with words, not fists."

3. Now, explore options with your child.

Guide him to think about other choices he can make should similar circumstances arise in the future. In the above scenario, Jack or Maria could ask Bradley, "What can you do differently next time your brother takes something of yours without permission?" Two possible solutions might be:

– Take a deep breath and then give him an "I message": "I'm really angry right now because you're not allowed to touch that toy without asking. Please put it down."

– Go for help. Tell Mom or Dad you're so angry you're afraid you'll hit. Ask them to help you solve the problem.

If necessary, have your child write down his or her options. Refer to this list and use it whenever you need to. When we discuss brainstorming in Chapter 8, we'll talk more about helping kids come up with solutions.

4. Find something to acknowledge your child for.

Maybe it's his or her willingness to look at solutions, acceptance of responsibility, good listening, or any positive behavior your child has exhibited in the process of working out the problem. However, you might not be able to do this right away. Your child might need time to cool off before you can even begin to discuss the problem. If that's the case, send him to his room for a while and then sit down and talk once he's calmed down. Looking for something positive to acknowledge reinforces positive responses or attitudes you observe and gives reassurance to your child that you still love him. A little caveat here: Only acknowledge him if it feels sincere to you.

Exercise:

What are some things you'd like to change about your children's behavior? List them.

Ask yourself this question: "Am I reinforcing any of these negative behaviors? If so, how?" Write about this.

Standards in Action

When my sons Mike and Tim were 10 and 7, Mike decided it would be cool to use put-downs against his brother. He'd been hearing a lot of put-down talk at school and on TV, so I wasn't completely surprised when he started using put-downs himself. The first time he did this I spoke to him firmly, starting from "I" (not "you"), telling him what he'd done was unacceptable and went against what we had agreed upon as a family. I told him firmly he needed to refrain from using put-downs in the future.

Unfortunately, he didn't. Here's how I handled it:

> **Me:** *"I'm really annoyed right now. Put-downs aren't allowed in this house and I've already asked you* not *to use them. What you said hurt Tim's feelings, and that's* absolutely unacceptable *to me. What's going on?"*
>
> **Mike:** *"He's a pain, Mom. He gets on my nerves."*
>
> **Me:** *"What's he doing that's bothering you?"* (trying to get to the bottom of the problem)
>
> **Mike:** *"Everything about him bothers me."*
>
> **Me:** *"Can you be more specific?"* (Continuing to delve without putting in my two cents yet. I wanted to gain some insight into what was motivating his behavior.)
>
> **Mike:** *"He acts like he's your little baby and he always tries to get me in trouble."*
>
> **Me:** *"Like this morning when he told me you took the TV remote away from him?"* (Remaining as detached as possible from my own reactions while trying to get to the cause of his actions.)
>
> **Mike:** *"Yeah, like that! I didn't take the remote. He put it down and I thought he was finished with it. Then he told on me!"*
>
> **Me:** *"You're angry with him because you felt like he got you in trouble, so you called him a name."* (reflective listening)
>
> **Mike:** *"Yeah. You always side with him."*
>
> **Me:** *"Do you feel I take his side because he's younger?"*
>
> **Mike:** *"You do!"*
>
> **Me:** *"You feel I care about him more?"* (empathizing)
>
> **Mike:** (filling up with tears) *"Yes."*
>
> **Me:** *"I'm so sorry if it seems that way, Mike. I love you both very much, and I care about you just as much as I do him."* (hugging him) *"I can understand your frustration if you feel I side with Tim more than I do with you, but that still doesn't justify putting your brother down. You're both very special to me, and I don't want either of you to hurt the other. I'm going to make a concerted effort to not take sides. What can you* do *the next time you're angry with Tim instead of calling him a name?"* (Moving into problem-solving. Please note that my boys and I had previously spent time talking about cooling off techniques and problem-solving, so this wasn't new.)
>
> **Mike:** *"I can give him an 'I message' about what's making me*

angry without using put-downs. If I'm too angry to talk, I can walk away and take some deep breaths first.

Me: *"Those are great ideas. You're going to need to remind yourself to do them next time you're angry with Tim instead of calling him names. You're also going to have to be aware that you'll be given a time-out if you choose to use put-downs again. Clear?"*

Mike: *"Will you be sure not to take Tim's side all the time?"*

Me: *"I will. Now, can I have your word there will be no more put-downs, even if it seems to you like I'm taking sides?"* Put-downs aren't allowed in our house.

Mike: *"OK." (a little reluctantly)*

Me: *"Shake on it?"*

Mike: *"Shake."*

Later that day when Mike got annoyed at something else his brother did, I watched him turn around, take some deep breaths, and tell Tim to cut it out without using a put-down. There was irritation in his voice, but he visibly resisted the urge to say something hurtful.

At that moment, I put my arms around him, gave him a warm hug, and whispered, "Mike, I'm so proud of you for using some restraint right now. I know it took a lot. Good for you." When Mike looked up at me, I could see the pride in his face in knowing he had made a much better choice than he had early in the day.

Did our agreement hold forever? I wish I could say it did without exception. What actually happened was that Mike's use of put-downs dropped dramatically after that day. Our talk strengthened his ability to control his impulses and make positive choices in the face of anger. He learned he could be true to himself, expressing his feelings through "I messages" rather than put-downs, and he realized when he was respectful, he felt better about himself. In essence, he learned there was an intrinsic reward for getting angry respectfully rather than abusively.

This never would have happened if I did not honor my own standard, "We don't hurt each other physically or verbally." It would have been a lot easier to let the incident go by because I was busy doing something else or because I didn't want to deal with Mike's reaction. But if I had, my boys would have gotten the message that Mom tells us one thing, but when push comes to shove, she doesn't follow through.

Another pitfall I avoided was losing my own temper, which only would have made the situation worse. What if I had yelled, "Darn it, Mike, you're being obnoxious! I told you yesterday to quit calling your brother names, and you're too stubborn to listen! No TV for a week!'"? Without question, Mike would have hurled a defensive response back at me. Before long, we would have become engaged in a tense verbal volley fueled by my irateness and his defiance, a lose-lose situation. Not to mention the pangs of regret I would have felt at taking away TV for a whole week (one or two nights would have been enough). But anger has a way of escalating itself, and too often when we succumb to it, our standards go out the window.

By honoring and modeling my own standards, I could stand tall in the knowledge that my behavior was congruent with the expectation I had for my son. In the process, Mike learned some invaluable skills that have stayed with him as he has grown into a caring, respectful, sensitive adult. And guess who his best friend is? That's right, his brother, Tim.

Why Set Limits?

Our children depend upon us to set limits and define standards, without which their lives would feel scary and unbounded. This doesn't mean we need to be autocratic dictators imposing rules arbitrarily. Instead, it means we can have a democratic family system where children have some input into what goes on, but that ultimately, we, the parents, set the limits for our children's behavior. In Chapter 4 we'll take a look at ways we can involve our children in creating "Guidelines for a Peaceful Family," giving them a voice in what goes on. Limit-setting, nevertheless, is still up to us.

By having clear, fair, consistent standards and limits, we help our children do better in life. Limit-setting helps children control impulses and delay gratification, two essentials of emotional intelligence. Daniel Goleman illustrates how our children's future success is deeply affected by their ability to abide by limits, control impulses, and delay gratification. In his book *Emotional Intelligence,* he shares the story of Dr. Walter Mischel from Stanford University, who began a thirty-year-long study in the 1960s now known as "The Marshmallow Test." In order to find out how young children handled delaying gratification, Dr. Mischel studied a group of 4 year olds of similar backgrounds. The children were individually brought into a room where a marshmallow was left on a table in front of them. The adult who brought them into the room told each child that he, the adult, had to step out for a little while. As soon as he came back, the child could have the marshmallow. If they waited, he said, they could even have two.

Two thirds of the 4 year olds did everything in their power to resist the marshmallow. They ". . . covered their eyes so they wouldn't have to stare at the temptation, or rested their heads on their arms, talked to themselves, sang, played games with their hands and feet, even tried to go to sleep." These children not only succeeded in resisting the first marshmallow, but also earned a second.

The remaining children, however, reacted in an entirely different way: Unable to abide by the limit set for them, they grabbed the marshmallow as soon as the adult left the room and stuffed it into their mouths. They couldn't control their impulses, in contrast to their peers, who were able to tolerate waiting and even developed strategies for enabling themselves to do so.

What's so significant about this study is that when these children were followed up in 10 years, the marshmallow resisters were better able to deal with life in a wide range of ways: They handled pressure better, were not stopped by challenges, and were actually more independent, assertive, reliable, and confident. The children who could not delay gratification had more difficulty in many areas of their lives: They lacked confidence and direction, had lower self-esteem, had problems making decisions, overreacted to stressful situations, and had more conflicts.

When the children were evaluated again at the end of high school, the results were even more startling: The children who had been able to resist the marshmallows at age 4 were more successful academically as well as socially.

One way we can help our children learn to delay gratification, control impulses, and follow rules is through the clear, consistent standards and the fair, reasonable limits we set for them. We help our children by saying no when we need to, even when they don't like hearing it. Psychologist Haim Ginott says, "A parent must like his children, but he must not have an urgent need to be liked by them every minute of the day." As we negotiate the rocky, complex, and sometimes confusing path of parenthood, there will be times we'll need to exercise our "enlightened" authority in the best interests of our children, even if they aren't thrilled with what we have to say.

Difficulties in Setting Limits

Sometimes we're uncomfortable doing things that make our kids unhappy, believing that saying no or setting limits will alienate our children from us. As one working mom said, "How can I say something I know will cause a power struggle with Stephanie? I already have so little time with her. Sometimes it's easier to just let her have what she wants."

Sure—if what Stephanie wants isn't really important to you, let her have it. If it is, you may need to tough it out. When we give in to demands we don't think we should give in to, we rob our children of one of the things they most need: dependable, consistent limits and the knowledge that we mean what we say. We also rob ourselves of something important: congruence with the standards we've set.

Many adults hesitate to exercise their authority because they don't want their children to view them the way they viewed their own parents. When most of us were kids, many of our parents wielded the club of arbitrary, capricious authoritarianism. Some of our parents' rules and punishments, many of which were doled out in reactive moments, didn't make sense to us. We grew up believing the word authority to be synonymous with autocracy. In our zeal to be democratic, we have relinquished too much of our own authority, leaving our children unsure of what their limits are.

A highly respected principal of a suburban elementary school sees this as a growing problem:

> On a number of occasions I've had to literally say to parents, "Be a parent." Many of them are so afraid of not being democratic, they are allowing children to make their own decisions in inappropriate situations. For example, there was one parent who was afraid to tell her child to do her homework. She didn't want to come across as autocratic or forceful, so she tried to negotiate the issue with her child.
>
> The child decided she just plain didn't want to do her homework, and the parent went along with her, saying this was the child's decision. I reiterated once again that the mother needed to "be a parent" and not be afraid to tell her child what to do. She could negotiate *when* the homework would be done, after school or after dinner, but not whether it be done at all. That decision was up to the mother. In telling her daughter to do her homework, this mother would build responsibility in her child and show her that the standards of the school needed to be supported as well.

It's time for parents to reclaim their role with "enlightened authority." This kind of parental authority has little connection to the negative authoritarianism we remember, rooted in our parents' desire to exercise control and compounded by their fear that children would run wild without arbitrary rules.

In contrast, enlightened authority is rooted in our ability to trust ourselves as adults, along with the belief that we have the right to make certain decisions in the best interests of our children, whether they like them or not. It is not our wish to dominate our children, but rather to help them grow into responsible, caring people with a good set of values and control over their impulses.

Authoritarianism breeds resentment, rebellion/passivity, and insecurity. Enlightened authority fosters trust, security, independence, and a sense of safety. It gives children the message that we are their parents and they can depend on us to make good decisions on their behalf, even if they don't agree with what we say. Our consistency and fairness tell children that they have a reliable structure in this complex world, and that we, their parents, are the keepers of that structure until they have the maturity to assume this role for themselves.

Are there some limits you find difficult to set for your children? For some parents, bedtime is the bane of their existence, fraught with whining and resistance. For others, limit-setting becomes challenging around issues of homework, eating habits, clothing, TV, requests for treats during shopping trips, what movies are appropriate to see, and more.

Think about your standards and values. Ask yourself where compromising might be more congruent with what's most important to you. Forcing the issue in certain situations might make things worse. For example, if you come home late one night with an overtired 6-year-old who refuses to brush his teeth, it probably would be best to just let it pass. Sometimes we can keep the peace and avoid power struggles by choosing our battles carefully.

Now picture a scenario where you might typically be tempted to let go of a limit *against* your better judgment. Ask yourself if "giving in" in this situation is counter to your standards and values or not. Reflect on this and see if a solution presents itself. Is there a way of responding to this situation that you haven't thought of before? Continue thinking about this and see if any new insights occur to you.

Exercise:

> *Are there any particular areas where I need to set clearer limits?*
> *What are they?*
> *What are my biggest blocks to setting limits?*
> *What can I do differently? Write about these.*

Limits and Standards in Action: George's Story

Limits and standards help children learn how to delay gratification and gain mastery over their impulses in school, too. Let me share with you a story about a little boy named George, whose teacher helped him succeed for the first time in his life by setting clear limits and standards.

When George transferred into a new second grade in the middle of the year, he was hyperactive, impulsive, and had always done poorly in school. His mind seemed more guided by his own thoughts, desires, and distractions than anything else. George would frequently glaze over when the teacher was speaking, or shout out answers inappropriately. He appeared to be unable to control his impulses and, as a result, had difficulty learning and getting along with others. Sadly, his history seemed as though it would become his future.

Luckily, the classroom George entered was a loving environment with clearly defined standards and limits. Aside from this, the teacher had worked hard to deeply ingrain peacemaking skills in all of her students. Consequently, the children had learned to be aware of the needs of others, exercise patience, wait their turns, and listen when others spoke. As young as they were, most of the children had already learned how to empathize with their peers.

For George, this was completely new, even somewhat bizarre. He had never before experienced an entire group of people with his best interests at heart who had the same expectation of him. He noticed that before speaking, each child would ask for the attention of the others, and would actually make sure they had it before they began. He also realized that his teacher was not going to let him ignore the standards of the class. With a combination of care and firmness, she consistently let George see that standards were standards, and George needed to abide by them along with everyone else.

Gradually, George started to change. With the support of his teacher and classmates, he became more aware of the other children and would catch himself when he would have otherwise interrupted. He started to look at his peers when they spoke and began listening to what they had to say instead of drifting back inside his own thoughts or disrupting the discussion.

Although George still had hyperactive tendencies, he eventually gained the ability to control his impulses. As a result, he started improving socially, emotionally, and academically. He had positive interactions with peers for longer and longer periods of time, engaged in fewer conflicts, and became a better student all around. For the first time ever, George started experiencing success.

George's story typifies what happens when children are given clear standards and limits in a framework of peacemaking. As difficult as it was initially for George, he eventually adapted, becoming happier and more productive in the process.

Modeling

Throughout this book, I will emphasize the importance of modeling whatever we want to teach to our children, since children learn more from our actions than anything else. When we live congruently with our highest convictions, our children gain strength and clarity from the example we set.

Harvard psychologist Robert Coles talks about this in his excellent book *The Moral Intelligence of Children*:

> The child looks and looks for cues as to how one ought to behave, and finds them galore as we parents and teachers go about our lives, making choices, addressing people, showing in action our rock-bottom assumptions, desires, and values, and thereby telling those young observers much more than we realize.

In our society's morally diffuse atmosphere, this is particularly important. Children aren't learning integrity from our nation's leaders, and they're bereft of true heroes. Parents need to be their children's role models and heroes.

Recap

Peaceful Parenting Key #5:
I am clear on the standards of behavior
I expect from my children. I honor those
standards and expect my children
to do the same.
~

•By examining our most important values and developing standards based on them, we lay the foundation for our children's good behavior. Our home will become more peaceful when we are clear with ourselves and with our children on what is acceptable and unacceptable behavior. Defining three or four basic standards is one of the keys to raising peaceful children.

•When a child ignores or defies a standard, you can do the following:

– Talk to your child and address what has happened.
– Next give a *fair, related* consequence or a firm reminder that one will be given if the behavior happens again.
– Explore options with your child, guiding him or her to think about other choices he/she can make should similar circumstances arise in the future.
– Affirm something positive about your child.

•Model the standards you set. Our children are guided primarily by our actions.

RESOURCES FOR PARENTS

Cecil, Nancy Lee and Roberts, Patricia. *Raising Peaceful Children in a Violent World*. Innisfree Press, 1995. Offers creative, practical ways to foster peace in the family and in everyday life. Provides action steps to help end violence and create a safer, more peaceful world for our children.

Coles, Robert. *The Moral Intelligence of Children*. New York: Random House, 1997. Building intrinsic morality, responsibility, and decency in children.

Dodson, Fitzhugh. *How to Discipline With Love*. New York: New American Library, 1987. Practical suggestions for positive discipline.

Faber, Adele and Mazlish, Elaine. *How To Talk So Kids Will Listen & Listen So Kids Will Talk*. New York: Avon, 1980. Dr. Ginnott's students give practical advice on effective communication with kids.

Ginott, Dr. Haim. *Between Parent and Child*. New York: Avon, 1965. A seminal piece of literature on parenting and discipline. A must-read.

Rolfe, Randy. *The 7 Secrets of Successful Parents*. Chicago: Contemporary Books, 1997. Core attitudes that empower parents, including setting limits.

Sears, William and Martha. *The Discipline Book*. New York: Little, Brown, 1995. Raising happy, well-behaved, well-adjusted children from birth to age 10.

RESOURCES FOR CHILDREN

Berenstain, Stan and Jan. *The Berenstain Bears Forget Their Manners*. New York: Random House, 1985. Rude behavior becomes rampant until Mama Bear comes up with a plan. (Grades K–3)

———. *The Berenstain Bears Get the Gimmies*. New York: Random House, 1988. The cubs are acting greedy, so Gran and Gramps come up with a plan to turn things around. (Grades K–3)

Moser, Adolph. *Don't Pop Your Cork on Mondays: The Children's Anti-Stress Book*. Landmark Editions, 1988. This is the first in an excellent series of books that help children cope with a variety of problems. Practical, appealing, and popular with kids. Suitable for all ages, his series also includes:

———. *Don't Rant and Rave on Wednesdays!: The Children's Anger-Control Book*. Landmark, 1994.

———. *Don't Feed the Monster on Tuesdays!: The Children's Self-Esteem Book*. Landmark, 1996.

———. *Don't Despair on Thursdays!: The Children's Grief-Management Book*. Landmark, 1996.

———. *Don't Tell a Whopper on Fridays: The Children's Truth Control Book*. Landmark, 1999.

CHAPTER 4

Raising Peaceful Kids

*Kids need to learn peacemaking when they're little,
so when they grow up they can teach their kids to be
peaceful!*
—Brianna, age 8

*If we were not so singleminded about keeping our
lives moving, and for once could do nothing . . .*
—Pablo Neruda

Peaceful Parenting Key #6:
*I provide my children
with empty spaces of time
during which they can just "be kids."*
~

It used to be a lot easier to find pockets of peacefulness in one's daily routine, especially if you were a kid. Not so long ago, life was simpler and there weren't as many pressures on children as there are now. Think back to when you were little.

When I was a child, we ate dinner together at 6:00 every night. This was as sure to happen as the sun rising in the morning and setting at night. My father would come home at that time, and all six siblings would gather round the dining room table, ready to eat together regardless of whatever activity we'd been involved in up to that point.

Although my family was nontraditional in many ways, dinner was dinner, and it was something we unquestionably shared with regularity. Our evening dinners were our touchstone, the time we melded our lives and shared the unspoken knowledge that no matter what else was going on, our family would be together night after night.

Sunday brunch was something else we all shared. Schedules and obligations never seemed to intrude, because our Sunday brunch together was another touchstone. No one questioned if we would have time to continue this steady ritual; we simply did.

I can still picture the food on the table and recall its delicious smells. Sundays were relaxed times for the whole family; somehow my father would always be in a good mood (after working all my adult life, I now know why). We would eat leisurely, joke, talk, and just *be together.*

I can't say I learned any important academic lessons during those times. Unlike the Kennedys, we were not expected to quote poetry or recount current events at our meals. There were no earthshaking discussions or didactic lectures, but there was a deeper lesson learned: We were part of a family and we could depend on each other to be there. Although I didn't realize it then, that message would stay with me for the rest of my life.

I also remember the sweet moments of free play after school, on weekends, and in the summer. What I'm talking about is *real* free play, not activities or sports that were organized by adults. I'm talking about "kid-play" like catch or hopscotch. If no one had a ball or a piece of chalk, we'd play tag or hide and seek. There were also times when we felt the need to be quiet, so we'd sit in the house or yard and draw pictures or read books for hours—simple, unstructured activities that we generated ourselves. We were free to use our ingenuity, imagination, and developing social skills to fill our time in the manner that *we* chose.

Back then, we seemed to have plenty of unhurried moments to connect with each other, talking, sharing, or simply deciding what to do next, something profoundly lacking in today's hurried society. Remember when time used to go on and on almost endlessly, especially in the summer? Now time is doled out in measured increments for kids, much the same way it is for adults. Many kids even have their own appointment books so they can keep track of all their activities and "play dates."

Who ever heard of play dates when we were little? If you wanted to play with someone, you'd knock on her door and ask her to come out, or you'd go outside and see who was around. Kids are losing the essential essence of childhood in all this overstructuring.

From preschools to boardrooms, people hurry from one activity to the next, bombarded by computer-generated images, regimenting their lives within rigid schedules—going, doing, and rushing, with little time for anything else. But with all this rushing, regimentation, and noise, we're missing the main point: **Kids need open spaces of time where they can just be kids.**

Psychologist David Elkind says we do our children untold harm by rushing and overstructuring their lives. He cautions that in the past few decades, we've adopted the unhealthy attitude that ". . . the years of childhood are not to be frittered away merely for fun. Rather, these years are to be used to perfect skills and abilities . . ." Then we wonder why so many kids are tense, hyperactive, lacking in inner direction, and have difficulty getting along with peers. Much as we haven't intended it to be this way, we've robbed our children of the open spaces of time they need to develop in these areas.

The gradual unfolding of such basic skills as compromise, empathy, and negotiation used to occur naturally in children through free play and their own devising of games and activities. Now the majority of kids' activities are planned, supervised, and scheduled by adults. Any free time children have is often spent alone in front of a computer, TV, or VCR.

Perhaps this is the reason so many teachers lament that today's children lack basic social skills. If children don't have free, unstructured time to play together, how can they learn to share, cooperate, resolve conflicts, and communicate with peers? When we don't give children time for pretending, making up games, relaxing, reading at their leisure, and plain old daydreaming, we rob them of many essential elements necessary for social, emotional, and even cognitive development.

What can we do to bridge the gap? How can we help our children develop positive social skills and peaceful ways of getting along with others? One way is to start now by providing empty spaces of time for our kids to just be kids.

Exercise:

Think about your schedule. Do your children already have some empty spaces of time where they can just be kids? If not, what can you rearrange to make this happen? Write about this.

Peaceful Parenting Key #7:
I hold regularly scheduled family meetings where my children have a voice in the workings of our family.

~

Peaceful Parenting Key #8:
I have set a foundation for peacefulness in our home by creating with my children "Guidelines for a Peaceful Family."

~

Family Meetings/Creating Guidelines for a Peaceful Family

Peacemaking is a family effort, and the most effective way I know to bring the skills of peacemaking to each member is by holding regularly scheduled family meetings. Family meetings are a way of building democracy within the family and allowing children to actively participate in decision making. This is another pivotal step in raising peaceful kids.

During your first family meeting, share your own commitment to having a peaceful family, and envision together what your family would look like if everyone in it treated each other with kindness, care, and respect. Ask your children how your home might be different if it were a more peaceful place. Ask them to envision how the people in your family would treat each other, speak to one another, and work out differences if they were all committed to having a peaceful home.

Invite your children to work with you in creating "Guidelines for a Peaceful Family." Work on developing the guidelines together so your family can put into practice the peaceful home they envisioned. By involving your children, the entire family will benefit. In his book *Teaching Children Self-Discipline,* Dr. Thomas Gordon outlines the top five positive outcomes of involving kids in this type of collaborative process:

1. Your children will be more motivated to live by the guidelines they have set.
2. They will learn to make better decisions.
3. You'll have closer, warmer relationships with one another.
4. Your children will develop higher self-esteem, self-confidence, and a sense of control over their lives.
5. Your children will develop a greater sense of personal responsibility and self-discipline.

As your children share their visions of a more peaceful family and the guidelines needed to make their visions a reality, record their suggestions and the things that are most important to you. Your children's input will make these guidelines far more meaningful to them than any rules or guidelines you might come up with on your own. Their active participation is what will motivate them to follow the guidelines that are set.

Here's why: By including your children, you give them a sense of ownership and responsibility toward the guidelines. The guidelines become their own. You're also helping build *intrinsic self-discipline,* the kind that comes from within, not from fear of punishment. Good behavior that's solely based on fear of punishment is transient and superficial. That's not the kind we're looking for. What we *are* looking for are positive behaviors that are their own reward; behaviors and choices that make kids feel proud of themselves.

When my boys were 6 and 9, we started having family meetings. Their father and I had separated around that time, and I would have been lost without the peacemaking skills that helped us get through this very rocky period. Our family meetings served to deepen our bond and strengthen trust while enabling my boys to channel their energies in a constructive direction. As time went on, our family meetings became a vital tool in building closeness and keeping open the lines of communication. Let me tell you how we started.

My boys and I had always had our best discussions on my large comfy bed, so that's where we came together on the wintry Saturday morning of our first meeting. I'd been telling my boys about the peacemaking program I'd been developing at school and asked them if they'd like to try some of the strategies. "This will help us all get along better and have a more peaceful home," I said. The idea appealed to them, so we got started right away. Making the setting warm, cozy, and comfortable helped set the tone.

We began by talking about how important it was for people to get along, and that our world was not such a peaceful place because so many people didn't know how to do this. I told my boys that I believed we each had the ability to make the world and our home much more peaceful places than they already were.

"How can we do that?" Mike asked.

"How do you think?" I asked.

"Maybe by not fighting ourselves," he answered.

"But how can that help the world?" Tim wondered.

"Because we are part of the world, and what we do affects the people around us." I went on, "Imagine if people in families all over started learning how to work out their differences without hurting each other. Imagine if people started treating each other with care and respect. Think about what kind of world we could have. This all starts right in our own homes."

"You mean like the Golden Rule?" said Mike.

"Exactly," I said. "Also," I added, "a very wise person once said, '"If you're not part of the solution, then you're part of the problem.'"

"What did he mean by that?" Tim asked.

"That means that if we sit back and do nothing about problems that exist, we enable them to continue."

"But I'm just a kid. I'm too small to do anything about problems in the world," he responded.

"That's not true, Tim. We all make a difference. Think of the kids in your school. The ones who misbehave make it harder on everyone. The ones who are helpful and caring make your school a better place. It's the same with the larger world."

"But grown-ups are the ones who really make a difference, much more than kids," Tim countered.

"All grown-ups were kids once," I responded. "Do you realize that you and other kids will grow up to be the leaders of this country someday, maybe even president? By learning how to be a peacemaker when you're young, you'll have the ability to make the world a better place right now *and* as you get older. What you learn when you're a kid, you'll take with you for the rest of your life."

"But what can we do here at home?" Tim asked. "Michael bosses me around all the time. That's not peaceful."

"That's exactly the kind of thing we can start with," I said. "In school we set up 'Guidelines for a Peaceful Classroom.' We can do the same thing here—'Guidelines for a Peaceful Home.'"

"You mean like rules?" Mike asked.

"Kind of," I said, "except we get to make them up together."

Mike and Tim both agreed they wanted to do this, so I asked them to envision what our home would be like if it were really peaceful. We each took some time to think about this, and then my boys and I talked about what we envisioned our home could be like if we all committed ourselves to making it a more peaceful place. Out of that conversation, we drew up a set of guidelines that combined all of our ideas, and then we all signed it like a contract. Here's what it said:

We agree to:

1. Treat each other with respect.
2. Not hurt each other physically or with words.
3. Listen to Mom even if we don't agree with what she says.
4. Be honest and kind.
5. Listen when someone speaks.

I posted our guidelines on the wall above the telephone, and we referred to it on a regular basis. We continued having our meetings, adding to the guidelines and talking about problem areas. Our Guidelines for a Peaceful Family served as a working document forming the basis for our interactions over time.

I made "the larger world" an integral part of this discussion because the ultimate goal of any work we do in the area of peacemaking is not to keep it confined to the small scope of our home, but to *live* the actions of peacemaking in the larger world. Children need to learn this perspective early on, as early as possible. Home is the place where this kind of thinking starts.

To paraphrase the renowned educator and author Vivian Gussin Paley, by inculcating our children with the broader concepts of peacemaking when they are young, we bring to life one of the ultimate goals of a democratic society: "helping children become kind and caring participants in a world that includes everyone."

Colette and Sam, the parents of two little girls, decided to introduce peacemaking to their family when their children were very young. Six-year-old Lara and 4-year-old Nicole became immediately engaged in the first discussion Colette and Sam had with them about having a more peaceful family.

When Colette proposed that they have a family meeting to create Guidelines for a Peaceful Family, both Lara and Nicole became very excited. Colette said, "It made my girls feel so grown-up." During their initial family meeting, Colette and Sam decided to start with only three guidelines, to make it easier for the girls to remember what they agreed to do throughout the week:

1. When Mom or Dad calls, we answer right away.
2. Whenever we can do something on our own, we should try doing it ourselves first before we ask for help.
3. We clean up our mess before starting something else.

Lara and Nicole signed the guidelines, along with Colette and her husband, and again, they felt very grown-up being asked to sign a paper that was hung up for all to see.

During the next family meeting, they talked about how each person had followed through on the guidelines they had set. Colette put a small dot by any guideline someone needed to work on. Next, they decided to expand their list and ended up with two more:

4. We won't disturb anyone when they need "peaceful time."
5. We won't interrupt when someone is on the phone.

Colette also initiated the beautiful ritual of having the family hold hands at the start of each family meeting, affirming each other and expressing their love toward each person in the family. She and her husband continue to meet with their girls on a regular basis and feel pleased that the girls are making a concerted effort to follow the guidelines they've set.

In fact, when Aunt Carol was visiting recently and she accompanied 4-year-old Nicole to her room to see the new toys she had gotten for her birthday, she was amazed when, after pulling out several toys, Nicole said, "I think I'll put these away before I show you any more." What struck Carol was the inner-directed nature of Nicole's comment.

Carol told Colette, "Your guidelines must really be working. My daughter *never* cleans up her toys unless I'm standing over her watching. Even then, she tries to get out of it."

Colette responded, "I think the fact that these guidelines came from *them* made a big difference."

Carol decided she would give this process a try in her home as soon as possible.

Exercise:

When do you plan to have your first family meeting? Where will you hold it? What do you hope to accomplish?

List some key topics you would like to cover at family meetings. Ask your children what topics they want to cover. You may also want to keep a log where you can record insights that come out of your family meetings.

Teach Your Child How to Cool Off When Angry

A chapter on raising peaceful kids wouldn't be complete without a section on cooling off. Although we'll be dealing with anger management strategies in depth later in this book, I want to give you a quick overview now so you'll be able to teach your children the process of cooling off right away.

We all get angry. Anger is a normal and natural human emotion. However, anger can lead to huge problems when we choose to react to it aggressively. Research has shown that when children are taught how to cool off and calm down, explosive episodes can be avoided.

Start by sitting down with your child at a neutral time when you're both feeling relaxed. Let your child know that you're going to help her come up with some constructive things she can do next time she feels angry. Tell her it's so much easier to solve problems when we cool off first; then we can sit down and talk about things calmly. Let your child know you've started using cooling off strategies in your life, and share some of your favorite ways of cooling off with her.

Now help your child identify things that help her feel calm when she is upset or angry, like deep breathing, counting to ten, going into another room, splashing cold water on her face, or writing down angry feelings in a journal. Be creative and don't discount any ideas your child comes up with. Sometimes unexpected ideas that come from children yield the best solutions.

When Barbara did this activity with 7-year-old Kim, here's what Kim came up with, "Hug my teddy bear, drink some apple juice, go into my room, put on my favorite tape, and 'squoosh' clay real hard."

So the next time Kim got upset, Barbara told her to stop, take some breaths, then look at her list to see what she could do to cool off. Kim went into her room, grabbed hold of her clay, and started rolling it out into a long rope. Before long, she became calm enough to talk over the problem with her mother. In the past, Kim would have gotten stuck in a pattern of whining and nagging instead.

Copy the following page so your child can make a permanent list of her cooling off strategies to post in her room for easy reference. Review your child's list periodically, and help her practice the techniques she has listed.

For example, if your child has said that counting to 10 helps her calm down, then the next time she is angry remind her of this technique, and even do it with her the first few times. Before long these skills will become automatic, helping defuse explosive feelings when they arise. We'll be talking more about this process in Chapter 7.

Cooling Off For Kids 🐱

Did you know there are lots of things you can do to calm down and cool off when you're angry, upset, scared, or worried? Sit down with Mom and Dad and list as many things as you can think of that make you feel better:

1 _____
2 _____
3 _____
4 _____
5 _____
6 _____
7 _____
8 _____
9 _____
10 _____

Hang up your list and use it whenever you need to. Cooling off is a cool thing to do! Don't lose your cool—cool off instead.

Below is an extended list of cooling-off possibilities for kids. After your child has listed all her own ideas, share what's on this list. Let it serve as a supplement for whatever ideas your child has already come up with.

Ways to Cool Off

wash your face	listen to music
draw	play an instrument
throw a ball	write an angry letter and throw it away
go outside and run	paint
build something	read
model clay	call a friend
jump up and down 50 times	clean your room

take a bath	jump on a trampoline
jump rope	cut and paste
clean out a drawer	sing
go outside and look at the sky	think of something funny
dig in the sand or dirt	ride your bike
go out and play	hug a stuffed animal

Closing Thoughts

Plant a seed and watch it grow. Notice it lift its face high toward the sun, ready to shed its own seeds. Each time we model peaceful behaviors, we plant seeds of peace within our children. And each time this happens, we nurture the souls of the human beings in whose hands the future rests. Keep this in mind as you continue to plant new seeds and watch them grow.

Recap

Peaceful Parenting Key #6:
I provide my children with empty spaces of time during which they can just "be kids."

~

Peaceful Parenting Key #7:
I hold regularly scheduled family meetings where my children have a voice in the workings of our family.

~

Peaceful Parenting Key #8:
I have set a foundation for peacefulness in our home by creating with my children "Guidelines for a Peaceful Family."

~

Downtime for kids enables them to think creatively if they're alone and to develop social skills when they're with other kids. Make sure your children have enough time like this in their lives.

Family meetings promote the democratic process in the home. Children benefit by having a voice, being heard, and participating in family decisions.

Allow your children to participate in developing guidelines to live by. Post your Guidelines for a Peaceful Family and review them on a regular basis.

Teach your child how to cool off when angry. Have him keep a list of all the things he can do to calm down when angry or upset. Post the list and help your child practice what is on it.

RESOURCES FOR PARENTS

Blustein, Jane. *The Parent's Little Book of Lists: Do's and Don'ts of Effective Parenting*. Deerfield Beach, Fla.: Health Communications, 1997. Simple, usable tips for raising happy, successful, confident children.

Crary, Elizabeth. *Kids Can Cooperate*. New York: Parenting Press, 1984. Helps parents deal with issues of conflict and cooperation with their children.

Elgin, Suzette Haden. *The Gentle Art of Communicating With Kids*. New York: Wiley, 1996. How to talk to your kids peacefully about anything and everything.

Ford, Judy. *Wonderful Ways to Love a Child*. Fine Communications, 1997. Sixty short essays that focus on ways to nurture the soul of a child and have fun in the process; teaches how to translate your deep love for your child into loving actions.

Gordon, Thomas. *Teaching Children Self-Discipline*. New York: Random House, 1989. More positive discipline strategies for parents.

Joslin, Karen Renshaw. *Positive Parenting from A to Z*. New York: Fawcett, 1994. Practical, age-related solutions to over 140 behavior problems.

Lewis, Sheldon and Sheila Kay. *Stress-Proofing Your Child*. New York: Bantam, 1996. Practical activities to alleviate stress in children.

Websites

Attention Deficit Order Home Page—www.attn-deficit-disorder.com
Information and resources on ADD.
Parenthood Web—www.parenthoodweb.com
Provides information for parents on a variety of issues and problems, including health, difficulties in school, and discipline.

RESOURCES FOR CHILDREN

Arnold, Eric H. and Loeb, Jeffrey. *I'm Telling! Kids Talk About Brothers and Sisters*. Boston: Little Brown, 1987. Real kids talk about what it's like to live with siblings. (Grades K–6)

Berry, Joy Wilt. *Let's Talk about Being Helpful*. New York: Scholastic, 1996. Opens discussion about acts of helpfulness in everyday life. (Grades K–2)

Carlstrom, Nancy White. *Kiss Your Sister, Rose Marie!* New York: Simon & Schuster, 1992. When a new baby comes into the family, Rose Marie experiences ambivalent feelings. (Grades K–4)

Clark, Emma. *The Story of Horrible Hilda and Henry*. Boston: Little Brown, 1988. Hilda and Henry are so bad their parents decide to give them to a zoo. See what happens after they meet the lion. (Grades K–3)

Cleary, Beverly. *Ramona, Forever*. New York: Avon Books, 1996. Third-grader Ramona has a lot to deal with, including conflict with a sibling, her mom not being home after school, teasing, and the prospect of a new baby. (Grades 2–4)

Cooper, Melrose. *I Got A Family*. New York: Henry Holt, 1997. A little girl talks about loving each of the different people in her family. (Grades K–4)

Hest, Amy. *The Mommy Exchange*. New York: Simon & Schuster, 1991. Two girls decide to switch their mothers and their houses and learn an important lesson along the way. (Grades 2–4)

Lalli, J. *Make Someone Smile and 40 More Ways to Be a Peaceful Person*. 1996. A lovely collection of multicultural photos and simple text with suggestions like: make friends, work together, sing, celebrate, and appreciate differences. (Grades K–2)

Munsch, Robert. *Love You Forever*. Firefly Books, 1988. A gentle affirmation of the love parents feel for their child throughout their lives. Touching. (Grades K–6)

Raschka, Chris. *The Blushful Hippopotamus*. New York: Orchard Books, 1996. Roosevelt has a big sister who says mean things to him. He learns to feel better about himself when he listens to a good friend instead. (Grades K–3)

Scholes, Katherine. *Peace Begins With You*. Boston: Little Brown, 1990. A simply written book on peace, conflict, and how to work out conflicts. (Grades K–2)

Simon, Norma. *Nobody's Perfect, Not Even My Mother*. Chicago: Albert Whitman & Company, 1981. The lesson in this book is that nobody's perfect and that's just fine. (Grades K–2)

Thomas, S.M. *Somewhere Today: A Book of Peace*. Albert Whitman & Company 1998. Text and photos show children from all parts of the world. Designed to inspire kids to take responsibility for making the world a better place.

CHAPTER 5

Strategies for Positive Discipline

Give us the strength to understand and the eyes to see.
—Sioux Prayer

Peaceful Parenting Key #9:
*I always remember
that I am the parent
and I deserve to be listened to.*
~

By now, you have begun looking at what your top priorities are as a parent, you've begun formulating positive goal statements, you've started setting standards for your kids, and perhaps you've even had your first family meeting. Congratulations. By doing all of this, you've put yourself on the path to raising peaceful kids.

But what about basic questions of discipline? Even in the face of peacemaking, discipline problems will come up. Certainly you will prevent many by pursuing the strategies in this book, but there will still be times when your child will act up, and you'll have decisions to make about how you're going to handle whatever the problem is. That's what this chapter is about.

Strategies for positive discipline are like the cement we pour to form a solid foundation when we build a home. Without these strategies, the building blocks of peacemaking will have nothing to stand on and the house will crumble.

When I lead workshops, one of the most frequent misconceptions parents have is that peacemaking means being "nice" all the time and never getting angry. My response to that is that peacemaking is a dynamic process wherein we seek positive solutions to problems while expressing our feelings *authentically* and *respectfully*. Disciplining, setting limits, and having standards to live by are all part of this process. We have the right to express anger, but must be absolutely vigilant about doing so in a respectful way. This is true for our children as well as ourselves.

Now let me share with you some steps you can take to foster positive discipline, lessen the incidences of power struggles, and help your children internalize intrinsic self-discipline—the ultimate goal.

Say "No" When You Need To, But Don't Overuse It

Even in the face of all the positive steps you are taking to have a more peaceful family, there will still be challenging moments we all dread: times when the kids just don't want to go to bed even after you've given them 10 more minutes and 10 more minutes, or when your 11-year-old daughter wants to wear eyeshadow to school, or when your 6-year-old begs for a new toy when you're shopping and you have no intention of buying him one.

These moments will still, unfortunately, occur at times, because life is imperfect and so are our children (and so, needless to say, are we!). The good news is that once the foundation for peacemaking has been set, those challenging moments will be fewer and your ability to handle them will be greater. Within this context, sometimes saying "no" to something your child wants will be the most helpful thing you can do to build positive discipline and curtail future power struggles.

Why does it work this way? Because, as we discussed before, children need limits and boundaries, and they depend on us to define them when they are too young to define their own. As we engage our children in the democratic process of family meetings and setting guidelines for a peaceful family, we build their sense of personal responsibility, self-control, and decision-making powers. However, our kids will still test us from time to time to see if we'll stand our ground and follow through on what we say.

As I said in the last chapter, there will be times you'll want to change your mind or compromise on something. That's fine, *as long as you feel good about what you've decided to compromise on.* But there will be other times when your gut will tell you that compromising is the wrong thing to do, and your child is hammering away at you anyway. These are the times when saying "no" is critical.

I remember when Michael was 10 and he wanted to be allowed to watch R-rated movies. I knew in my gut this wouldn't be a good thing for him. He pulled out all the big guns and worked on me relentlessly: "All the kids can watch R-rated movies but me," "I'm the only one in the neighborhood who can't watch R-rated movies," "You're trying to keep me a baby, and I hate it!" and—are you ready for this one?—"I know what all that sexy stuff looks like anyway, so what are you trying to protect me from?"

By the time he was finished, I really did wonder if I was the only parent in the entire neighborhood who didn't have the good sense to let her 10-year-old watch R-rated movies! So do you know what I did? I said no anyway, because that's what my gut told me to do. Afterward, I was glad I did.

Now let's take a look at how one husband and wife supported each other in saying no to their child when they knew it was the best thing to do:

Bill and Kathy have three children, ages 11, 7, and 5. Eleven-year-old Raymond tends to be high-strung and is very much influenced by his peers; there are times he tries to push his parents to their limits. Bill and Kathy are skilled parents and have agreed there are going to be times they'll choose to compromise with Raymond, but this will only happen if they believe compromising is truly in his best interests and their own. Bill and Kathy also know there will be other times when they'll choose to say no and deal with Raymond's reactions.

The issue of bedtime on weekends has been a rough one with Raymond. In fact, Bill and Kathy tried to compromise on this issue with him last Saturday night, and they realized afterward it was a big mistake. After agreeing to let him stay up until midnight, they woke him for church the next morning at 7:30. Raymond was so tired he could barely get out of bed. He argued with Bill and Kathy in the morning, begging them to let him miss Mass, something their family never does, and he ended up being cranky and irritable for the rest of the day. Bill and Kathy saw that Raymond was the kind of child who needed his sleep, regardless of his protestations.

The following Saturday night, Raymond was on the internet sending messages back and forth to his friends. At 10:30, Bill came into the room and said, "You need to turn the computer off now. It's time for bed and we all have to be up early for church tomorrow."

"What?" responded Raymond irately. "You're treating me like a baby. All my friends are gonna be on the internet without me. They're allowed to stay up as late as they want on weekends!"

"Sorry, Ray," Bill said gently but firmly. "We tried that last weekend and it was a disaster. You need to go to bed."

"I hate this!" yelled Raymond. "I'm the only kid on the block who has a bedtime on the weekends. Everyone else can stay up as late as they want except me! The other kids are gonna think I'm a loser!"

"I'm sorry you feel that way, Raymond, but you still need to go to bed. Remember last Sunday how exhausted you were and how much trouble you had getting up for church? In fact, you were tired the rest of the day."

"So? I don't care if I'm tired," Raymond said. "I just want to stay up now! Mom, what do you think?" He appealed to Kathy, hoping he could use the divide-and-conquer technique.

"Sorry, Ray. No is no, and that's that. Turn off the computer and go to bed," Kathy said in a no-nonsense voice as she looked Raymond square in the eye.

Raymond, realizing this was a lost cause, begrudgingly turned off the computer and headed for the bedroom, all the while complaining about how unfair his parent's were and how all the other kids were allowed to stay up late. Bill and Kathy held their ground, difficult as it was, and within moments of getting into bed, Raymond was fast asleep.

By holding their ground, Bill and Kathy had accomplished a number of important things:

– They didn't relinquish what they believed was in the best interests of their child, despite his protestations.
– They'd reinforced their parental authority in a firm but loving way, neither of them getting "hooked" by Raymond's reactions.
– They'd set a solid foundation for the future, showing their son they would stand by their decisions and by each other.

As Raymond gets older and is faced with things like driving a car and going to parties where alcohol might be available, Bill and Kathy will have set the stage for Raymond to understand that his parents mean it when they say no. As family therapist Renee Kevlis says, "It's a lot easier to say no to a defiant 11-year-old than to a six-foot-tall adolescent who's used to getting his way. If we don't exercise our authority when our kids are young, it's almost impossible to do so later."

Kevlis has seen many cases in which kids were completely out of control during their adolescence because they did not have consistent standards to live by when they were younger, and "no" didn't hold when it needed to.

"Without standards, limits, and the ability to say no, our children can get lost," she cautions.

On the other hand, if we say "no" too often, it loses its power. We run the risk of being tuned out, and we create an atmosphere of negativity. In order to save your no's for the times you need to use them the most, try the following options:

Give choices when you can.

"Adam, your room needs to be cleaned."

"I don't feel like cleaning my room today. Can I do it tomorrow?"

"It needs to be cleaned today. Would you like to do it before lunch or after?"

In this scenario, Mom does not say no to Adam's request to not clean his room. Instead, she lets him know that the job needs to be done, yet he has some choice as to when this will happen. Sometimes giving kids just a little extra leeway will help avoid a power struggle.

Provide alternatives to what your child is asking for.

"Mommy, can I have some cookies?"

"It's so close to dinner. Cookies aren't a good idea right now."

"But I'm hungry."

"How about an apple or some cheese to hold you over?"

"I really want cookies."

"Cookies aren't allowed before dinner. I can offer you fruit, cheese, or carrot sticks. Which would you like?"

By responding in this way, we can avoid rendering a flat-out no. At the same time, we're helping our children see what the acceptable alternatives are.

Help your child envision options for himself.

"I want to go in the pool now. Will you come outside and watch me?"

"I'm right in the middle of feeding the baby, so now isn't a good time. Maybe in 20 minutes."

"But I don't have anything to do."

"What else can you think of that would interest you until I can go outside and watch you?"

"I can't think of anything."

"What are your top three favorite things to do when you're by yourself?"

"Legos, video games, or playing with my Beanie Babies. But I don't want to do any of them. I just want to go in the pool."

"Tell you what. I'll set the timer for 20 minutes. Choose one of those activities just till the timer goes off, and then we'll go straight to the pool. Being able to wait will make me very proud of you."

Helping our children envision options is a creative process, one that will aid them in other parts of their lives. When you consistently encourage your children to think creatively and look for options, they begin learning how to do this on their own.

Grant in fantasy what you can't in reality.

This is a wonderful technique developed by child psychologist Haim Ginott. Here's an example of this in action.

"I really want to get Play Station. All the kids have it. Will you buy it for me?"

"Play Station is very expensive, and right now we can't afford to buy it for you."

"But I really want it. All my friends have it, and I feel bad that I don't."

"I wish I had all the money in the world so I could buy you whatever you wanted. I'd go out right now and buy you *two* Play Stations if I could."

By granting in fantasy what we can't in reality, we're letting our child know we understand her desires and would love to grant them if we could. This gives an entirely different message than a flat-out no.

Exercise:

Are there particular times when you have trouble saying no? Why?

Are there any particular issues that are more difficult to deal with in this regard (bedtime, meals, cleaning up, friends, etc.)?

Envision yourself handling difficult situations more effectively. Write about what you envisioned.

Following Through on What We Say

Consistency in following through on what we say we're going to do creates solid ground and sends a clear message to our children: I am the parent, and I expect you to listen. When we crumble, the ground beneath our feet becomes shaky, fault lines develop, and power struggles result.

Sandra and 5-year-old Amy had a lunch date with Sandra's friend Clarissa and her 6-year-old daughter Sophie. Although Amy behaved well throughout most of lunch, when dessert time came along, things began to change. Sandra told Amy she could have a small ice cream sundae if she would promise to eat it carefully and not get any on her new white shirt. Amy quickly gave her promise, but when the sundae was delivered, she abandoned her spoon and began dipping her index finger into the chocolate syrup.

"No fingers, Amy. Use your spoon," Sandra cautioned. "If you don't eat carefully, I'm going to take the ice cream away."

But as soon as Sandra turned around, Amy quietly dipped her finger back into the chocolate syrup, which started to drip down her hand.

A moment later, when Sandra caught sight of the chocolate syrup dripping down her daughter's wrist, she was livid. Not wanting to provoke Amy, she stuffed down her feelings and tried to ignore what was happening. She prayed Amy would stop by herself, but Amy didn't. Finally Sandra turned to her with a mixture of fury and trepidation and said, "OK, Amy, that's it. No more ice cream."

"Don't take my ice cream away," squealed Amy in a loud voice. "I'll use my spoon, see?" she added, picking it up.

Not wanting to cause a scene, Sandra reluctantly relented again. "All right, Amy, one more chance," she said. But before long, as Sandra drifted back into relaxed conversation with Clarissa, Amy stuck her finger right back into the ice cream.

"Amy, didn't I say I was going to take that ice cream away if you didn't use your spoon? Do you want me to do that?" said Sandra, wanting to shout, but letting the words hiss out of her instead, like steam from a radiator.

"OK, OK, I'll use my spoon. Do you have to be so mean?" responded Amy.

"You'd better," barked Sandra as she turned back to Clarissa one more time, attempting to pick up her lost thread of conversation.

Fully in control now, Amy used her spoon for about two minutes, but as she and her friend Sophie giggled, she very subtly put her spoon back on the table and very lightly put her finger back into the sundae. Chocolate fingerprints appeared all over her new white blouse.

When Sandra looked up and saw this she finally lost her cool. "That's it, Amy, I'm taking the ice cream away. Give me that bowl!" she yelled, reaching toward it.

Amy grabbed the bowl tightly and held on to it with both hands. "Please let me keep my ice cream!" she wailed. "I'll be good, I promise!"

Sandra, not wanting to prompt any more of a scene, gave in against her better judgment, allowing Amy to keep the ice cream despite her continued threats and warnings.

By caving in, Sandra enabled Amy to win the battle—for the moment. But in the long run, Amy actually lost. Here's why: By relinquishing her parental authority, Sandra guarantees future power struggles with Amy. Someday, this may lead to out-of-control behavior on Amy's part. Amy could end up crossing boundaries as an adolescent that might have serious repercussions in her life.

The message Amy gets each time Sandra ignores her own threats is that if she persists in her defiance, she will eventually wear her mother down. Thus Amy's manipulative behavior is reinforced. By allowing Amy to ignore what she says, and by ignoring her own admonitions herself, Sandra is setting herself up to relive the above scenario over and over again.

By the time Amy is 15, Sandra will have very little power, if any, over Amy's behavior—and that's a scary prospect. Hard as it is to say no to our kids and follow through, it is absolutely essential that we do so when the situation warrants. Ultimately, when we stand by our convictions about the limits of acceptable behavior, we help our children become responsible, respectful people.

Now let's see how the above scenario may have turned out had Sandra handled it differently. Imagine for a moment that Sandra has gained some insight into what it takes to become a peaceful parent and raise peaceful kids. She's clear on what her standards are and has made her standards clear to her children. Sandra also has become comfortable setting limits and following through on what she says.

Aside from this, Sandra has begun having family meetings where she and her children have set Guidelines for a Peaceful Family. In fact, by now Sandra's family is regularly expressing their growing commitment to peacemaking.

Imagine that in the face of all these changes, Amy, who has always been strong willed, is now starting to become less resistant, more cooperative. Sandra still occasionally questions her ability to set limits for Amy, but her confidence in doing so is growing. Her positive goal statements have helped: "I trust what I need to do in managing my children's behavior." Let's see how the scenario plays itself out now.

Amy: *"Mommy, I'd like a chocolate sundae for dessert."*
Sandra: *"I know how much you'd enjoy that, but you're wearing your new white shirt. Maybe vanilla would be a better choice."*
Amy: *"I promise to be careful, Mommy."*
Sandra: *"OK, but I expect you to be extra careful, because chocolate stains."*
Amy begins eating her ice cream with a spoon but before long dips her finger into it, testing her limits.
Sandra responds immediately with a balance of firmness and gentleness. She turns her body to face Amy, looks directly into her eyes, and clearly says, "Amy, the ice cream must be eaten with a spoon."
Amy once again begins eating with her spoon but then tries dipping her finger back into the ice cream, all the while watching for her mother's reaction.
Sandra gives her a warning this time. Once again she looks directly at Amy and says firmly but calmly, "Amy, I'm going to take the ice cream away if you put your fingers back in it again."
Amy, wanting to see if Sandra will actually follow through on what she said, tries one more time to eat the ice cream with her finger. This time, Sandra quietly lifts the bowl off the table and signals for the waitress to take it away.
Amy bursts into tears and wails, "I want my ice cream back!"
Sandra: *"Sorry, Amy, you didn't listen."*
Amy: *"But I'll use my spoon. I promise."*
Sandra: *(lowering her voice, and looking directly at Amy with conviction)* *"Sorry, Amy. You can't have the ice cream."*
Amy: *(getting louder)* *"But I wasn't finished. There's still half a bowl left!"*
Sandra: *(calmly, firmly, maintaining a tone of evenness and conviction)* *"Sorry, Amy, you can't have it back. You didn't listen, and we're not discussing it anymore."*
At this point Sandra turns her back to Amy and decides to let her wail a little. She makes sure to completely ignore her as she does.
Amy continues to cry and complain, but soon Sandra looks directly into Amy's eyes and firmly says, "That's enough. If this goes on much longer I'm taking you to the car."
Sandra turns away from Amy and continues her conversation, ignoring any further protestations. She is fully prepared to carry Amy

out to the car and let her cry there if necessary. Amy finally calms down, realizing that her mom means what she says.

In time, Amy will start giving up whining, begging, crying, cajoling, and any other kind of manipulative fussing, because they never seem to get her what she wants. She is learning that Mom follows through, and the next time Mom tells her to do something, she will listen a little better.

Exercise:

How are you at "following through"? Are there any issues you have trouble doing this with? Write about them and reflect on what you can do differently.

If Your Child Ignores What You Say

If this happens, first make her aware in a firm but nonpunitive way she is doing something wrong. Avoid put-downs, labels, or any kind of derogatory statements. Just state the facts firmly, clearly, and respectfully, as Sandra did in the second scenario: "The ice cream is supposed to be eaten with a spoon, not your fingers."

If your child continues to misbehave, give a warning and state what the consequences of her action will be if it happens again: "I'm going to take the ice cream away if you put your fingers back in it again."

At this point, if your child chooses to ignore what you have said, then it is crucial for you to follow through. If you say you're going to take away the ice cream, then do it the first time your child sticks her fingers back into the ice cream after your warning. *No second chances now.*

If you keep giving second chances, you'll encourage manipulation and will give your child the message that if she whines and fusses enough, you'll back off. Not a good thing for her, and an even worse thing for you.

Also, be brief. Don't let your child pull you into long protracted dialogues. Say what you need to say, listen to what she has to say, discuss it briefly, and then stop. If your child continues nagging at you after that, make a simple statement like, "That's it. The discussion is over," and then ignore her.

If she really starts getting on your nerves, send her to her room when possible, or walk away. Engaging in long verbal volleys only increases power struggles and encourages your child to carry on more. If you try all these things consistently and your child is still openly defiant on a regular basis, you may want to consider seeking outside help—a perfectly viable and respectable option, an option I've chosen in my own family when it's been warranted. More on this in Chapter 10.

Trust Your Own Judgment

As parents we need to recognize that *we* are the adults and we know what's best for our children. We must be careful not to allow our child's resistance to cause us to doubt ourselves. Remember, setting limits will help our children become better people. If you have any doubt about this, think back to the story of the marshmallow test.

A cautionary note here: Please don't link the concept of limit-setting with the kind of authoritarian parenting that says "I'm the parent and what I say goes" under all circumstances and in defiance of reason. If we believe compromising is the best choice in a particular circumstance, we can certainly compromise, but there will be other times our best judgment will guide us toward setting a limit. If we do so, it doesn't mean we're being dictatorial.

A wise father of five grown children recalled what he told them when they were young: "Some things are nonnegotiable. That's the way society is. There are laws you will have to live by in life, and learning how to do so starts right here in our home." He and his wife trusted their judgment, not allowing their children to negotiate issues they deemed nonnegotiable. By being firm, fair, and loving, they allowed their children to grow up to be effective, successful people.

Trust your own judgment, and your children will too.

Compromise When You Believe It Is the Best Thing to Do

As I've said, there will be times when you'll decide that compromising is the fair and appropriate thing to do. The caveat here is that we mustn't let our children force us into compromising when we feel that doing so would be inappropriate. This isn't compromising, it's giving in against our own better judgment because our child has worn us down—always a mistake.

As psychologist Haim Ginott says, "When a child is allowed behavior that he knows should not be tolerated, his anxiety mounts." There will be times, however, when compromise is a reasonable option. Let's take a look at such a situation.

> *Carlos and Maria have told 9-year-old Jaime that he needs to do his chores every Saturday morning before going out to play with his friends. Jaime generally collects all the trash and puts it outside and he helps with the vacuuming. He is usually pretty good about his chores, but one Saturday morning he woke up and started watching a special show on TV. Carlos popped his head into the den at 10:00 and said, "OK, Jaime, time to start your chores."*
>
> *"I'm watching this show, Dad, and it's really good. Can't I keep watching it?"*
>
> *"I don't think so, Jaime. You have soccer practice at 12:30, and you have to get your jobs done before you leave," answered Carlos.*
>
> *"But my show will be over at 11:00 and I could help vacuum then," pleaded Jaime.*
>
> *"What about the trash? The garbage truck will be here before you know it," Carlos responded.*
>
> *"Can't I skip the trash just this once? Maybe I could do something else. This show is about whales, and you know how much I love whales. What do you think, Dad?" Carlos looked at Maria, and by the expression on her face, he could tell that what Jaime said was OK with her.*
>
> *"OK, Jaime," Carlos said. "But at 11:00 sharp, the TV goes off and the vacuum goes on. You can help me in the basement after that in place of the trash."*

Compromising in this case reinforced Jaime's sense of responsibility. He found a way to do his chores plus watch the show he wanted so badly to see. Carlos and Maria realized this, and rather than being stuck in a rigidly defined routine, they allowed Jaime the freedom to renegotiate his jobs. **Peaceful parenting thrives on the balance between authority and compromise.**

Keep Your Cool in the Face of Resistance

I'm going to share with you a highly effective technique to use when your child is resistant to something you've said and you don't feel that compromising would be appropriate. It's called "The Broken Record Technique." Explain to your child why you have made the decision you did, then make a simple declarative statement expressing your point: "Nine o'clock is your bedtime, and you need to go to bed now."

Repeat your statement without further explanation, *calmly and firmly* each time your child tries to argue, but don't let it go on too long. By using the broken record technique, you avoid engaging in a verbal power struggle while reinforcing your point.

The key here is to remain calm, firm, and unshaken by your child's resistance. And if you don't feel calm, fake it. That's right, "Fake it 'till you make it," as the saying goes, or, to borrow another cliche, "Never let them see you sweat." Teachers do this all the time. Inside your heart might be pounding a mile a minute, but you still somehow manage to project a cool exterior. After a while it gets easier.

Try practicing this technique ahead of time in front of a mirror, watching your body language and facial expression. It's essential that you feel (or at least appear) in control of your own reactions when you respond to your child, conveying to him or her that you are the parent and you have made your decision. You can say, "There will be other decisions you will get to make, but this isn't one of them." Here's an example of this technique in action:

> *Eleven-year-old Lisa has been invited to her friend's birthday party. "All my friends are allowed to wear makeup to parties and I want to wear it, too," Lisa says to her mom, Margie.*
>
> *Margie and her husband are both teachers, and they have very strong feelings about this, having seen too many kids growing up too fast, moving from makeup to "making out" and more. Margie and Ken want their children to maintain their innocence as long as possible.*
>
> *Margie decides to hear her daughter out first, letting her express her feelings and showing that she is listening. "I know how much you would like to wear makeup to the party, especially seeing your friends being allowed to wear it."*
>
> *Lisa replies, "Please, Mom. I don't want to feel like I'm the only one who can't, like I'm a baby or something."*
>
> *"I understand how you feel," Margie says gently, "but makeup isn't allowed in our house till you're a little older."*
>
> *"But, Mom, all the girls will be wearing it," appeals Lisa.*
>
> *"Sorry, Lisa, but makeup isn't allowed in our house till you're older."*
>
> *"You're treating me like I'm a baby!" Lisa says.*
>
> *"I'm sorry you feel that way, but makeup isn't allowed in our house till you're older, and that's it."*
>
> *At that, Lisa stomps off into her room and sulks for about 15 minutes. Before long, Margie overhears her on the phone with one of her*

*friends saying, "I'm not allowed to wear makeup either." Margie is
glad she stood her ground.*

To use the broken record technique effectively, it's essential to stand
confident in the knowledge that you are the parent and your decision is in
the best interests of your child. Margie knew that allowing Lisa to wear
makeup would not be a good thing for her. She felt bad that Lisa was as
concerned as she was about what her friends might say, but this was all the
more reason to stand by her own convictions. She thought ahead to other
decisions Lisa would be confronted with in the face of her peers, and realized this would be the first of many as Lisa walks the bumpy path toward
adolescence.

Try this: Close your eyes and picture yourself standing tall and firm in
the face of your child's objections to something you have said no to. Picture
yourself owning your full parental authority and calmly reiterating what
you told your child without reacting. Imagine yourself feeling whole,
strong, and confident in your decision. Picture your child benefiting from
your ability to do this, now and as life goes on.

Peaceful Parenting Key #10:
I have fair, reasonable consequences
for negative behaviors
which I only use when necessary.
~

Using Consequences

*Four-year-old Tamera is a dawdler. Her mother, Joyce, is con-
stantly struggling to get Tamera to do the things she's supposed to do
on time.*

*This is particularly frustrating when Joyce has to get right out the
door, like today. While Joyce dresses 2-year-old James for his doctor's
appointment, she calls into the next room to remind Tamera to hurry
up and get her shoes on.*

"OK, Mommy," calls Tamera.

*However, when Joyce appears at Tamera's door, baby in her arms,
ready to start putting coats on, Tamera is still sitting on the floor
playing with Barbies, her shoes at her side.*

"Tamera, if you don't get your shoes on this minute you're not

going to Kara's birthday party later! Did you hear me, Tamara? I mean it! I'm sick and tired of your constant dawdling, and I'm not going to put up with it anymore!" shouts Joyce.

Tamera bursts into tears and starts pleading to be allowed to go to her friend's party.

As Joyce looks at her daughter, red-faced and distraught, she realizes immediately she has made a threat that she in no way wants to follow through on. She realizes, too, that she was reacting in haste and not thinking clearly.

Had she taken a moment to cool off, Joyce might have told Tamera she wouldn't be able to watch TV later, or better yet might have taken away her Barbies for the rest of the day. Each of these consequences would have been far more fair and reasonable than the one she had so impulsively levied.

We can avoid this kind of scenario by taking the following steps:

Using Consequences Effectively

Prepare ahead of time.

Think about what consequences you might use in a variety of situations. You can even do this with your children. Sometimes kids come up with far more stringent consequences for themselves than parents would ever think of. But that's not what we're after. We want our children's involvement so that any consequences they are given are meaningful and help build a sense of responsibility.

Let your children know what kinds of behaviors will generally warrant a consequence.

Eric and Evelyn sat down and talked to their children about what standards of behavior they expected of them. They were very clear on what was acceptable and unacceptable. Eric said, "We let the kids know that there's no talking back to mom or dad, no physical fighting, and no saying no when mom or dad tells you to do something. We talked about this at one of our family meetings, and we let the kids know there would be a loss of privileges if any of these things happened."

They even asked the children to suggest what kinds of privileges could be taken away as a consequence. The children came up with dessert, TV, and staying up later on weekends.

Stop, breathe, and "chill out" before reacting to your child's negative behavior.

By giving yourself some distance from your emotions, you will substantially cut down on your own chances of overreacting. If you have to walk out of the room for a minute before saying anything, do it. *This will enable you to address your child's negative behavior from a base of internal control.* In doing so, you'll ameliorate further escalation of the problem while providing valuable role modeling.

Don't ignore behaviors that warrant a consequence.

As we talked about before, sometimes we let things go by that we shouldn't. Each time we do so, we reinforce negative behaviors in our children.

Before they came to an understanding of this, Eric and Evelyn found themselves reinforcing defiance in their 9-year-old son, Sean. For example, one night Sean said to his mother, "No, I'm not going to do my homework."

Evelyn let it go, not wanting to engage in a power struggle. The following night, however, the same thing happened. By allowing Sean to say no to her without a consequence, Evelyn enabled him to lay his first building block in a foundation of resistance.

Eric and Evelyn decided to have a family meeting about this. They told Sean saying no to his parents was absolutely not allowed and would be punished by the loss of all computer privileges for a whole day should it happen again.

Testing his limits, Sean tried saying no to homework once again the following week. This time Evelyn followed through with the consequence, even though Sean complained. After that, homework became less of a problem, and Sean's defiance lessened. The more Eric and Evelyn held their ground, the more Sean came around.

Make sure the consequences you have laid out are fair and reasonable.

If possible, consequences should be related to the behavior that's being punished. For example, if your 10-year-old didn't pick up his clothes after you asked him to do so three times, grounding him for a week would be excessive. More appropriate would be having him clean his room instead of going outside. Follow the three R's of consequences by making them *re*asonable, *re*spectful, and *re*lated.

Exercise:

What are some reasonable consequences you might have in your home? Write about this.

Concluding Thoughts

Raising peaceful kids requires a balance of wisdom and judgment. We can trust ourselves to make good decisions about disciplining our children when our actions are guided by love, compassion, fairness, respect, and integrity.

Recap

Peaceful Parenting Key #9:
*I always remember
that I am the parent
and I deserve to be listened to.*
~

Peaceful Parenting Key #10:
*I have fair, reasonable consequences
for negative behaviors
which I use only when necessary.*
~

Using the following strategies will help build positive discipline:

– Say no when you need to, but don't overuse it.
– Avoid overusing no in the following ways:
    Give choices when you can.

Help your child envision options for himself.

Grant in fantasy what you can't in reality.

– Follow through on what you say you're going to do.

– Compromise when you believe it is the best thing to do.

– Mean what you say.

– Trust your own judgment.

– Keep your cool in the face of resistance.

– Have fair, reasonable consequences for negative behavior.

– Use consequences effectively by:

Preparing ahead of time.

Letting your children know what kinds of behaviors will generally warrant a consequence.

Stopping, breathing, and cooling off before reacting to your child's negative behavior.

Not ignoring behaviors that warrant a consequence.

Making sure the consequences you have laid out are fair and reasonable.

RESOURCES FOR PARENTS:

Adams, Christine. *Parenting*. New Harbinger, 1996. Discover why children act out and behave aggressively. Find out how to build cooperation, self-control, and respect.

Clark, Jean Illsey. *Time-In: When Time-Out Doesn't Work*. Parenting Press, 1999. Offers insights into what children need from adults in their lives; provides four components of a "Time-In" system.

Coloroso, Barbara. *Kids Are Worth It! Giving Your Child the Gift of Inner Discipline*. New York: William Morrow, 1994. How to enhance your child's internal motivation and develop a nurturing atmosphere in the home.

Gordon, Thomas. *Teaching Children Self-Discipline*. New York: Random House, 1989. Strategies for helping children internalize self-discipline.

Whitham, Cynthia. *Win the Whining War & Other Skirmishes: A Family Peace Plan*. Los Angeles: Perspective Pub., 1991. Concrete suggestions for handling bad behaviors in an assertive, effective manner.

Wolf, Anthony E. *It's Not Fair, Jeremy Spencer's Parents Let Him Stay Up All Night!* New York: William Morrow, 1995. Practical strategies for positive discipline. Engaging and humorously written.

RESOURCES FOR CHILDREN

Crary, Elizabeth. *Children's Problem Solving Series.* Seattle: Parenting Press, 1996. Each book in this series helps children find solutions to common problems:

I'm Lost — *I Want It*
I Can't Wait — *I Want to Play*
Mommy Don't Go — *My Name Is Not Dummy*
(Grades K–3)

————. *Dealing with Feelings Series.* Seattle: Parenting Press, 1994. Each book in this series helps children discover acceptable, creative ways to express their feelings:

I'm Mad — *I'm Furious*
I'm Frustrated — *I'm Scared*
I'm Proud — *I'm Excited*
(Grades K–3)

Danziger, Paula. *Everyone Else's Parents Said Yes.* New York: Delacorte Press, 1989. Matthew uses practical jokes to get revenge for things he finds unfair. (Grades 2–5)

CHAPTER 6

Fostering Good Listening Skills

*When someone deeply listens to you
it is like holding out a dented cup
you've had since childhood
and watching it fill up with
cold fresh water.*

—John Fox, *Spiritual Literacy*

Peaceful Parenting Key #11:
***I listen with all my heart to what
my children have to say, and teach
them to be good listeners for others.***
~

Listening is a gift we can give our children anytime we wish. Each time we give the gift of listening, we build our children's sense of self-worth. By being good listeners ourselves, we model for our children the most essential part of good communication. Listening forms the basis for positive relationships throughout life. When we truly listen to our children, listening with all our hearts, we strengthen their loving connection to us over time.

A good friend of mine once told me how she'd always felt valued and loved in the presence of her father. She said he'd had a way of treating her that made her feel very special.

"What was it about him that made you feel that way?" I asked.

Thinking for a moment, she replied, "It was the way he used to listen:

> *I remember one time my father came into my room to say 'Good night.' As he sat on the edge of my bed, I started talking to him about my day and told him some things that were bothering me at school. My father sat quietly and just listened, soaking in every word. He didn't seem distracted, he didn't interrupt, he didn't give advice, he simply listened with his fullest attention. When I was finished talking he said, 'I liked hearing about what was on your mind, and I hope tomorrow you'll tell me more.'*
>
> *I remember being so touched by my father's interest in me. The way he listened to me had such depth. And the fact that he wanted to hear more . . . His words have remained in my mind even now that he is gone. His intense listening to the simple details of my day, I'll never forget that."*

How many of us have had this kind of experience? Probably not many. Here's an experience that might be more familiar. In describing a recent visit with her mother, Cara said:

> *I'm never comfortable around my mother. Every time I tell her something, she either gives me her opinion or takes my words and turns them into a story about herself. Like the other day, I was telling her about a trip I just got back from. Instead of listening, she just interrupted and started talking about a trip she had taken. Each time I tried to tell her more, she would interrupt me and talk about herself. Finally I gave up. Afterward I thought about how discounted I usually feel in my mother's presence, almost invisible.*

Does this sound more familiar? I have had many experiences like Cara's, and can fully identify with her feelings of near invisibility in the presence of someone who doesn't listen.

Sometimes people listen for a while and then feel compelled to give an opinion or advice of some kind. In this vein, Jack had the following story to share:

> *I finally stopped telling my father about problems I had. He would never fully listen to me, and he'd constantly offer opinions. Sometimes I just needed to get something off my chest and then figure out the solution for myself. When my father would jump in and tell me what to do, it was like he was trying to tell me I couldn't figure things out for myself. I'd always walk away feeling a little less adequate.*

As psychologist Michael P. Nichols, author of *The Lost Art of Listening*, says, "Speaking without listening, hearing without understanding is like snipping an electrical cord in two, then plugging it in anyway, hoping that something will light up." This type of listening builds chasms rather than bridges.

Think about your own life. Have you ever noticed that the people you like to be with the most are the people who take an interest in you? And how do they express that interest? By listening with care and openness, not just by simply hearing your words. They stay focused on you, making full eye contact, often nodding as you speak. They don't interrupt—in fact, just the opposite. When you're finished, it's almost like they want to hear more. These are the people we all like to be around the most, and these are the people we most need to *be* for our children.

People, particularly children, want more than anything to be listened to fully, completely, and without judgment. When we sincerely listen to our children, it gives them a sense of being loved, validates their personhood, and builds their self-esteem. Why? Because true, deep listening conveys to our children that they are worthy of being heard and that what they have to say is important.

How do we listen fully? How do we teach our children to listen this way, too? By modeling, practicing, and teaching the following five steps:

Give the person who is speaking your full attention.

Make good eye contact and don't allow yourself to be distracted. Turn your body toward the speaker. Let your body language show that what the person is saying is of prime interest to you.

Listen with all your heart.

Make what the other person is saying your fullest priority. Don't allow your thoughts to drift to what you are going to say next, what you have to do later, or what you did before. Stay focused on the other person.

Don't interrupt.

So often when someone else is speaking, we want to jump in and say what's on our mind. Resist that temptation. It only serves to make the speaker feel frustrated. Let the person finish before you start to speak.

Practice active listening.

When the other person speaks, nod your head and show interest. Then reflect back what they said by paraphrasing what you just heard. This simple technique builds empathy and trust.

Don't judge what the other person has said.

Allow them to have their own opinions, insights, and perceptions. You might not agree with everything they say, but you need to grant them their right to say it. When you do so, mutual trust and communication increase.

Teachers around the country have seen that when they teach and practice these five simple principles, the overall climate in the classroom improves and incidents of conflict lessen. By consistently practicing and reinforcing these skills, you'll find the same results in your home.

Exercise:

> *How do you feel when you are truly listened to? Write about this. In what ways can you improve your listening?*

The Good Listening Game

How can we teach and reinforce good listening in our children? Here's a great activity your whole family will enjoy and learn a lot from. In this game, you will get to demonstrate the difference between good listening and bad listening by acting each out for your children. Here's how:

At a family meeting, talk about what it feels like when we're truly listened to. Encourage your children to describe experiences of being listened to and experiences of the opposite. Tell your children you're going to demonstrate bad listening for them (have fun with this). Ask your spouse or one of your children, "What's your favorite place you've ever been to?" Then ask him to describe this place, telling you about the last time he was there.

As you demonstrate bad listening, be sure to do the following things:

– don't pay attention
– interrupt

- change the subject
- don't make eye contact
- act disinterested
- cross your arms and legs so you look unreceptive
- turn your body slightly away from the speaker
- fidget
- ask questions about things they already told you
  ("Where did you say you went?")
- think about what you are going to say next

After you're finished, ask your family what "bad listening" behaviors they observed. Ask the person you role played with how it felt to not be heard. List all the bad listening traits your family observed, then ask people if they recognize themselves in any of these traits.

Next, role play good listening. Ask the same question you did before, but this time be sure to use the following good listening strategies:

- look directly at the speaker
- make good eye contact
- have your body language be open and receptive
- suspend your own thoughts and focus intently on what the speaker is saying
- don't interrupt or tell stories of your own
- ask relevant questions at appropriate times
- nod as the person speaks
- encourage the speaker to tell you more
- sit still and lean forward, toward the speaker
- if distracting thoughts come into your mind, let them go and bring your attention back to the speaker

Now ask your family to identify all the things they noticed you doing as a good listener. Talk about how this scenario differed from the first. Ask the person you role played with what it felt like to be truly listened to. Discuss all these questions at length. *Let your children know that good listeners have more friends, do better in school, and generally get along better with the people they know.*

Good Listening Chart for Adults:

The Ten Elements of Good Listening

1. Look directly at the speaker.
2. Make good eye contact.
3. Have your body language be open and receptive.
4. Suspend your own thoughts and focus intently on what the speaker is saying.
5. Don't interrupt or tell stories of your own.
6. Ask relevant questions at appropriate times.
7. Nod as the person speaks.
8. Encourage the speaker to tell you more.
9. Sit still and lean forward, toward the speaker.
10. If distracting thoughts come into your mind, let them go and bring your attention back to the speaker.

Good Listening Chart for Kids:

Here's What Good Listeners Do:

1. Look at the person who is speaking.

2. Think about what he or she is saying.

3. Don't interrupt.

4. Keep focusing on the speaker and don't let yourself get distracted.

Fostering Good Listening Skills in Your Children

After you've begun the practice of family meetings, played The Good Listening Game, and modeled good listening for your children, how do you help them maintain good listening skills as a lifelong habit? Here are four ways to encourage your children daily:

Eye contact

Eye contact sets the stage for what is going to be said and gives the speaker a sense of being recognized.

One way to help your child develop the habit of making good eye contact, is by giving good eye contact yourself and asking him to do the same. If your child tends to look away when you speak, gently take his chin and turn it toward you, and begin speaking when you have his full attention. Remind him each time to look directly at you, and when he starts to do so on his own, acknowledge him specifically with loving praise.

If your child is uncomfortable giving eye contact, tell him it's OK to look at your mouth or chin instead. Some children need to build up to looking directly at the eyes. Each time he makes any kind of eye contact, even if for a brief moment, compliment him. Let him know how good it makes you feel when he looks at you. Also, touch him while he talks to help him feel more comfortable. Hold his hand, stroke his shoulder, or touch his knee.

Good eye contact is particularly important when emotions like anger and upset are present. The first thing people usually do to break or hinder communication is look away, yet when they're accustomed to giving and receiving eye contact, they are less likely to remove it in the face of conflict.

By helping your child develop the habit of making good eye contact, you'll insure that the first step toward communication already is in place when conflicts arise. Believe it or not, the simple act of looking at each other is one of the first steps toward resolving conflicts. More on this in Chapter 8.

Body Language

Body position and body language are critical forms of nonverbal communication, as well. When our body language is open, it enhances communication; when body language is closed, communication shuts down. Let me reiterate for a moment what open body language looks like:

- You are positioned in the direction of the other person.
- Your arms and legs are uncrossed.
- Your head is tilted toward the other person.

– You are leaning slightly toward the other person.
– Your hands and feet are relatively still, not fidgety.

Sometimes it's unrealistic to face your children as they talk to you, like when you're doing the dishes or throwing in a load of wash, but whenever possible, turn your body toward them, look directly at them as they speak, and ask that they do the same for you. Check in with yourself from time to time to notice if your body language remains open or tends to close off.

If you're preoccupied or rushed, your body language may be closed without your even realizing it. If you see this happening, readjust the way your body is positioned and shift your thinking into a listening mode. What's interesting is that your children will unconsciously mimic your own body language. Modeling receptivity toward your children's words will teach them to be receptive toward your words and the words of others.

Ask Them to Listen

When you give the gift of your own listening, it's easy to ask your children to give this gift back to you. As soon as they begin talking, you can start doing this. "Please look at me and listen to what I have to say," is a request you can make frequently. Let them know how good you feel when they listen to what you have to say. Your smiles and attention will continue to reinforce the habit of good listening.

At family meetings, it is particularly important that each person listen to the other. A technique that some parents and teachers use to foster this is called "Hold the Ball." Get a ball of any size (you can substitute any object you like) and tell your family that each time a person gets a turn to speak, she will hold the ball. As long as the speaker is holding it, everyone else needs to look at her, listen to what she's saying, and not interrupt. When she is finished speaking, she passes the ball to the next person.

This technique is highly effective, because it provides a visual reminder for other family members to wait their turn, suspend their own thoughts, and focus on the speaker. When your child sees the ball in her brother's hand, she will have an immediate signal to do all of these, and so will you.

Affirming

Catch your child in the act of good listening and affirm him for it *immediately, specifically,* and *sincerely*. By doing so, you'll reinforce good listening habits and help insure that they continue.

"I'm so pleased with the way you're listening to what I have to say.

You're looking directly at me, and you seem to be concentrating very hard on what I'm talking about. That makes me feel you care. I really appreciate being listened to the way you're listening to me right now." This kind of acknowledgment is worth a thousand reprimands and will help bring about more of the positive behavior you just praised.

Here's why: Each time you affirm, you enable your child to see her own positive qualities and behaviors. Your child's self-esteem grows, and she begins internalizing the intrinsic reward of being a good listener.

> **Exercise:**
>
> *Which of the elements of good listening do your children need to work on most (focusing, not interrupting, etc.)?*
>
> *How do you plan to help your children improve their listening skills? Write about this.*

Reflective Listening

When you want to make your child feel truly understood, try this: listen very carefully to what she has to say. When she is finished, paraphrase what you heard and say it back to her. Don't include advice, judgments, or related stories. Just listen, focus, and paraphrase.

This may be hard to do, especially if your child has a problem. Often we want to jump in and fix whatever the problem is, but providing a solution isn't always the most effective way to help. What will help is listening with an open mind, reflecting back what we hear, and guiding our child toward her own solutions whenever possible.

Through this process, children get to vent feelings, examine options, engage in critical thinking, and problem solve. Thus we empower them to think critically and to think for themselves. The outcome is responsibility, autonomy, and independence.

Beyond all else, the simple act of reflective listening helps our children feel understood. Here's an example:

> ***Paul:*** *I had the worst day ever at school. First, I thought I forgot my homework and the teacher yelled at me. The whole time it was in my book bag. Then I banged my knee on my desk. But the worst thing was that I had an argument with Matthew and now he's not talking to me.*

Mom: It sounds like it was an awful day between your homework, your knee, and Matthew. That's a lot.

*Paul: It **was** awful. I wish I'd never gone to school at all today!*

Mom: You wish you could have just missed this awful day?

Paul: That's right. Now I'm afraid Matthew won't make up with me.

Mom: You sound pretty worried.

Paul: I am. We've never had an argument like that before.

Mom: (intuiting that this would be an appropriate time to ask a question, but ready to back off if Paul's response indicates that it's not) Want to tell me what happened?

Paul: Well, we were playing basketball on the playground and when I went to make a shot, I accidentally elbowed Matthew in the nose. Then his nose started to bleed and he started yelling at me like I did it on purpose! But I didn't. It was an accident! And now he doesn't want to talk to me.

Mom: (resisting giving advice) I can see why you're so upset. What do you think you can do?

Paul: I guess I can try to talk to him tomorrow, maybe on the way to school, if I can get him to walk with me.

Mom: What might you say? (instead of suggesting something)

Paul: I could say I'm sorry and I didn't mean to hurt him and I just want to be friends.

Mom: Sounds good, Paul. How do you think he'll react if you say that? (encouraging him to perceive the outcome)

Paul: He'll probably still be a little miffed, but I bet he'll at least listen to me. I think he knows I would never do anything to hurt him on purpose.

Mom: Especially after you've been friends for so long. So you'll give it a try?

Paul: Do you think I should?

Mom: It sounds pretty reasonable to me. What do you think?

Paul: Might as well. He's already not talking to me. At least this might make things better.

Mom: I bet it will. Let me know.

By simply listening and reflecting back what she heard, Paul's mom opened the doors to communication and trust, eventually guiding Paul to his own solution. If she had jumped in too quickly with her own suggestions, she would have hindered Paul's opportunity to think for himself and come up with a logical solution to his problem.

What if Paul's solution doesn't work? Then Paul and his mom will probably engage in a similar discussion, this time looking at alternative solutions. In any event, Paul will be encouraged to think for himself, perceive outcomes, and engage in critical thinking, skills that will help him succeed in life.

Paul will most likely continue confiding in his mom because she listens empathically, without judging. In doing so, she opens the doors to trust and communication. There are times she may bite her tongue and hold back from giving advice so as not to shut her son down. By simply listening with an open heart and reflecting back what she hears, Paul's mom will continue to set the stage for deeper levels of communication and for his openness to her counsel when he needs it.

Teaching Kids Reflective Listening

Did you know children as young as five are being taught how to use reflective listening in schools where peacemaking is taught? With good listening, relationships thrive and kids have fewer conflicts, so schools are better able to do their jobs. Less time is then wasted on fights, arguments, and tattling—all of which take valuable time away from learning.

Here's a fun way to teach your children how to use reflective listening. It's a game for two players called "I Heard You Say . . ." Take turns being the speaker and the listener. The listener asks a question from the list below. The speaker answers; then the listener reflects back what was said, starting with the phrase, "I heard you say . . ."

Each time the listener accurately reflects back what he heard, the speaker gives a thumbs up. If the listener paraphrases incorrectly, then he must repeat the question, listen once again, and paraphrase correctly. This is also a great game for spouses to play. You'd be surprised how much your relationship will improve when you each listen more deeply and more empathically to the other.

"I Heard You Say . . ."

(Try to keep your answers relatively brief, or break them into parts that can be paraphrased a little at a time.)

What's your favorite thing to do when you have free time?
What is your earliest memory?
If you could be anything you wanted, what would you be and why?
What's your favorite holiday and why?
What's your favorite book and why?

What is something that really gets on your nerves and why?

If you could go anywhere in the world, where would it be and what would you do there?

Who is someone you really admire and why?

You can add your own questions to the list, but make sure they require more than a yes or no answer. Each time you play this game, you'll help your child master the complex skill of reflective listening while doing the same for yourself. You'll also be developing a great tool for resolving conflicts. More on this is in Chapter 8.

Open Listening

Have you ever noticed that some people listen with an open mind, but others, who appear to be listening, are really just waiting for their turn to speak? And some people listen but then close down communication by the way they respond. Open listening is actually based on a commitment to showing care toward another. Open listeners suspend their own agenda and allow themselves to be fully in the presence of the other person, just like my friend's father was—the one who sat on the edge of her bed and listened to what she had to say.

You always know when you're with someone who is an open listener because you feel good in her presence and you want to be around her more. How does an open listener listen? With sincere attention, empathy, care, and lack of judgment. An open listener develops the ability to suspend his or her own thoughts so they can fully listen.

As Michael P. Nichols says in *The Lost Art of Listening,* "To listen well we must forget ourselves . . ." Good listeners have the ability to do this. They have the confidence and patience to know that they'll get their turn to speak, and that by listening well, other people will take a greater interest in what they themselves have to say.

The Seven Biggest Blocks to Communication

The purpose of good listening is to open communication, build trust, and express care for the person being listened to, all essentials in peacemaking. Unfortunately, most people don't listen in this way. How do many people listen? Here are a few classic negative patterns, things to avoid especially when you listen to your children. Remember, too, that listening habits are like genes—we pass them on to our kids.

Criticizing

> **Nicole:** *(age 11, dressed in tight hip huggers, a midriff top, and lots of jewelry)* I'm going to Janie's house to hang out for a while. I'll be back before dinner.
>
> **Mom:** You're wearing **that**?
>
> **Nicole:** What do you mean **that**? I like what I'm wearing. It's cool.
>
> **Mom:** Young lady, you march right upstairs and change this minute. No daughter of mine is going out of the house dressed like some singer from MTV. Where do you think you are—at a nightclub?
>
> **Nicole:** What are you talking about? All the kids dress this way!
>
> **Mom:** Well you're not all the kids. If their parents let them going around looking cheap, that's their business. You're not leaving the house that way. Go up and change that disgusting outfit right now!
>
> **Nicole:** *(starting to cry)* **Cheap**! How could you call me that? You just don't want me to be cool like the other kids, that's all! You're the meanest mom on this whole block!

We all get upset when we see our children trying to grow up too fast. Power struggles like this one often surface in transitional periods like the one Nicole is going through. Nicole's mom is understandably upset, which is why it's especially important for her to back away from her immediate emotional reaction before responding to her daughter.

What Mom needs to do is stop, take some deep breaths, repeat a positive goal statement in her head, like "I remain calm in the face of problems," and then respond. *It's essential that she reclaim her bearings before saying a word.*

Instead of blatantly criticizing Nicole's outfit, Mom needs to make an "I statement" like, "I'm not comfortable seeing you in that outfit, Nicole. It's not appropriate. I'd like you to choose something else before you go to Janie's house." This is far less inflammatory than the statement she originally made. Nicole still might not like what her mother has to say, but her reactions will be less defensive and less emotional.

By choosing to communicate in a more neutral way, Mom will create a greater possibility of being able to maneuver Nicole into changing her clothes. Criticizing creates and intensifies power struggles, as we saw above.

Opinion-giving

> ***Sara:*** *(age 8) I'm worried about the spelling test we're going to have tomorrow.*
>
> ***Mom:*** *Don't be silly. You're good at spelling.*
>
> ***Sara:*** *But it's on all the words we've had this whole marking period.*
>
> ***Mom:*** *Did you study for it?*
>
> ***Sara:*** *I studied hard, but I'm still worried.*
>
> ***Mom:*** *Well, if you studied hard, you shouldn't be worried.*
>
> ***Sara:*** *But I can't help it. Tests scare me.*
>
> ***Mom:*** *Then just put it out of your mind and do something constructive like play the piano or read a book.*
>
> ***Sara:*** *But I don't want to play the piano or read a book. My stomach is in a knot.*
>
> ***Mom:*** *Oh, Sara, you're such a worrier. Isn't she a worrier, Henry?*

You be the judge—did this conversation help Sara? Will it enable her to cope with her fears or find a solution she's comfortable with? Will Sara be likely to go to her mother next time she's worried or upset about something? Will conversations like this deepen their relationship?

If you answered no to all of these questions, you're right. Sara's mom shut down communication and made Sara feel invalidated. Now Sara's worries about her test are compounded by two other negatives—bad feelings about herself for worrying too much, and irritation toward her mother. Sara might not even be consciously aware of the latter, or she may have vague feelings of annoyance around her mother and wonder why.

In a situation like this one, Sara's mother needed to hear her daughter out and encourage Sara to talk about her feelings, using reflective listening to validate them. She might have asked Sara what she could do to calm herself before the big test. After Sara fully expressed herself, then her mom could offer some helpful advice and soothing words—if Sara was open to them. Unsolicited opinions and advice are one of the biggest blocks to communication.

Preaching

> ***Daniel:*** *(age 6) I had to put my head down in school today.*
>
> ***Dad:*** *What did you do wrong?*
>
> ***Daniel:*** *Nothing. I just talked to the kid next to me during reading group.*

Dad: *You know you're not supposed to talk during reading group. Reading group is for reading, not for talking.*

Daniel: *But the book we were reading was* Frog and Toad, *and I have the same one at home. That's all I wanted to tell Jason.*

Dad: *Well, you must have interrupted the other kids, and you shouldn't have done that. Now the teacher is going to think you're a troublemaker. When I was your age, I never had to put my head down.*

Like Sara, Daniel will now think twice before confiding in his father, and if his father continues to interact with Daniel in this way, Daniel will soon start avoiding conversations with him altogether, noticing that somehow he feels bad about himself when he talks to his dad.

Fixing

Sejal: *(age 10) The kids were making fun of my snack today.*

Mom: *Why would they do that?*

Sejal: *Because it was different than the snacks they had.*

Mom: *Well, you just tell them to mind their own business.*

Sejal: *I can't do that! They'll think I'm mean, and then they'll be mean back to me.*

Mom: *Then I'm calling the teacher. I'm not going to let a bunch of fresh kids make fun of my daughter's snack.*

Sejal: *No, Mom! That would be awful. Then everyone would know you called and I'd really feel embarrassed.*

Mom: *Well then, you just march in there and tell the teacher yourself.*

Sejal: *(crying now) No! I'm not gonna do that, and if you do I'll never speak to you again!*

What Sejal needs here is to be supported in finding a solution she feels comfortable with. Although Sejal's mother has her best interests at heart, she's expressing them in an intrusive way that isn't helping Sejal come up with a workable solution. If Sejal wants her mother to intervene, she will let her know. For now, more than anything Sejal needs to be heard, understood, and empowered to seek solutions for the problem she's faced with.

Comparing

Tommy: *(age 9) I just found out I'm going to get a D in math.*

Dad: What? No one in our family has ever gotten a D before. Didn't you pay attention in class?

Tommy: I tried my best, but math is hard this year and I'm not good at long division.

Dad: Your brother had long division and **he** never got a D. You could learn something from him.

Tommy: No, I can't. I'll never be as good in math as he is. I'm not smart enough.

Tommy's feelings of inadequacy are being reinforced by his father's comments. Here again, a problem is compounded. Tommy feels bad about getting a D and worse that he can't be as smart as his brother. In this case, Tommy's dad needed to encourage Tommy to express his feelings of disappointment and then explore ways to help him do better in the future.

Denial

Ivan: (age 6) Daddy, I'm so mad at Ari, I could punch him in the nose. He spilled juice all over the best drawing I ever made, and it's ruined! I can't stand that baby!

Dad: You know you don't mean that, Ivan. Ari is only three. He didn't mean to spill juice on your picture.

Ivan: (raising his voice) I do mean it! If I wouldn't get punished, I'd beat him up right now. I really can't stand him. He always ruins things!

Dad: Come on, Ivan, you don't feel that way. You love your brother, so stop saying mean things about him.

Ivan: How do you know how I feel? You're not me!

This conversation is leaving Ivan feeling confused, guilty, and even more angry, because right now he really *can't* stand his brother. What Dad needs to do is acknowledge Ivan's feelings and let him feel what he feels in this moment. Dad needs to have faith in Ivan, and know that when he calms down, he'll realize for himself that he really doesn't hate his bother.

By validating Ivan's feelings, Dad would have gotten a better response:

Dad: I see you're very angry with Ari right now. You really loved that picture and now it's ruined.

Ivan: That's right. I'll never be able to draw one like it again. How could Ari be so dumb?

Dad: Did he realize he was going to knock the juice over?

Ivan: He wasn't paying attention, and now my picture is ruined. I can't stand him!
Dad: You're really upset with him, aren't you?
Ivan: I really am.

Here Dad is validating Ivan's feelings, which is exactly what Ivan needs so he can move beyond them.

Sometimes parents can be very uncomfortable about their children's negative feelings, especially toward a sibling. The fact remains, however, that we all have these feelings from time to time. Children need to express what they feel without hurting the person. Sometimes we can be a sounding board for this, and by doing so, we help our children let go of the anger that might eventually cause them to hurt one another.

Taking the focus away from the speaker and putting it on yourself.

Nina: (age 10) Guess what? I made the junior cheerleading team! Isn't that great?
Mom: That's great! I remember when I made cheerleading in high school. They didn't have junior cheerleading back then. Anyway, I was so excited because all the girls tried out and only a handful got picked and I was one of them. We had the best uniforms . . .
Nina: (trying to get a word in edgewise) Our uniforms are pink skirts and sweaters, with purple pompoms.
Mom: I remember when I got my first uniform. It was . . . (and so on)

By now the air has been taken out of Nina's sails, and the moment she was looking forward to—coming home and telling her mom about becoming a junior cheerleader—has been diminished. She has lost her moment to shine.

If you have seen yourself in any of the above scenarios, take heart. We all make mistakes, even in the face of good intentions. Each day is an opportunity for change and growth, and that's why you're reading this book. Be gentle with yourself and acknowledge yourself for any steps you are taking to shift negative patterns. Share your changes with your children. This will make it easier for them to come to you and share changes they're making. And always keep in mind that the path to peacemaking is nonlinear. As we move along it, we wind and weave into a new way of life.

Exercise:

Are there any blocks to communication that you find yourself doing? Write about this. After you do, picture yourself letting go of old patterns.

Effects of Good Listening in School

Lois, an elementary teacher for twenty-five years, became very animated when asked to talk about the impact good listening has in the classroom. Here's what she had to say:

> *Repeatedly over the years, I have noticed that kids who are good listeners do better in school. They are better able to take in information and process it, and they are better able to comprehend what is being taught. Good listeners internalize information and absorb details with greater ease. Even their friendships are positively impacted by their ability to listen. Because they listen to their peers, they are more equipped to work out problems and cooperate in group situations. Good listening is one of the most important skills a child can have.*

Lois's comments mirror hundreds I have heard from teachers around the country. By teaching good listening at home, we help our children as peacemakers and as students, giving them skills they will use for the rest of their lives.

Closeness Counts

When we listen to what our children have to say, we build closeness—something absolutely critical to their healthy development, particularly as they grow into adolescence. Did you know that family closeness helps teens resist the demons we fear most: drugs, alcohol, teen pregnancy, and more?

Peaceful parenting opens lines of communication, builds trust, and strengthens bonds. The resulting closeness is crucial in helping adolescents resist the "big demons." This was revealed in the largest study of its kind ever conducted: The National Longitudinal Study on Adolescent Health, which surveyed approximately 90,000 children ages 12 and up.

According to a *New York Times* article on the study's results, "The most significant finding is that the teenagers who reported feeling close to their families were the least likely to engage in any of the risky behaviors studied . . ." Dr. Robert Blum, director of the Adolescent Health Program at the University of Minnesota and a researcher for the study, said, "You need to give your kids the message that when they need to talk to you, you're available, even if it's by phone, and that they matter."

Of all the factors studied, *family closeness and the emotional connection between parent and child were the most significant in influencing adolescent behavior.* So next time you think you're too busy to listen to your child, remember this. Over the long run, it may be the most important thing you can do.

Recap

Peaceful Parenting Key #11:
I listen with all my heart to what my children have to say, and teach them to be good listeners for others.

~

Remember that listening is a gift we can give our children anytime we wish.

To model good listening:
– Give the person who is speaking your full attention.
– Listen with all your heart.
– Don't interrupt.
– Practice active listening.
– Don't judge what the other person has said.

To foster good listening skills in your children, do the following:
– Teach them to make good eye contact.
– Model receptive body language.
– Ask them to listen.
– Catch them in the act of good listening and affirm them immediately, specifically, and sincerely.

Teach and practice the art of reflective listening.
Be an "Open Listener."
Avoid the seven biggest blocks to communication:
– criticizing
– opinion-giving
– preaching

– fixing
– comparing
– denial
– taking what your child says and making it about yourself

Remember that good listening helps kids succeed in school.

RESOURCES FOR PARENTS

Burley, Allen and Madelyn. *Listening: The Forgotten Skill*. John Wiley and Sons, 1995. Excellent techniques for mastering the essentials of good listening.

Faber, Adele and Mazlish, Elaine. *How to Talk So Kids Will Listen & Listen So Kids Will Talk*. New York: Avon Books, 1982. Communication skills based on the work of Haim Ginott. Dialogues, anecdotes, and good sound advice.

Nichols, Michael, *The Lost Art of Listening*. New York: The Guilford Press, 1998. If you're going to read one book on becoming a better listener, read this one. Excellent, well-written, and practical.

Tannen, Deborah. *You Just Don't Understand: Women and Men in Conversation*. New York: Random House, 1991. An acclaimed sociologist tells us why men and women have trouble communicating and what we can do about it.

Van Pelt, Nancy. *How to Talk so Your Mate Will Listen, and Listen so Your Mate Will Talk*. Baker Books, 1989. Since modeling is key, find out how to employ listening and communication skills in your relationship with your partner.

RESOURCES FOR CHILDREN

Adams, Lisa K. *Dealing With Someone Who Won't Listen*. The Rosen Group, 1998. A book that tells kids what they can do when someone in their lives doesn't listen to them. (Grades K–4)

Baylor, Byrd. *The Other Way to Listen*. New York: Simon & Schuster, 1997. Focuses on the wisdom of listening fully to the world around us. (Grades K–3)

Conrad, Pamela. *Blue Willow*. New York: Putnam, 1999. Kung Shi Fair lives on the banks of the Wen River. Her rich father realizes too late that he should have listened to her wishes. (Grades 1–5)

Cosgrove, Steven. *Gabby*. New York: Putnam, 1986. Dealing with challenges and looking for solutions, listening being a part of the answer. (Grades K–4)

Estrin, Leibel. *The Story of Danny Three Times*. Hachi Publishers, 1989. Danny's parents have to say everything to him three times before he will listen. (Grades K–2)

King, Mary Ellen. *A Good Day for Listening*. Morehouse Publishing, 1997. Theodore the teddy bear is a good listener but his brother is not, so he misses out on a lot of good things. (Grades K–2)

Lester, Helen. *Listen, Buddy*. New York: Houghton Mifflin, 1997. A funny story about a bunny who never seems to listen until he realizes the consequences. (Grades K–2)

Micallef, Mary. *Listening: The Basic Connection*. Good Apple, 1996. This nonfiction book gives children basic advice on good listening. (Grades K–6)

Reardon, Ruth. *Listening to the Littlest*. C.R. Gibson Company, 1986. This book expresses, through the voices of children, the need to learn from them by listening. (Grades K–2)

Showers, Paul. *The Listening Walk*. New York: Harper Collins, 1993. Father and daughter go on a listening walk and hear the wonderful sounds around them. (Grades K–2)

CHAPTER 7

How to Deal With Anger— Your Own and Your Child's

*Anger, like a hurricane, is a fact of life to be
acknowledged and prepared for. The peaceful home,
like the hoped-for warless world, does not depend
on a sudden benevolent change in human nature. It
does depend on deliberate procedures that methodi-
cally reduce tensions before they lead to explosions.*
—Haim Ginott

Peaceful Parenting Key #12:
I teach my children how to handle anger in nondestructive ways and I model this consistently.
~

*"Jeffrey, put that bottle of soda down right now!" snaps Audrey to
her 10-year-old son as he reaches to pour himself another glass of
soda after being told he can't have any more.*

*"Come on, Mom. Let me have some more. What do you think, I'm
gonna drink the whole bottle or something?" Jeffrey retorts sarcasti-
cally.*

*"Don't get smart with me, young man! Now put that bottle down
this minute!" Audrey feels her face getting red and her heart pounding. In her mind is the thought,* I can't let him get away with this.
He'll be harder to control if I do. *Beneath this thought is Audrey's
unconscious belief that she'll have no power as a parent if she lets her
child be fresh to her. "Put that soda down this minute!" Audrey is
yelling this time.*

"You can't make me!" Jeffrey yells back.

"That's it," Audrey shouts, yanking the plastic soda bottle out of

his hands and pushing him out of the room. "Wait till your father gets home—you're going to be in big trouble! Just wait!" she shouts, her heart beating a mile a minute.

Does this episode sound familiar? We all get angry. Anger is a natural part of being human and a natural part of parenting. Our children will bait us, test us, and push us toward our last limits, sometimes purposely and sometimes not even realizing what they're doing. As a parent once said to me, "Tara has a way of getting on my last nerve!"

We will never be able to eliminate anger from our lives, but by understanding the nature of anger and its effect on us, we'll be able to gain some mastery over our reactions to it. One thing to remember is: *Anger itself doesn't necessarily cause problems. The way we choose to respond to anger does.*

I stress the word "choose" here, because we do have choices in the face of anger, and that's what this chapter is about: making new choices when dealing with anger and helping our children do the same.

What Happens When We Get Angry?

Our brain is the source of all thoughts, decisions, and emotional reactions. Our most intense emotions arise from a part of the brain called the amygdala, two small almond-shaped structures that lie on either side of the brain near our temples. The amygdala are triggered very quickly in the face of anger or fear, causing the surge of adrenaline that often makes us feel so out of control.

When Jeffrey spoke defiantly to Audrey, her amygdala sent out a surge of adrenaline, causing her to jump into a reaction. What Audrey didn't know was that even though her amygdala was triggered, the rest of her brain was still functioning, and with those *other* parts she could have made a more rational decision about how she would respond.

It's too bad Audrey didn't know that a little cooling off would have left her with a lot more choices.

The part of our brain that helps us make rational choices is the neocortex. The problem is, our amygdala responds much faster than our neocortex. In the words of Daniel Goleman, the amygdala "hijacks" our reactions, causing us to feel intense emotion very quickly, rendering us unaware that we, in fact, do have the ability to control our responses. I'm not talking about repressing what we feel and then seething inside, but rather, detaching from momentary surges of intense emotion and *choosing* our responses instead of letting our responses choose us.

Audrey, not realizing she had this ability at her disposal, allowed her anger and its accompanying thoughts to throw her into an "automatic reaction." This happens to all of us from time to time, and we usually feel bad afterward. As Audrey said later that day, "I can't stand the way I reacted with Jeffrey. There's got to be a better way."

There is. Now let's find out all about it.

Choice and Anger

There's a wide range of choices available to us when we get angry— choices we might not even be aware of. Most of us react automatically when anger takes hold, just as Audrey did. We may have the same style we did as children, or perhaps the same style our parents had.

"How far back does the cycle go?" we might ask ourselves, shuddering at the thought of becoming our parents when we get angry. Janie, a single parent of two young children, said, "I can't help myself. When the kids start driving me crazy I act just like my father used to, rageful, blaming and scary. I can't stand acting this way, but I don't know what else to do."

That feeling of being out of control is directly linked to the amygdala, the source of quick intense reactions. But, we *do* have the ability to gain control over the overwhelming responses we feel in the face of anger, and we have the ability to help our children do the same.

Know Your Anger Style and That of Your Children

We each have our own unique ways of reacting to anger. You do and so do your children. Take a look at the six most common anger reaction styles and see if you can identify the styles of each member of your family. By understanding your anger styles and what you can do to shift them, you'll be taking the first crucial steps in relinquishing anger's power over you:

Explosive

People with this anger style are short-fused and immediately reactive. They blow up quickly and often calm down just as fast. Explosive people often wonder why others are still mad at them after they've gotten over it. They don't always realize the things they say and do when they explode can be very hurtful and sometimes frightening to the people in their lives.

When explosiveness crosses the line into rage, it becomes very destructive. Even if nothing physical happens, words spoken in rage leave a shattering imprint. *Rage is never acceptable.*

Shifting this anger style: When you first start feeling anger beginning to build, immediately catch yourself. Inwardly say, "Stop!" Be forceful with yourself and don't give the anger a chance to overflow. Remind yourself that you *can* stop yourself from doing something you will later regret.

Be aware of your personal signals—pounding heart, sweaty palms, or whatever physically happens to you when anger starts to rise. Be aware of the thoughts that pop into your mind when anger builds, like "I'm not gonna let him get away with that!" Replace those thoughts with statements like, "Calm down," or, "I refuse to let my anger get the best of me." Move yourself away from the source of anger, take some deep breaths, and do one or more of the cooling off techniques you are going to read about in this chapter.

Most of all, do not act on your impulses. Realize instead that your reaction to anger is a choice and you *can* choose to act differently than you have in the past.

Repressive

People who repress their anger hold it in, either pretending that they're really not mad, or silently seething inside but feeling unable to express it. People who repress their anger are usually afraid of what they feel or are afraid of the response their anger might elicit in another person. Consequently, if this is your style, you probably have conditioned yourself to keep your anger in at all costs. That's why this anger style can lead to ulcers or other physical illnesses.

Shifting this anger style: If you tend to repress your anger, your first job will be to simply notice when you are starting to feel angry. Your next step will be to notice what's going on inside of you in that moment.

Colleen, who was raised in a home where anger was never expressed, noticed this about herself as an adult: "In the beginning of my marriage, if my husband started yelling at me, I would feel myself disappearing and going numb. All there would be was an absence of feelings and an extreme sense of detachment. Only after some counseling did I begin to make some connection between my sense of detachment and my feelings of anger. Then, during arguments with my husband, I'd say to myself, 'Look at how he just spoke to me! How could I not be angry right now?' After a while, I started noticing an extreme sense of irritation beneath the numbness. Once I could identify the irritation, I began to understand that I really was angry and that I needed to express it. And it's funny—once I started expressing my own anger, my husband toned his down."

If you're like Colleen, try to notice what you do when faced with anger, and look for the feelings underneath. Try writing down what you notice so you can begin unearthing your authentic feelings in the face of anger. Then try choosing a more assertive way to respond.

Passive-aggressive

People who are passive-aggressive claim not to be angry but do quietly aggressive things like forget to take out the garbage or let slip some hostile remark about the person who is the source of their anger. They indirectly express their anger and, in doing so, incur the wrath of those they are angry at. There's an aggressive edge to the seemingly benign things they do. "Oh, I hurt your feelings?" asks a passive-aggressive person with a look of complete innocence. "I was only teasing. You take things much too seriously."

Shifting this anger style: Les realized he had a passive-aggressive way of handling his anger after Ginger repeatedly pointed out to him that he would often "forget" to do the things she asked or didn't "hear" her when she spoke to him after they had an argument.

"Last week I asked Les if he picked up the tickets to a show we decided to see," said Ginger.

"Did you ask me to do that?" said Les. "I guess I didn't hear you. Sorry. You can pick them up yourself after work tomorrow."

Ginger was incensed.

Les had grown up in a home where he was made to feel ashamed of angry feelings. Consciously and unconsciously, he had learned ways to show his anger indirectly. What can he do now to shift this pattern?

First, he can begin by understanding that **it is healthier to express anger honestly as long as it doesn't hurt other people, property, or oneself.** Les also needs to start telling Ginger when he's angry, using "I messages" instead of avoiding his feelings and then undermining Ginger after the fact.

Ginger can help by encouraging Les to say what's on his mind when he's angry, making it safe for him to do so, and letting him know when he's indirectly hurting her. By communicating honestly and respectfully with one another, Les and Ginger can work to redirect Les' pattern of passive-aggression.

Withdrawing

People who withdraw in the face of anger get very quiet and sulky after an argument. They feel hurt, wronged, or threatened by the other person's reactions and retreat to lick their wounds. They don't always realize that behaving in this manner can be a way of trying to gain control over the other person.

Shifting this anger style: Ten-year-old Monica would shut herself in her room every time she had a fight with her mom, Alana. She'd stay there for a long time, and then when she'd come out, she'd be cold and uncommunicative for hours, sometimes even days.

This drove Alana crazy. Alana wanted to resolve the problem and move on, but Monica acted like a brick wall. It seemed that every time there was an argument, the rest of the day would be ruined.

Alana decided it was time to help Monica change her style of excessive withdrawal. During a neutral time, Alana sat down with Monica and said, "Monica, I understand that you need some space and time to cool off when you're angry, but taking too long makes the bad feelings hang on, and that isn't healthy for you or for me. Next time you're upset, I'm going to give you some space for about a half hour, but then you'll need to come out of your room so we can talk the problem over. I love you too much to let bad feelings ruin our time together."

By firmly and respectfully stating her expectation, Alana enabled Monica to have some time for cooling off, yet provided limits so the cooling-off time wouldn't drag on indefinitely. This helped Monica begin to realize that she had to exercise some self-control over the time she took to withdraw. She actually began to feel better when she didn't let herself stew for so long. Monica eventually found that clearing the air was preferable to staying in her room and sulking.

Self-defeating

People who possess this style redirect anger toward themselves by either assigning self-blame or engaging in self-destructive behaviors like overeating, drugs, alcohol, or guilt. People who turn their anger inward often have a tendency to become depressed.

Shifting this anger style: If you believe you have a self-defeating anger style, here's what you can do. First, try getting in touch with the feelings that come up when you are faced with anger—your own or someone else's.

Candace, age 10, was overweight. What came out when she worked with her school guidance counselor was that each time her father yelled at her she felt afraid—afraid of him and afraid of the angry feelings she had toward him. So she ate.

When her father yelled, Candace would go to the kitchen, grab a bag of cookies, sit down in front of the TV, and gobble down the cookies along with her bad feelings. Of course, this didn't work, because the bad feelings would still be under the surface, and on the surface was Candace's steady weight gain.

Things started to change when Candace's father, Hal, went into school with her to talk to the guidance counselor. Hal acknowledged that he had a bad temper, just as his father had had, and he felt guilty for yelling at Candace the way he did. The guidance counselor taught Hal how to disengage from his anger, and at the same time she taught Candace how to express her feelings through "I messages." Hal learned it was crucial that he help Candace feel safe around him, especially when he was angry.

Candace started learning how to own her angry feelings and express them without fear. When that happened, her need to use food as a crutch lessened.

Assertive and compromising

This anger style strengthens relationships, increases communication, and builds self-esteem. Assertive compromisers talk about problems soon after they occur and look for ways to work things out fairly and equitably. They are assertive without being aggressive, honest without being hurtful, and direct without being blameful. They respect the dignity of others and they respect themselves.

Assertive compromisers take responsibility for their role in conflicts and try to gain insight into the other person's point of view. They see conflict as something to be resolved rather than won. The ability to have a peaceful family rests on each person's willingness to be both assertive and compromising. This is the anger style we will be aiming to create throughout this chapter and the next.

Exercise:

Which anger style typifies you? Many of us combine several anger styles, but usually have one we lean toward most heavily. Think about this, and write down what you believe is your most common anger style. Where did it come from? What keeps it in place? How do you feel about this style? Does it work for you in some way? If so, how? Does it work against you? How? Does it work for the people in your life? Would you change this style of responding to anger if you could? Reflect upon these questions as you write, remembering that reflection is the first step toward change.

Now think about the anger styles of your children. What have you observed in them? Consider the questions above as you write about your children's responses to anger.

My Anger Style _____

_____

_____

My Children's Anger Styles _____

_____

_____

Making New Choices

Regardless of the anger styles we have had until now, we all have the ability to change. Being a parent may make us more aware of this need; after all, we don't want to pass on to our children negative anger styles we might have inherited from our parents, and they from theirs.

If we're open to change, sometimes we can learn lessons from our children, too.

Robin, a loving and devoted mother, knew she had a tendency to explode when she got angry, even though this ran counter to the lessons of peacemaking she had been teaching her children. Robin had been working hard to reinforce the peacemaking skills and understandings her children were learning in school, and her children, particularly 5-year-old Zoe, had been eagerly absorbing these lessons. There were still times, nevertheless, when Robin would lose her temper and respond to her children in ways she later regretted. Things started to change when Robin learned an important lesson from Zoe, one she would never forget.

It happened on a day when Robin felt completely overwhelmed by stresses at work and at home. What triggered Robin's temper on that

particular day was the mess Zoe had left in the bathroom after play-
ing in the mud: mud was all over the counter, the soap, the towel, and
Zoe's mud-caked sneakers sat in the middle of the bathroom floor.

Robin walked into the bathroom, took a look at the mess, and blew
up. "Haven't we been through this bathroom discussion a million
times already?" she shouted, her eyes narrowing. "This time I've had
it! You're a complete slob, and I'm sick of it! Now get back in there,
clean up the mess you made, and don't come out till it's perfect!"

As she shrieked at Zoe, Robin felt completely out of control.
Expecting Zoe to either burst into tears or shout back at her defen-
sively, Robin was stunned at her daughter's response.

Zoe calmly turned to her, looked directly into her eyes, and said,
"Mommy, you don't have to yell like that. I'll clean up the bathroom.
But you can say it in a nicer way. You don't have to shout at me to
make me do it. You just have to ask."

Robin was speechless. Her daughter's self-possessed reaction
spoke volumes about the lessons of peacemaking she had absorbed. In
that moment, Robin realized how inappropriate she must have
sounded and felt deeply touched by her daughter's presence of mind
in the face of her own outburst. At the age of 5, Zoe was able to do
what many adults can't: remain calm in the face of anger.

Robin realized there was something important here to learn from
her daughter. She bent down and hugged Zoe tenderly, apologized,
and thanked her for her calmness and wisdom.

For weeks after that, Robin thought about what Zoe had said, re-
alizing that she never again wanted to allow her anger to get out of
control. She also realized that as young as Zoe was, she understood
that human beings have the ability to choose their behaviors, even in
the face of anger. After all, Zoe had done this herself.

Sometimes our children can be our greatest teachers. Their hearts, not
yet hardened by the ways of the world, are more open to the lessons of
peacemaking, and if we're open, we can learn from their clear perceptions.

Zoe's response exemplifies what author Carol Tavris says about choosing
not to act on our lowest impulses when we are angry. Tavris cautions, "We
do not need to deny our mammalian, primate heritage, but we do not need
to reduce ourselves to it either. Judgment and choice distinguish human
beings from other species; judgment and choice are the hallmarks of
human anger."

In other words, we have the ability to exercise judgment in the face of anger. Rather than acting out the rage we feel in an angry moment, we have the ability to choose a more civil way of responding. Zoe was lucky enough to have learned this lesson at the age of five.

As human beings, we *can* gain mastery over feelings of anger. When we allow ourselves to rage at others, we indulge our "primate" emotions. We might justify our behavior with an excuse—"He made me lose my temper"— as though someone else can reach inside our brain and reconnect the synapses in such a way that we lose all sense of good judgment and rationality.

Not true. *No matter how out of control our emotions might feel to us, **we** ultimately choose how we're going to respond.*

Sometimes our reactions feel so instantaneous we don't even know other choices are available. The surge of adrenaline triggered by the amygdala strikes like a bolt of lightning, and, boom, we react.

What we don't realize is that by backing away from that instantaneous response instead of moving toward it, we can regain control. Stepping back, removing ourselves from the situation for a moment, taking deep breaths, and repeating a calming statement in our heads allows the part of our brain that makes rational decisions to do its job.

When we allow ourselves to express rage, we indulge ourselves, like children throwing a temper tantrum, and we pass this pattern on to our own children. The message we need to give instead is: **We have the capacity to make rational choices no matter how angry we feel.** Peaceful parenting depends, in part, upon our ability to do this and teach it to our children.

Strategies for Detaching From Anger

There are concrete steps we can take to help us change the way we respond to anger. This applies to our children as well. By practicing the anger management strategies below, you will learn how to distance yourself from your automatic reactions and change the way you've responded to anger in the past. Try practicing these strategies alone, then teach them to your children. The more you and your children become comfortable with these techniques during neutral times, the easier it will be to apply them when faced with anger.

Abdominal Breathing

When we breathe deeply, we send oxygen to the brain and enable ourselves to think clearly while calming the body. When this happens, we can more easily detach from feelings of anger, hurt, or upset. The pulse slows, the body relaxes, and before long we feel more in control. *This is an invaluable tool for coping with whatever life throws at us.*

Practice deep abdominal breathing with your children daily, and encourage them to use it initially just to relax. Before long you both will be able to use this technique when faced with anger—your own or someone else's. Use the following text to teach abdominal breathing to your children and your entire family:

Exercise:

Do you know that the simple act of breathing deeply can help you feel calm and relaxed? You can actually use deep breathing to calm yourself when you are upset, angry, frightened, or nervous about practically anything. Many well-known people do deep breathing before giving speeches, acting in plays, singing on stage, or participating in sports. Olympic athletes do deep breathing before their competitions. Now you can do it, too. Here's how.

First, sit up tall and put your hand on your abdomen (the lower part of your stomach). Imagine that this part of your stomach is like a balloon that you can fill with air. Try taking in a nice, slow deep, quiet breath and imagine the air going right down to your abdomen. Then let the breath rise up into your chest, letting your chest gently expand as you do this. Hold the breath for a moment, and gently let it out through your mouth. As you do, deflate your stomach.

Now try it again. Breathe in slowly, deeply, and gently. Let the air fill your stomach and then move up to your chest. Feel the air inside your body and hold it there for a moment. Now let it out, slowly, gently, and quietly.

Now try this with your eyes closed. Breathe in slowly and gently through your nose. Bring the breath deep inside you and expand your abdomen as you do. Hold the breath for a moment and then let it out gently through your mouth. How did that feel? Does your body feel more relaxed now? Does your mind? Try this whenever you need to. Doing deep breathing can even help you relax before going to sleep. Just think—this is something you can do that's absolutely free and will always make you feel better.

Positive Self-Talk

Anger is magnified by the thoughts we think. Researchers have found we actually heighten our own reactions to angry situations by the negative statements that come into our minds. A parent might think, "These kids are driving me crazy! I'm not cut out to be a mother." A child might think, "Jennifer took my favorite doll again. I wish she was never born!"

As we discussed earlier, our bodies react to anger, giving us uncomfortable sensations like a rapidly beating heart or a dry mouth. These physical sensations are then compounded by the thoughts we allow into our minds, sometimes unbidden. The combination of tense physical reactions and negative thoughts can create a volatile situation.

The good news is we *can* gain control over our negative reactions by replacing angry thoughts with positive ones. This, combined with deep breathing, will help restore us (and our children) to a place of sanity in the face of anger.

Think about the last time your were angry. What thoughts crossed your mind? Now think about a statement you could have made to yourself that would have been in direct contrast. "These kids are driving me crazy," could be changed to, "I can calm myself down right now." My personal favorite is, "I can handle this." I like the generic nature of this statement, the fact it can be applied anywhere.

Positive self-statements should start with "I can" rather than "I can't" or "I'm not." "I'm not going to let them get the best of me," has a negative overtone. "I can handle this," is proactive in a positive way.

Exercise:

Write down a few positive self-statements you can make in the face of anger. Practice saying them in your mind as you replay angry situations you've dealt with in the past. Picture yourself standing tall, looking strong, breathing deeply, and saying one of your statements. Next time you get angry, try putting this into practice. In doing so, you will unhook yourself from angry thoughts and empower yourself with positive ones.

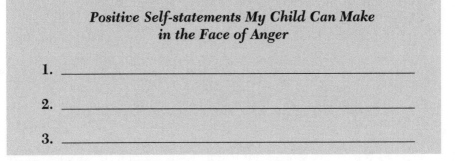

Positive Self-statements I Can Make in the Face of Anger

1. _____

2. _____

3. _____

Try this with your children. Have them write down some positive self-statements they can make in the face of anger. Just like you did, have them picture an angry situation they were involved in and then have them imagine themselves taking a deep breath and replacing the negative thoughts with positive ones. Have them practice this mental exercise so they can apply it when the need arises.

**Positive Self-statements My Child Can Make
in the Face of Anger**

1. _____

2. _____

3. _____

Stop, Breathe, Chill

Teach your child these three words and have him repeat them. Have your child picture the last time he got angry and ask him to replay the scenario in his head. Have him look at the way he originally responded to anger, and then ask him to replace this picture with another, this one showing him stopping—instead of reacting—breathing deeply, and repeating a calming statement in his head.

Rehearse the stop, breathe, chill strategy, and have him picture himself applying it in other angry situations he's experienced. Make sure your child has memorized his calming statement, too, because when the next surge of anger kicks in, he won't have time to look it up. Let your child know that once he's detached from that initial surge of anger, he'll be better able to work out the problem.

The next time you see anger building in your child, say the words firmly: *Stop, breathe, chill.* Do this for yourself, too, whenever you need to. This is your turning off signal, the one that will allow you to detach from the swift reaction of the amygdala. Now you'll be able to access the rational part of your brain. Stop, breathe, chill. Don't forget it.

Guided Imagery

Your mind is like a river. If the river is clear and unpolluted, it flows freely, filling you with a sense of well-being and nurturing the environment of your body. In stressful times, however, pollutants are perpetually tossed into the rivers of our minds, hampering the flow and threatening our sense of well-being.

Picture all the debris that floats around in your river at any given moment—worries, tensions, fears, "what-ifs." Check in with yourself right now. What specific debris do you have floating around in the river of your mind? In a moment you'll discover another way to let go of it.

Children, even at early ages, have already started accumulating debris in the rivers of their minds. When asked about the kinds of things that preoccupy him, 7-year-old Jason said, "I worry that bad people will come to my school and start shooting the children. I worry about kidnappers. I think about my family and hope that nothing bad will ever happen to them. I think about all the animals that might become extinct too, and it upsets me." Even at the age of 7, Jason's mind has absorbed the polluting fears of our society.

Fear leads to stress, stress leads to anger, and anger leads to violence. By offering ourselves peaceful images, we can slow down racing thoughts, lessen fears, and alleviate tensions. We can actually start depolluting our rivers by moving out the debris and replacing it with calming images. In doing so, we help insulate ourselves against overreacting toward the many sources of anger we face in life. A tense mind is the breeding place for impulsive reactions. A quiet mind can reason more clearly.

Try teaching your child the following guided imagery technique to calm the mind, replenish the spirit, and reduce tension. Do it yourself, too.

Start by having your child lie down or sit in a comfortable spot, relaxing his body completely. Tell him you're going to read something that will make him feel very calm and relaxed inside. Encourage him to concentrate on the soothing sound of your voice and to bring his attention back to it if any extraneous thoughts come up.

Now begin reading, and be sure to use your most calm, relaxed, soothing voice. This is a time for you to relax, too. Children as young as 3 years old can engage in this exercise.

Exercise:

Close your eyes and let go of any thoughts or feelings you might have in this moment. Take a slow, deep breath in through your nose and out through your mouth. Breathe in slowly, deeply, and gently. Imagine the air you breathe being able to go right down to your stomach. Gently expand your stomach as you breathe in. Let your stomach release as you breathe out. That's it. Keep breathing slowly, deeply, and gently.

Now pretend your mind is a movie screen and the screen is blank. Just look at your blank screen for a moment. A beautiful picture is about to come on. Keep watching your screen and notice your screen has become blue, a deep, soothing blue like the sky on a warm, sunny day. Keep watching your screen. Look, your screen has turned into the sky! A clear, brilliant, sparkling blue sky filled with fluffy white clouds.

Imagine yourself walking over to the sky and touching one of those clouds. It feels soft, cottony and soothing. Look, the cloud is strong enough to hold you, just like a bed of cotton. Climb onto the cloud and lie down. Relax back into the softness of the cloud and rest. Let the cloud support you and lift you up into the sky. Lean back into the fluffy white cloud and let it protect you as it lifts you higher and higher into the sky. The air is so clear up here—warm, soothing and clear. A soft breeze gently caresses you. Lie back deep into your cloud and let the breeze touch your face, your arms, your eyelids, your legs.

The cloud is moving softly across the sky now, and you feel safer and more comfortable than you ever have before. All is well. You are completely safe, happy, and relaxed.

Keep resting on your cloud and letting it float you through the sky. I'm going to stop talking for a few minutes, and in the quiet I want you to keep picturing yourself floating on this fluffy white cloud.

(Let your child envision this image for the next few minutes or longer. You can close your eyes at this point and picture yourself on a cloud, too.)

After a few minutes, say: Your cloud is bringing you back to earth now. Feel yourself floating down. Feel yourself getting up and climbing off the cloud. Picture yourself walking back into the room.

When I ask you to open your eyes, you will feel safe, happy, and relaxed, as though the magic of the cloud is now inside of you.

Open your eyes.

Welcome back.

Do this as often as you like. The more often you do this exercise with your child, the easier it will be for him to absorb the mental processes of relaxation and imagery. Before long he will be able to call the images to mind on his own and relax without your help.

Unguided Imagery

Every person alive has the capacity to dream, especially children. I remember when I was small, I used to dream I lived in my very own house. I could picture every room and every detail, right down to the swimming pool in the backyard. This image accompanied me to bed every night. It was calming, relaxing, and empowering. The empowering thing about it was that I could call it to mind whenever I wanted. It was my image, and I had the power to make it visible in the recesses of my imagination.

Help your child tap into the power of her own images by doing the following exercise.

Have her sit in a comfortable spot. Ask her to close her eyes and think about a place she's been to that makes her happy to think about. Say, "It can be as simple as your own backyard or as far away as Disney World."

Have your child focus on that image, picturing herself in it. Keeping her eyes closed, have her think about the following questions: "What are you doing in this special place? Are you alone or with other people? What do you see? What else do you want to do when you are there?"

Say, "You can go anywhere you want in this image. It is your very own, and you have the power to make it be exactly the way you want it to be."

Allow your child to quietly let the image expand and grow.

Let your child know she can call this image back whenever she wants. Say, "You can do this just for fun, or you can do it to bring back happy feelings if you're sad or nervous or angry. This image will always live in your heart and mind, and all you need to do is close your eyes and imagine it.

You can have your child make a list of several favorite places to envision. That way she'll have a choice as to where she wants to go next time she decides to do some imagery. She can draw, paint, or write about the places she envisions, and hang up whatever she creates to remind her of the power of her imagination.

Magic Box

Some children worry that they'll forget their image once they stop envisioning it. If so, here's a technique children love.

Say, "Pretend you have a magic box small enough to hold in your hand.

Open your hand and take a look at your magic box. There it is. Now put your magic box down for a moment and picture a place that makes you feel happy, safe, and calm. This is your peaceful place. Picture yourself being there, and imagine doing whatever you'd most like to do. Picture every detail you can about your peaceful place. Now take your peaceful place out of your head and shrink it down until it's very tiny. Open the lid of your magic box and put your peaceful place inside. Now close the lid and put your magic box in your pocket, and if you don't have a pocket, put it in your shirt. You can take out your magic box whenever you want to be in your peaceful place. It is always there for you, no matter what."

This technique, like the last two, helps quiet the noise of the mind and relieve stress while giving children a sense of safety. These are buffers against the tension that can ignite into anger, and they provide children with a calm place to go that is uniquely their own. Children who practice these techniques on a regular basis are less likely to be quickly triggered by stressful situations.

Physical Activity

There is nothing more effective to release anger than physical exercise. Aside from the obvious health benefits, physical exercise releases endorphins, which give us a calm, upbeat feeling. We can actually reverse an angry mood by engaging in some form of physical activity.

Help your child list at least five physical activities she can do when faced with anger. Some things she might include are: bouncing a ball, running around the yard, climbing, jumping on a trampoline, tumbling, or doing jumping jacks, sit-ups, or bent knee push-ups. Post this list next to her cooling off list and encourage her to refer to either of these lists when she is angry. Remind your child that she'll feel better if she does something physical. Model this by letting your child see you releasing anger through physical activity. Remind your child—and yourself—to try not to focus on angry thoughts while doing the physical activity. Instead, focus on the release of energy and other physical sensations you're experiencing.

Once the anger has been released, then you can talk about the problem. In Chapter 8, we'll be looking at a wonderful strategy you can use to resolve any conflicts that arise in your lives.

Distraction

This is another technique the experts recommend for unhooking ourselves from the grip of anger. When we practice the technique of distraction, we purposefully engage in an activity that takes our energy away from the source of anger and enables us to channel it elsewhere. Participants in the workshops I lead have come up with a wide range of distraction techniques, including: clean the house, bake cookies, go down to the basement and build something, rake the yard, take a ride, go shopping, organize a closet, and more. Children have come up with: build blocks, play with the dog, straighten my room, count up my baseball cards, color, and go on the swings.

Many of the cooling-off techniques you thought about earlier probably fell into the category of distraction. These are particularly helpful when we can become completely absorbed in what we are doing. Once again, a trap to watch out for is physically engaging in the distracting activity while mentally focusing on bad thoughts about the person who angered us. If we're going to practice distraction, then we need to engage our minds as well as our bodies.

Humor

Sometimes we can unhook from angry reactions by interjecting humor. I'm not talking about teasing or joking at the expense of the other person. I'm talking about the kind of humor that releases tension and makes you realize the problem might not be as big as you thought it was.

Husband and wife Lyndie and Fred use humor with each other when the tension starts to build. Lyndie said, "Sometimes Fred and I will get into an argument, and then one of us will make a joke. The next thing I know, we'll be laughing and realizing what we were arguing over wasn't that important."

Lyndie and Fred's 5-year-old son Zack sees his parents doing this, and he's learning from them. One day Lyndie was reprimanding Zack for leaving his toys all over the floor, and he said with a twinkle in his eyes, "A little man must have come in and put those toys there, Mommy, 'cause I know better than to leave a mess like that." Lyndie couldn't help but laugh, and when she did her annoyance subsided.

When we model using humor to dispel anger, we help our children learn to let go of bad feelings quickly and invite good feelings in their place. As we noted before, anger and other bad feelings are contagious. By using humor to dissipate anger, we can spread good feelings, which are contagious, too.

Journaling, Drawing

One of the best gifts you can give your child is a journal. Set aside a time when your child can write or draw in her journal for even as little as ten minutes a day.

By building the habit of journaling, you will help bolster your child's good mental and physical health. That's right. Research has shown that the simple act of journaling helps people acknowledge, express, and release their feelings, forming the basis for both mental and physical health. Through self-expression, the immune system is actually supported.

If your child is angry, encourage her to write or draw about it. Let her know that the feelings she has are legitimate simply because they are hers. Tell her, "Feelings are neither right nor wrong. They just are," and be careful never to judge her feelings or your own.

Impress upon your child that her journal is private and that no one is going to see what she wrote. Her journal is her special place for letting out whatever is inside. Angry feelings and other feelings can be released, examined and soothed through the process of journaling.

As with all anger management techniques, after we have calmed down, we need to talk to the other person and work out our differences. Sometimes with children, the need to talk things out practically disappears once they are calm.

Nine-year-old Chad and his 8-year-old brother Vincent got into a tussle about which show they were going to watch at 8:00. Alan, their father, said, "OK, boys, this isn't working. Go to your rooms and choose something to do on your cooling-off lists. In a little while I'll come and get you so we can talk this over."

When Chad looked at his list, he decided to spend some time with his fish, feeding them, skimming the tank, and watching them swim around. Vincent went into his room and decided to work on a jigsaw puzzle he had started weeks ago. Both boys became completely engaged in what they were doing.

Twenty minutes later, when Alan asked the boys to come out of their rooms to talk things over, the problem seemed to have disappeared. Both Chad and Vincent had an entirely new perspective. Distracted by the activities they had gotten involved in, they both realized that the TV show really wasn't worth fighting over.

"I'm not angry at all anymore," said Chad, giving his brother a gentle smile.

"Neither am I," said Vincent.

"How about if we play Uno at 8:00 instead of watching TV?" said Chad.

"Fine with me," said Vincent. "Sometimes TV is boring."

"Hey, wanna come see my fish?" said Chad to his brother. "I think the big one's going to have babies." The two boys walked over to Chad's room, completely free of the conflict they had had earlier.

Note: Make sure your kids are sincere if they say they're not angry anymore. Some children let go quickly when they are distracted from the source of the problem. Others hold on a little longer but are reluctant to admit it. If you sense this is happening with one of your children, help him engage in a conversation to work it out rather that letting him shrug it off.

Exercise:

Which anger management strategies do you plan to use? When do you intend to practice them? List which days of the week and times you plan to designate for practice. Post these dates and times you have listed.

Which anger management strategies do you plan to teach your children? When? Write about this.

Forgiveness

No book about peacemaking would be complete without some words about forgiveness. Martin Luther King once said, "Forgiveness is not an occasional act; it is a permanent attitude." The only way children can learn the habit of forgiveness is by seeing us, their parents, forgive others and forgive ourselves.

Minister Fredrick Buechner says, "When you forgive somebody who has wronged you, you're spared the dismal corrosion of bitterness and wounded pride. For both parties, forgiveness means the freedom again to be at peace inside their own skins and to be glad in each others' presence."

The freedom to be at peace in our own skins—that's what forgiveness allows. We relinquish this freedom when we hold onto anger and resentment. Enormous amounts of energy are wasted when we hold back our love, hold on to hate, and harbor acrimonious feelings. The only remedy is letting go, accepting what is, and forgiving.

Psychologist Robert Enright of the University of Wisconsin says, "People who forgive . . . reap huge emotional rewards. They have less hostility and anxiety and have a better chance of suffering fewer stress-related health problems. When you forgive, you also become more hopeful about the future and your self-esteem rises."

But even more difficult is forgiving without reconciliation: forgiving for the mere purpose of forgiving. Certainly, what we strive for is to reconcile all conflicts, clear the air, and understand one another. But there are times this is impossible—with a parent who has passed away, with someone who has wronged you and is long gone, with someone who is unwilling to communicate. These are the times we must dip deep into our own souls and see if we are willing to forgive anyway.

I have on the bulletin board above my desk a yellowed article written by the scholar and Holocaust survivor Elie Weisel in 1997. I have never taken this article down, and I never will. In it, Elie Weisel expresses the most profound act of forgiveness imaginable. It is here that Elie Weisel expresses forgiveness toward God for the Holocaust.

In the article, Weisel asks God the question he has struggled with all his life: "Where were you, God of Kindness, in Auschwitz?" Weisel had never been able to understand how a loving God could have allowed the Holocaust to exist. But out of the question that has tormented him for fifty years, Weisel gleans a sudden insight: "Watching your children suffer at the hands of your other children, haven't you also suffered?"

In this moment of compassion, Weisel is finally moved to offer God his forgiveness: "Let us make up, Master of the Universe," he says. "In spite of everything that happened? Yes, in spite. Let us make up: for the child in me, it is unbearable to be divorced from you for so long."

This story is a reminder to me that *forgiveness and compassion are essential and possible under all circumstances.* For the child in all of us, we must learn to forgive. And for the sake of the children we love with unparalleled ferocity, we must model the most magnanimous and humbling of all acts—the act of forgiveness.

Exercise:

Is there someone you need to forgive? Write about that person and the circumstance below. Are you ready to forgive him or her? If so, go on to the next step.

Complete the forgiveness statement below.

I _____ *do   hereby grant forgiveness to* _____ .

I forgive you for _____

_____

_____

_____

Here's what I need to communicate so that my offering of forgive-ness will be complete: _____

_____

_____

_____

_____

Talk to your child about the importance of forgiveness. Ask him if there is anyone he needs to forgive. If so, copy the above forgiveness statement, and have him fill it out.

Recap

Peaceful Parenting Key #12:
I teach my children how to handle anger in nondestructive ways and I model this consistently.
~

We have the capacity to make rational choices in the face of anger.

By knowing our anger style, we can discover ways to gain mastery over it.

You can use the following strategies to detach from anger and help your child to do the same:

– stop, breathe, chill
– deep breathing
– guided imagery
– unguided imagery
– magic box
– positive self-statements
– physical exercise
– distraction
– humor
– journaling/drawing

Learning to forgive is essential. Practice the art of forgiveness and teach it to your children.

RESOURCES FOR PARENTS

Carter, Les et. al. *The Anger Workbook.* Thomas Nelson, 1992. A 13-step interactive program that helps identify the best ways to handle anger and eliminate the myths that perpetuate it.

Eastman, Meg and Rozen, Sydney Craft. *Taming the Dragon in Your Child: Solutions for Breaking the Cycle of Family Anger.* New York: Wiley, 1994. Shows parents how to deal constructively with their children's anger in a variety of situations from temper tantrums and pouting to sarcasm and sibling rivalry.

Ellis, Albert. *How to Make Yourself Happy and Remarkably Less Disturbable.* Impact Publishers, 1999. Ellis shows how to use our natural constructive inclinations to overcome negative patterns; includes how we can move beyond inherited and acquired tendencies to become anxious, depressed, and enraged.

Lerner, Harriet. *The Dance of Anger.* New York: Harper and Row, 1985. Insightful book on sources of anger and what to do about them.

McKay, Patrick et. al. *When Anger Hurts Your Kids: A Parent's Guide.* Fine Communications, 1996. Explains why parents get angry, how children are affected, and suggests how to gain control of angry emotions.

Paul, Henry A. *When Kids Are Mad, Not Bad: A Guide to Recognizing and Handling Your Child's Anger.* New York: Penguin Putnam, 1998. Anger in children can manifest as tantrums, hostility, sarcasm, depression, and more. Parents learn to interpret the messages a child may be sending and handle anger in a loving, constructive way.

Tavris, Carol. *Anger: The Misunderstood Emotion.* New York: Simon & Schuster, 1982. Learn more about anger triggers, their roots, and what to do about them.

Weisinger, Hendrie. *Anger at Work.* New York: William Morrow, 1995. Practical strategies for dealing with anger.

Whitehouse, Elaine and Pudney, Warwick. *A Volcano in My Tummy: Helping Children to Handle Anger.* New Society Publishers, 1998. Helps parents show children how to handle their anger so they can live healthily, happily, and nonviolently; full of stories and easy-to-use games and exercises.

RESOURCES FOR CHILDREN

Bang, Molly. *When Sophie Gets Angry—Really, Really Angry.* New York: Scholastic, 1999. A little girl doesn't know how to manage her anger; she learns how to take the time to cool off and regains her composure. (Grades K–2)

Berry, Joy Wilt. *Let's Talk About Feeling Angry.* New York: Scholastic, Inc., 1996. Part of the "Let's Talk About" series. Explains how to handle even the toughest situations and emotions in a clear, simple language. Other titles include: *Let's Talk About Feeling Afraid, Let's Talk About Needing Attention,* which addresses temper tantrums, and *Saying No,* which illustrates when saying no is appropriate and when it is not. (Grades K–2)

Blumenthal, Deborah. *The Chocolate Covered Cookie Tantrum.* New York: Houghton Mifflin Company, 1999. Sophie finds out that throwing a tantrum will not get her what she wants. (Grades K–2)

Everitt, Betsy. *Mean Soup.* New York: Harcourt Brace, 1995. Horace has had a very, very bad day and is feeling grumpy. His mother helps him find a cure. (Grades K–2)

Gardiner, Barbara and Aaron, Jane. *When I'm Angry.* Western Publishing, 1998. Children learn how to deal with anger. Includes a parents' guide in a question-and-answer format. (Grades K–2)

Hopper, Nancy J. *Ape Ears and Beaky.* New York: E.P. Dutton,1984. A boy with a bad temper learns not to overreact. (Grades 2–6)

Lindgren, Astrid. *Lotta on Troublemaker Street.* New York: Macmillan, 1984. Lotta has a bad temper. After running away, she gains insight into a conflict. (Grades 2–6)

Mayer, Mercer. *I Was So Mad.* Western Publishing Company, 1985. A young child tries a variety of ways to let go of anger. (Grades K–2)

McGovern, Ann. *Scram, Kid!* New York: Viking, 1974. Joe isn't allowed to join the baseball team. He reacts to being rejected. (Grades K–3)

Merrill, Jean. *The Pushcart War.* New York: Atheneum, 1987. Conflict on the streets of New York and how it gets solved. (Grades 2–6)

Minarik, Else Holmelund. *No Fighting, No Biting.* New York: Harper Collins, 1978. Rosa and Will hear the story of two alligators who argue until they meet a big hungry alligator. (Grades K–2)

Moser, Adolph. *Don't Rant and Rave on Wednesdays!: The Children's Anger-Control Book.* Landmark Editions, 1994. Children find out how to control anger and express feelings appropriately. (Grades K–6)

Naylor, Phyllis. *King of the Playground.* New York: Atheneum, 1991. A little boy gets bullied and learns how to deal with the problem. (Grades K–2)

Simor, Norma. *I Was So Mad!* Albert Whitman, 1991. A look at situations that make children angry, including sibling rivalry, annoyance with parents, school problems, and more. (Grades K–2)

Udry, Janice May. *Let's Be Enemies.* New York: Harper Trophy, 1988. When John sees James as bossy, he decides that they are enemies. They eventually become friends again. (Grades K–2)

Van Leeuwen, Jean. *Amanda Pig on Her Own.* New York: Puffin Books, 1994. Amanda has to solve some problems, deal with angry feelings, and meet other challenges when she is by herself. (Grades K–3)

Waber, Bernard. *But Names Will Never Hurt Me.* Boston: Houghton Mifflin & Company, 1994. A little girl with the unlikely name of Alison Wonderland deals with teasing. (Grades K–2)

Walker, Alice. *Finding the Green Stone.* San Diego: Harcourt Brace Jovanovich, 1997. Johnny loses both his green stone and his sense of joy after talking mean to the people in his life. As a result, he learns some important and life-changing lessons. (Grades 2–4)

Walter, Nancy and Patfield, V. Lin. *Seemor's Flight to Freedom*. Rosemount, MN: Nan Publishing, 1996. Poignant story of a nearsighted seagull's struggle with anger; includes questions for discussion between parents and children about how our brains process anger. (Grades K–2)

Wells, Rosemary. *Benjamin and Tulip*. New York: Dial Books, 1977. Tulip beats up Benjamin. They eventually come to a truce. (Grades K–2)

Zolotow, Charlotte. *The Quarreling Book*. New York: Harper & Row, 1982. A chain reaction of angry feelings occurs when Dad forgets to kiss Mom good-bye in the morning. (Grades K–2)

CHAPTER 8

Six Steps to Resolving Conflicts

The only way our culture of violence will change is if we teach this generation to develop the skills needed to resolve conflicts. Only then can we become more hopeful as a society. We must make these changes when our children are young, for this is the time of greatest impact.

—Patricia Vincent
Director of Elementary Education
Hamilton Twp. Schools

Peaceful Parenting Key #13:
I resolve conflicts peacefully and teach my children to do the same.
~

How lucky we are that in recent decades strategies for resolving conflicts have been developed and old myths are being laid to rest. Not too long ago, people believed that human beings were, by nature, adversarial and that peaceful resolution of conflicts was beyond our reach.

When I started leading conflict resolution workshops in 1982, it wasn't unusual for participants to say, "People aren't wired up to resolve conflicts—they need to fight," or "Conflict resolution is unrealistic. Kids will never buy into it." As we learned in the last chapter, it *is* possible to make positive choices in the face of anger.

Similarly, **people, especially children, *can* resolve conflicts with-**

out fighting. The skills needed to do this can be taught. This is great news for all of us, and in this chapter you will learn proven ways to resolve conflicts and how to teach your children to do the same.

Creating Willingness

Before anyone can successfully use conflict resolution strategies to mediate conflicts, two critical factors must be present:

the willingness to work out problems
and
an openness to compromise

Every previous chapter has been preparation for this. By living and modeling the concepts you've learned so far in this book, you've been setting the groundwork for your family to resolve conflicts peacefully. Use the following questions to see if each of you is ready:

– Am I willing to listen to what the other person has to say?
– Am I open to his or her point of view?
– Am I willing to take responsibility for my part in the conflict?
– Can I let go of being right and concentrate instead on working things out?
– Am I committed to finding a fair solution, one that satisfies each of us?
– Am I amenable to compromise?
– Am I willing to forgive?

Let these questions be your companion as you seek ways to resolve the conflicts in your own life and teach your children to do the same. Remember, *your children will learn more from your example than from anything else*. As you work to resolve conflicts with friends and family, your children will follow your lead.

In the words of an experienced school social worker, "It has to be 'do as I do,' not 'do as I say.' Children pick up so many cues from our actions. We have to make sure we're acting in concert with what we want our kids to learn."

Learning how to resolve conflicts isn't easy, especially when we first start. It's like learning how to ride a bike. At first it feels awkward and shaky, but the more you do it, the easier it becomes.

Sharing honestly with your children about the challenges you face in resolving conflicts will provide great insight for both of you. Learn together, learn as you teach your child, and don't be afraid of the bumps in the road. I have fallen many times on the road to peacemaking, and I still do.

The point is to pick ourselves up and keep going, no matter what. If our commitment is strong enough, somewhere along the way, the road will smooth out beneath our feet. Before long we'll find ourselves coasting along in harmony with the wind, negotiating the turns and bumps along the way.

Using the Win/Win Guidelines

When the willingness to compromise is present, it's time to introduce the Win/Win Guidelines, a six-step approach to resolving conflicts that has been successfully used by adults and kids in schools throughout the nation and beyond for the past fifteen years. Take a look:

The Win/Win Guidelines

1. Take time to cool off.
2. Take turns stating the problem as you see it, using "I messages." No put-downs, blaming, or name-calling.
3. Take turns stating the problem as the other person sees it, reflecting back what you have heard.
4. Take responsibility for your role in the problem.
5. Brainstorm solutions together, and choose a solution that satisfies both people, a win/win solution.
6. Affirm, forgive, or thank each other.

(Look for the Abbreviated Win/Win Guidelines at the end of this chapter, formatted for easy use.)

In previous chapters, you've learned how to cool off (step 1), how to give "I messages" (step 2), and how to do reflective listening (step 3). In this chapter, you'll learn how to introduce these and other steps of the Win/Win Guidelines to your children, and you'll find out how to apply them in conflict situations. When we help other people work out conflicts using these steps, it's called mediation.

There are two ways that conflicts usually get peacefully resolved in the home. The first is when parents mediate their kids' conflicts, and the second (which only happens after you've done the first for a while) is when your children mediate for themselves, applying the steps of the Win/Win Guidelines independently. That's the ultimate goal.

How do you begin? First by introducing the Win/Win Guidelines ahead of time, not during a conflict, and then by helping your children mediate conflicts on the spot. After a while, your children will assimilate the process and become comfortable with it.

You don't have to do every step every time. With very young children, 4 and 5 year olds in particular, you'll want to keep it very simple. Just have them cool off, give "I messages," and brainstorm solutions. Have them talk directly to each other, giving eye contact, and work together to solve their problem.

With children of all ages, encourage them to come up with their own solutions. This is critical, because the process is meaningful only when children have ownership of it. If conflict resolution is something you perform on your kids, like a tonsillectomy, it'll feel just about as good. When children come up with their own solutions, they're empowered, and the process of problem solving becomes one they'll want to repeat again.

Be sure also to introduce the Rules for Win/Win, which your children must agree to follow before you begin mediating any conflict:

Rules for Win/Win

We agree to do the following:

1. Tell the truth.
2. Treat each other with respect.
3. Attack the problem, not the person.
4. Wait for our turn to speak. No interrupting.
5. Be willing to compromise.

A Conflict Mediation

Now let's see what it looks like to use the Win/Win Guidelines in a conflict situation:

Liz, age 10, and Jay, age 8, are sitting on the floor in the family room playing Monopoly. All of a sudden their voices start to rise, shouts echo, and Jay starts to cry. He runs into the kitchen to tell on Liz.

Jay: *Mommy, Liz just threw a hotel at me!*

Mom: *What are you talking about?*

Jay: *We were playing Monopoly and she threw a hotel at me and she almost hit me in the eye!*

Mom: *(taking a very deep breath, checking Jay and seeing he's really not hurt, and resisting the impulse to just plain yell at both of them) Jay, just stay right here. Liz, come in here so we can talk about what just happened.*

Liz: *Don't get mad at me, Mom. He stole $500 and he wouldn't give it back!*

Jay: *Did not! She's lying, Mom!*

Mom: *(maintaining her cool by continuing to breathe deeply and repeating one of her goal statements in her head: "I remain calm no matter what") OK, OK. STOP! Both of you. We're not going to attempt to talk about this until you cool off. (She gives each child direct eye contact, stands tall, and keeps her voice steady but firm—a no-nonsense stance.) I'd like you to go to separate parts of the house and keep away from each other until I call you, do you understand? And while you're apart, do something on your "cool off" lists.*

Jay: *But, Mom . . .*

Mom: *No buts, just go!*

Liz: *(under her breath) He's an idiot.*

Mom: *No put-downs, Liz. Now go before you end up losing TV.*

Liz goes to her room and turns on some music and Jay goes into the basement to jump on his pogo stick. When Mom calls them together in twenty minutes, they're both visibly calmer. Liz still looks a little annoyed, but Mom decides to begin mediating the conflict anyway, knowing she'll stop the process if either child is too angry to talk things over in a civil way.

Mom knows it's not the job of the mediator to force the mediation to work. There has to be willingness on the part of the disputants for a conflict to be resolved successfully.

Mom: *Are you two cooled off enough to talk this over in a respectful way?*

Jay: *If she is.*

Liz: *I guess.*

Mom: *Well, if you're not, we can't do this, so you'd better be honest with yourselves. Will you be able to follow the rules for Win/Win that we talked about at the family meeting? (Mom gestures toward the rules, which are posted on the refrigerator next to the Win/Win Guidelines.)*

Liz: *OK, let's just get this over with.*

Mom: *Do you both agree to be honest and not use put-downs of any kind?*

Jay: *OK.*

Liz: *(sulkily) OK.*

Mom: *(She positions Liz and Jay at the kitchen table facing each other and she sits on the side. This is important, because the disputants need to be able to make eye contact.) OK, Liz, you can go first. Look at your brother and tell him why you got so angry. Make sure to use "I messages."*

Liz: *(looking at her mother) I didn't like it when he took that $500 bill and wouldn't put it back when I asked him to.*

Mom: *Liz, you need to look at Jay and tell him, not me.*

Liz: *(turning toward her brother a little begrudgingly) I got really angry when you took that $500 from Free Parking and said it was yours.*

Jay: *I didn't take it!*

Mom: *(looking directly at Jay) Just say back what you heard. You'll have a chance to give your side of the story next. Look at your sister.*

Jay: *(begrudgingly looking at Liz) I heard you say you think I took the $500 from Free Parking, but I didn't.*

Mom: *Is that your "I message," Jay, that you didn't take the $500?*

Jay: *(looking at Liz, but then looking down) I didn't take the $500.*

(Liz makes an irritated sound.)

Mom: *Liz, say back what your brother just said.*

Liz: *(annoyed) I heard you say you didn't take the $500, but I don't believe you. He's lying, Mom, I swear!*

Jay: *I had the $500 from the beginning of the game!*

Liz: *But you spent it when you bought houses, then you snuck it out of Free Parking when you thought I wasn't looking, but I was!*

Mom: *(continuing to keep her cool, and trying to be as objective as possible) Well, I wasn't there, so obviously I didn't see what happened. We seem to have two very different versions of this story, and I just want to caution you that we aren't going to be able to work this out unless you both tell the truth. That was the first rule we agreed to.*

(She looks both children in the eye and waits. The table becomes very silent for a few minutes.)

Mom: *Well, do you want to continue or not?*

Jay: (*tears coming into his eyes*) OK, I took it! There, are you happy now? But she shouldn't have thrown that hotel at me. She could have taken my eye out with that thing!

Liz: (*looking at her mother*) See, I told you.

Mom: (*trying to get them back on track*) So you were both responsible in your own way for this conflict, weren't you? Jay, how were you responsible?

Jay: I shouldn't have taken the money.

Mom: How else?

Jay: I shouldn't have lied about it.

Mom: That's right. I'm glad you realize it. (*turning to Liz*) How about you? How were you responsible?

Liz: OK, I guess I shouldn't have thrown the hotel at him. I was just so mad when he wouldn't put the money back!

Mom: But does that justify throwing something at him? Didn't we agree we wouldn't do things to hurt each other?

Liz: (*lowering her head*) I know.

Mom: So what can we do to prevent this problem from happening again?

Jay: I guess I shouldn't take money and then pretend I didn't.

Mom: That's right. Dishonesty never works, and I hope you'll never do that again. Liz, how about you?

Liz: I guess I need to control my temper a little better.

Mom: That's right. Hurting isn't allowed. What can either of you do next time you get angry? Let's brainstorm.

Liz: I can walk away until I calm down.

Jay: Or ask for help.

Mom: What else?

Liz: I can take deep breaths like you were just doing before.

Jay: Count to ten.

Mom: What else is on your cooling off lists?

Liz: Walk out the door and get my bearings.

Mom: How about you, Jay?

Jay: Pet the dog.

Mom: I have to compliment you both. You did a great job of working out this conflict, and I'm very proud of of you. Jay, I know it took a lot of courage to tell the truth about what you did. I'm especially proud of you for that. And, Liz, I'm proud of you for being able to sit and talk this over even when your brother hadn't told the truth yet. That took a lot, too, and I'm proud of you. Now could the two of you affirm, forgive, or thank each other?

Liz: *OK. I forgive you, Jay, and I hope you'll tell the truth from now on.*

Jay: *Thanks, and I forgive you and I hope you'll never throw anything at me again.*

Liz: *(smiling at her brother) I won't.*

Mom: *Do you want to shake on it?*

They shake hands and give each other a smile.

Does mediation take the place of consequences? No. If Liz had really hurt her brother, she should have been punished before the mediation even started. Sometimes we have to give a consequence and then mediate afterward. One thing shouldn't replace the other. If we skip the mediation and just give a consequence, then the underlying problem will likely recur because it was never resolved to begin with.

Should you mediate every conflict that comes up? *No,* or you'll be mediating all day. Just work on the ones that are either constantly recurring or seem to be of greater importance. When you take steps toward creating a peaceful family, many of the little conflicts that come up will blow over or get worked out simply.

Does mediation always work? Nothing works every single time, but using this process will help tremendously. Just make sure your children are cooled off before you begin. If they're not, the mediation won't get off the ground. If necessary, you can even wait till the next day to mediate.

However, if you think your children are just being difficult or stubborn, give them a consequence and let them know you expect their cooperation. Sometimes kids need to be "nudged" into this process. If they'd rather stew or hold a grudge than work out the problem, you may need to force the issue a little bit until they see the value of it themselves.

I remember my son Michael being resistant to mediation initially. At those times, I'd give him a choice: You can either choose to work out your conflict peacefully or you can choose no TV for tonight. Which one will it be? That's actually how I got him started with mediation. And now—well, you'll see when you get to the end of the chapter.

Introducing Win/Win Step-by-Step

Now let's take a look at how to introduce the Win/Win Guidelines to your children, one step at a time.

Step 1—Take time to cool off.

Don't skip this step. It's impossible to resolve conflicts when people are hot under the collar. Think about it. If your friend tried to force you to calmly talk out a problem when you were on the verge of exploding, you'd probably feel like exploding at her! As we learned in the last chapter, human beings aren't wired up to detach instantaneously from intense emotions. We need a little distance from them in order to "unhook." Only then can we think clearly and gain control over our reactions.

Take a look at the following anecdote to see how cooling off helps:

Jackie, a single mom, had attended a peacemaking workshop where she learned about cooling off strategies. As soon as she got home, Jackie shared what she'd learned with her two children, Kenny, age 10, and Jessie, age 7. When she asked what would help them cool off, both children agreed that the most important thing was distance from each other. Another top item on both of their lists was taking deep breaths. Jackie tucked away this information but had little idea how much it would soon help her.

The power of cooling off revealed itself a few days later, when Jackie and her children were on their way to a family gathering. They were driving along a busy highway, and before long the familiar sound of bickering rose up from the backseat.

Kenny, who had been having difficulties in fourth grade, had just told his sister he might have to go to summer school. Her response was, "Good! That way I can have the house all to myself and I'll get to play while you have to work all day!"

Shocked and inflamed by his sister's remark, Kenny shouted, "You think you're so great, huh? Well, I'll show you!" and he landed a swift punch on her upper arm. At that, Jessie punched him back, and within seconds the car was filled with shouts and shrieks.

"Stop!" Jackie yelled, as she tried to figure out what to do. Normally she might have pulled over, yelled at the kids, and threatened them with their lives, but this time, pulling over wasn't an option. They were on a three-lane highway with no shoulder. Moreover, since attending the peacemaking workshop, Jackie wanted to handle this dispute differently.

Thinking quickly, she remembered cooling off. That's it! *she said to herself,* Instead of yelling at them and fueling the tension even more, I'll try having them cool off. What do I have to lose?

"OK, you two," she said forcefully without shouting, "I want you

to separate right now. Jessie, you stay on one side of the car. Kenny, you move over to the other. No talking and no touching," she added, *"and don't look at each other, either."*

"But . . ." Kenny started objecting as he moved closer to the window on his side.

"No talking," said Jackie with firmness in her voice. *"I just want you to sit quietly, breathe deeply, and cool off just like we talked about a few days ago. And when you feel a little calmer, you can think about ways to work out the problem you were just fighting over. **I'll** let you know when it's time to talk again."*

"But, Mommy . . ." Jessie whined, attempting to sidetrack Jackie.

Again Jackie stood firm. *"No talking until you've cooled off. Now take some deep breaths and don't stop until you feel a little calmer,"* she reiterated with a clear sense of purpose.

Seeing Jackie's resolve, the children stayed on their respective sides of the car, took deep breaths, and mulled over the problem in silence. Jackie watched them through the rearview mirror, and was surprised to see them sitting as quietly as they were, each gazing out a window deep in thought. Before long, Jackie noticed the children's faces soften and their bodies start to relax. They didn't look as stiff and angry as they had a few moments ago.

Jackie gave them a little while longer to cool off and then said, *"OK, I'm going to give each of you a chance to say what's bothering you. Just remember, no put-downs or blaming. Kenny, I want you to start."*

"I've been really upset about school. I'm worried about my grades and lately everything Jessie does annoys me. I guess I've been acting kind of mean to her."

Jackie asked Jessie to speak next.

*"Kenny **has** been acting mean to me. He always tells me to get out whenever I come into his room and he gives me dirty looks all the time. That's why I talked to him like that before. I really don't want him to have to go to summer school."*

Jackie could feel the ice breaking. The cooling off period had worked, allowing time for Kenny and Jessie to calm down and reflect. As a result, they started gaining insight into each other's behavior and their own. Kenny described the pressure he'd been under at school and how it had been affecting him. Jessie listened intently to her brother's concerns, and through the rearview mirror, Jackie could see compassion in her eyes.

Before the ride ended, Jackie asked the children to talk about al-
ternatives to hitting, and she emphasized she didn't want them ever
to respond to conflicts by hurting each other. Both Kenny and Jessie
agreed that fighting was a bad thing and that they'd cool off the next
time they got angry instead of bombarding each other with put-
downs or punches.

Jackie and the children arrived at the family gathering with
warmer feelings toward one another and new insights. Jackie smiled
as she reflected on the power of "cooling off." She knows that in the
future she will continue to use this process with her children and in
her own life.

Introduce cooling off at a family meeting. Reiterate your commitment
to having a peaceful family and let your children know how *you've* been
cooling off when faced with conflicts. Review some of the strategies your
children put on their cooling off lists (from Chapter 3) and see if there are
any more they want to add.

As time goes on, encourage your children to talk about how they are *ap-*
plying the strategies on their lists. This is important, because kids are very
good at parroting back what they think we want to hear. But in order for
any strategy to work, it has to be put into practice. By cooling off each time
he gets mad, your child will learn a lifelong skill.

Here's what my son Tim told me about how cooling off helped him get
a handle on the bad temper he'd had as a little boy:

When I was little I had a bad temper. I would yell and throw
things when I got angry, and my face would turn all red. But when
you taught us how to cool off I remember starting to change. If
Michael got me upset, instead of reacting to him I would go to my
room and listen to music. Or sometimes I'd go for a bike ride. Then
the problem wouldn't seem so bad and I'd start to forget about it.

That's the way I started to gain control over my temper—by get-
ting away from the source of the problem and cooling off. I started to
realize there was nothing to gain by giving in to my temper. But by
not letting it get the best of me, I was in control. That made me feel
good, so good that I kept on cooling off each time I got angry. After a
while, my temper was no longer a problem. I'm really glad I learned
that when I was little.

Tell your children Tim's story. Let them know it really *is* possible to cool
off, even if you have a bad temper. As a family, have each person make a

commitment to **stop, breathe, and chill** whenever any of you get angry. Model, reinforce, and affirm this behavior each time you see it. Catch your children in the act of cooling off and acknowledge them immediately, specifically, and sincerely. But above all, let your children see *you* cooling off each time you're angry.

Step 2—Take turns talking it out using "I messages." No put-downs, blaming or name-calling.

There are two excellent ways to introduce this step: through puppets if your kids are younger, or by staging a conflict between you and your partner if your kids are older. I've seen puppets work with older kids when they get to hold them and do the talking. Try this any way you think will work with your kids. As you read on, for the sake of ease, I'll refer primarily to the puppet method, so adapt this in your mind if your planning to introduce "I messages" another way.

At a family meeting, introduce the Win/Win Guidelines. Tell your children this is a proven method for resolving conflicts and is used by adults and kids all over the country. Go over each step and tell your children you'll be working on step 2, giving "I messages" today. Let your kids know you'll be using the puppets to teach them how to use "I messages" when they have conflicts of their own.

Tell them that conflicts are a natural part of being human, but it's the way we handle our conflicts that can be a problem. Tell your kids we always have a choice as to how we're going to behave, and discuss some of the negative choices people make when they have a conflict: hitting, screaming, cursing, pouting, using put-downs, throwing tantrums, saying mean things that they regret later, and any others your family can think of.

Now ask your children why these choices aren't good ones. Talk about the natural consequences that arise when we choose to handle conflicts in a negative way: damage to relationships, feeling bad about yourself, getting punished, disappointing your parents, being disliked, gaining a bad reputation, retaliation from others, guilt, and more. *Encourage your children to come up with as many natural consequences as possible.*

Let your children know there are also positive choices we can make when we're faced with conflicts. Cooling off, talking it over, asking for help, and forgiving are some of them. Stress that when we make positive choices, we generally get positive results: feeling good about ourselves, preserving our relationships, making our parents proud, getting along with others, and being a role model for others. See if your children can think of some others.

Now have the puppets act out a conflict typified by statements like, "He took my toy," "she called me a name," "he came in my room without asking," etc. (If your children are old enough, they can do the play acting.) Have the puppets do whatever your children normally do when they have conflicts, including calling each other names or hitting each other. (Your children will love this part!)

Now ask your children what the puppets can do to resolve their conflict peacefully. Guide them to come up with statements like, "use words instead of fists," "talk it over," or "work it out." Encourage your children to focus on the fact that people need to be respectful and not hurt each other when they have conflicts, even though they're feeling angry.

Have your children decide what the puppets can say to each other to work out the conflict they just had. Young children will immediately come up with, "They should say they're sorry." Let your children know that "I'm sorry" can come later. For now, the puppets need to talk about what's on their minds in a respectful and honest way. Tell them that in order to clear the air and understand how each of them feels, the puppets will need to discuss the problem first. Let your children know that the best way to do this is to start from the word "I" as opposed to the word "you." Model this.

Have your children come up with several "I messages" the puppets can give to each other. Talk about the "I messages," making sure they are not blameful or aggressive. Remind your children that the tone of voice we use when giving an "I message" is just as important as the words we use. Let them know that the look on our faces, the way we hold our bodies, and the way we say our words convey a message, too. Emphasize that *our goal is to solve the problem fairly, not to place blame or determine who's right and who's wrong*. This is also very important for you to remember when you're helping your kids mediate their own conflicts.

After your children have helped the puppets talk out their conflict using "I messages," follow up with an "I message" exercise similar to the one you did in Chapter 1. Read your children the following scenarios and have them turn the "you messages" into "I messages."

Scenario 1: *You're playing by yourself and your brother is in the same room having a snack. You get up to get a drink, and when you come back your brother has started playing with the toy you just had. This bothers you.*

"You message": *You better put that down right now. That's mine!*

"I message":

Here are some suggested "I messages" you can read to your children *after* they have come up with their own:

– I was just playing with that toy and I'd like it back.
– I wish you'd ask me before playing with a toy I'm in the middle of using.
– I don't like that you took the toy. Please give it back.

Now have your children role play this scenario using any "I messages" they came up with. Have one person play the role of the sibling who had the toy first. Have someone else be the brother who picked up the toy. After the initial "I message" is delivered, have the second person think of an "I message" as a response. Here's an example:

> **Person 1:** *"I didn't like it when you took the toy I was playing with. Please give it back."*
> **Person 2:** *"I didn't realize you were still playing with it. You got up and left the room."*

After the role playing, talk about how it felt to deliver "I messages" and then go on to the next scenario:

> **Scenario 2:** *Your best friend has just come over. Your little sister wants to play with the two of you. You don't want to include her because you find her annoying.*

"You message": *You're a pain. Go away and leave us alone.*

"I message":

Have your children come up with their own "I messages" first. You can share the following ones with them afterward:

– I know you'd like to play with us, but we're going to play by ourselves this afternoon.
– I don't want to hurt your feelings, but we're not going to play with you today.
– I don't like it when you always try to play with my friends and me. It annoys me.

Once again, have your children role play this scenario, each giving "I messages" to the other. Talk about the role play when they are finished. Remind them that the purpose of the "I messages" is to say what's on their mind but to do so respectfully. *Emphasize the importance of compassion balanced with authenticity.*

Scenario 3: *You lent your sister your new CD. She lost it. You're livid.*

"You message": *You lost my new CD? How could you be so careless! That's the last time I'll lend you anything!*

"I message":

Suggested "I messages":

– I'm *really upset* that you lost my CD. It was brand new!
– I can't believe this happened! I'd like you to buy me a new CD with your allowance.
– I'm so angry. I asked you not to take my CD out of the house! I think you should replace it.

Scenario 4: *Your mother has just made an embarrassing comment about you in front of your friends.*

"You message": *You made me feel like a complete idiot! How could you have said that about me in front of my friends?*

"I message":

Suggested "I messages":

– I'm completely humiliated right now! What you said was *so embarrassing* to me!

– I don't want you to talk about me like that in front of my friends. Don't you realize how embarrassing that is for me?

– I'm really angry right now. My friends are probably laughing at me because of what you just said!

Scenario 5: *Your family has agreed that there will be no physical fighting. This is part of your Guidelines for a Peaceful Family, plus an important standard your parents have. However, today your older brother is in a really bad mood. You accidentally step on his foot and he turns around and pushes you into the refrigerator.*

"You message": *You jerk! You know pushing isn't allowed. You're in big trouble now, because I'm telling!*

"I message:"

Suggested "I messages:"

– I'm *not* going to get into a fight with you. It's not worth it.

– I *don't* want to be treated that way, do you understand?

– As much as I'd like to push you back right now, I'm not going to. We made an agreement as a family and I intend to honor it.

This situation is a lot harder, because most children's automatic response to pushing or hitting is to push or hit back. Kids, especially boys, don't want to appear weak or vulnerable. The urge for retaliation can become very strong in these moments. **We need to address this with our children and let them know that regardless of the circumstance, it's neither "cool" nor acceptable to fight or use put-downs.**

You're probably wondering right now: "What if my child is out on the playground and some bully attacks him? Shouldn't he defend himself?" That's a valid question, one parents often ask. You don't want your child to get in fights, but you don't want him to be taken advantage of, either. Yet did you know it is often petty fights that lead to violence? That's right. The majority of violent acts children perpetrate against each other often start with benign things like name-calling, dirty looks, or teasing. Staying out of a fight may actually save your child's life.

Those of us leading peacemaking workshops around the country are strongly recommending that instead of fighting, we must teach our kids to stand tall, look the other person in the eye with conviction, and say firmly, "This isn't worth fighting over," then walk away with dignity. Reiterate to your children that standing tall and looking the person directly in the eye takes more strength and courage than fighting back. Often, bullies will back down when confronted assertively like this. If not, your child should immediately seek the help of an adult.

Tell your children when someone makes them angry enough to hit, they themselves have actually lost. By hitting, we show we've lost control of our good judgment. If your children have a tendency to fight at home, tell them the best thing they can do when a fight starts brewing is *immediately separate, take a deep breath, and then give an "I message."*

Have your kids practice standing tall and making assertive statements like those above while looking someone directly in the eyes. Let them role play this scenario and really spend time discussing it. See if you can get your children to the point where they'll agree to stop themselves from giving in to the impulse to physically hurt each other. Emphasize the need to stop, breathe, and chill the minute the impulse to fight comes on. Remind them, too, that it is critical to talk things out afterward.

If your kids have a lot of physical energy they need to release with each other, roughhousing sometimes will do the trick. Boys, especially, use roughhousing as a way to bond. *As long as they agree not to purposely hurt each other,* roughhousing can provide them with the physical outlet they need.

Caution them, however, that they must be vigilant not to let roughhousing cross over the line into aggression. Tell them as soon as either of them senses this happening, they must say "Time out" and separate.

Step 3—Each person states the problem as the other person sees it, reflecting back what they have heard. (Note: This is also called "Say back.")

Once again, introduce this step to your children with puppets and/or role play. In Chapter 5 we played "The Good Listening Game" and "I Heard You Say." Both are excellent preparation for using reflective listening in conflict situations. Now take a look at how to apply this strategy in a role play using puppets:

Let your children know you'll be practicing step 3 of the Win/Win Guidelines today. Have the puppets engage in another conflict. Ask your children to suggest ways the puppets can cool off and "I messages" they can give. After one puppet gives an "I message" have the other puppet paraphrase what he has just heard, like in this example with my two favorite puppets, Froggie and Alf:

> **Froggie:** *I'm mad because you sat in my chair.*
> **Alf:** *You're angry with me because I sat in your chair?*
> **Froggie:** *That's right. I was just about to sit down and you were in it.*
> *(Now the other puppet gives his "I message.")*
> **Alf:** *I didn't realize it was **your** chair. I just thought it was a plain old chair!*
> *(Now Froggie reflects back what Alf just said.)*
> **Froggie:** *So you didn't realize it was mine?*
> **Alf:** *No, and I didn't mean to get you angry, either.*

I've had people in workshops ask, "How can young children possibly do this? It seems too hard." Believe it or not, children as young as kindergarten have successfully learned to do reflective listening. I've gone into kindergartens where I've heard children say things like, "I didn't like when you took my doll," to which the other child has responded, "I heard you say you didn't like when I took your doll. Here, you can have it back." It's easier for children to learn this strategy when they're young. The younger the better, as a matter of fact, because young children have so much less to unlearn.

Now, back to our role play. You don't need to resolve the whole conflict yet. Just practice reflective listening, and later we'll put all the pieces together. Continue with the following scenarios and have your children think of "I messages" and reflective listening statements for each.

> **Scenario 1:** *You were just about to eat the last slice of pizza in the box. Your brother grabs it first.*
> *Person 1 gives an "I message":*
> *Person 2 paraphrases what was said:*
> *Person 1 acknowledges being heard correctly or not (saying either "That's right," or "No, what I meant was . . ."):*
> *Person 2 gives an "I message":*
> *Person 1 paraphrases what was said:*
> *Person 2 acknowledges what was said (saying either "That's right," or "No, what I meant was . . ."):*

Scenario 2: *Your little sister squishes toothpaste on your hand and thinks it's funny. You don't think it's funny at all.*
Person 1 gives an "I message":
Person 2 paraphrases what was said:
Person 1 acknowledges being heard correctly or not (saying either "That's right," or "No, what I meant was . . ."):
Person 2 gives an "I message":
Person 1 paraphrases what was said:
Person 2 acknowledges what was said (saying either "That's right," or "No, what I meant was . . ."):

Scenario 3: *Your dad just yelled at you for playing your music too loud. You don't think it's loud, plus you don't like the way he just talked to you.*
Person 1 gives an "I message":
Person 2 paraphrases what was said:
Person 1 acknowledges being heard correctly or not (saying either "That's right," or "No, what I meant was . . ."):
Person 2 gives an "I message":
Person 1 paraphrases what was said:
Person 2 acknowledges what was said (saying either "That's right," or "No, what I meant was . . ."):

Your kids may wonder why they need to reflect back what the other person says. When we say back what we heard, we show we're really listening to the other person and not just thinking about what we're going to say next. That makes the other person more willing to listen to what *we* have to say.

Also, we are sometimes mistaken in our assumptions, and reflecting back ensures that we really *do* understand how the other person feels. Research indicates that 85% of all conflicts come from miscommunication. That's right, 85%! Reflective listening enables us to understand what went wrong and clear things up.

Beyond all else, good listening is a sign of respect. When we show respect, it's easier to solve problems.

Step 4—Each person takes responsibility for his or her role in the conflict.

The essence of conflict resolution is taking responsibility. Looking to assign blame or trying to figure out who started it is counterproductive.

Nobel Peace Prize nominee Thich Naht Hanh says, "Like a fireman, we have to pour water on the blaze first and not waste time looking for the one who set the house on fire . . ."

You'll notice that after you've taken the time to build a foundation of peacemaking, your children will be more apt to take responsibility for their roles in conflicts. Therefore this step is optional. Practice it with your children anyway, because there still will be times they'll resort to blaming, and this step will help them get back on track.

Once again, use puppets or role play to introduce this step. Start by letting your children know that in the majority of conflicts, *both* people are responsible in some way. It is only in bullying situations where one person is completely at fault and the other is absolutely innocent. Sometimes conflicts can even arise out of not being assertive when you need to be, as you'll see in the following puppet scenario.

> *Background: Alf played with his friend all morning and didn't include Froggie. Froggie felt left out and hurt. Instead of saying anything, Froggie waits until the friend leaves, and then purposely trips Alf as he walks by.*
>
> **Alf:** *Hey! What did you do that for? That was mean. (Alf pushes Froggie as he says this.)*
>
> **Froggie:** *Get your hands of me, you idiot! (pushing Alf back)*
>
> **Alf:** *You started it! (pushing Froggie one more time)*

Ask your children to "advise" the puppets on how to work out their conflict. By now, your children should easily suggest cooling off, "I messages," and reflective listening statements. After they do this, ask the question, "How was each puppet responsible for the conflict?" Talk about this with your children and have them suggest alternative ways each puppet could have responded.

Now try the next scenario and go through this process again:

> *Alf is playing Nintendo and he wants it all to himself. Froggie walks in.*
>
> **Froggie:** *Alf, will you share the Nintendo with me?*
>
> **Alf:** *No, I want to play by myself.*
>
> **Froggie:** *Well, I'm not gonna be your friend anymore! (He stomps off.)*

Be sure to have your children determine how each puppet was responsible for the conflict and what Froggie and Alf could have done differently.

Now ask your children to think about a conflict they've had with each other. Make sure the conflict they come up with is one that involves no more than two children.

Role play the conflict and then have your children suggest ways they could have cooled off, "I messages" they could have given, and reflective listening statements they could have made. Stop when you get to step 4 of the Win/Win Guidelines, "taking responsibility." Encourage each child to say how they were responsible for their role in the conflict. If they take responsibility, affirm them for their honesty and maturity. If not, tell them that it takes a big person to admit a mistake and to "own" what they might have done wrong. Let them know that they'll feel proud of themselves when they do this, and you will too.

Step 5—Brainstorm solutions and choose one that satisfies both parties, a win/win solution.

To practice brainstorming, refer back to the puppets' conflict over the Nintendo. Have your children come up with as many ways as possible for the puppets to solve their problem. Don't eliminate any ideas and don't let your children censor each other. Let them know that sometimes the best solutions come out of what seem to be outlandish ideas.

List your children's ideas on paper and encourage them to keep coming up with more, even after they think they've exhausted every possibility. The reason for doing this is to let your children see that *there are many, many possible solutions to problems,* and that working out conflicts is a creative process.

After your children finish brainstorming, have them choose one or two solutions they think will be fair and acceptable to each puppet. Let them know they can combine solutions, too.

Note: This particular conflict provides an opportunity for you to bring up the concept that, much as we don't like it, people do have a right to say "No." After your children have come up with solutions for the puppets' conflict, have them look and see what options Froggie could have exercised if Alf had, point blank, refused to share with him. Let your children know that although it's always preferable to share, sometimes it's not realistic to expect others to do so every time we want them to. When another person won't share with us, we need to find alternatives so we don't end up in a funk over their decision.

Back to brainstorming. Remember the other conflict your children just role played, the one they actually had together? Now have them brainstorm solutions to this conflict, coming up with as many solutions as possible. List their solutions and then have them choose one or a combination of several. Let them know this is the process you want them to use whenever a conflict arises. Make sure their solutions are their own, not yours, except if your children are 5 and under.

Step 6—Affirm, forgive, or thank.

Congratulations! You have just helped your children mediate a conflict. Affirm yourself for the great job you did. Now it's time for the good part: Affirm your children for the great job *they* did and have them affirm each other.

In some conflicts, affirming might not be the thing to do. Forgiving, thanking, or saying "I'm sorry" might be more natural. Sometimes a hug or handshake is all that's needed. Have your children do what feels right to them. Sometimes kids will choose to apologize at this point. If apologizing seems like the appropriate thing to do, encourage it, but don't push too hard. Closure and acknowledgment are what this step is about.

A Lifelong Strategy

Now let me share with you a story about my son Michael, now 25—the one who had initially resisted conflict resolution.

I asked him what lessons of peacemaking he applies in his life as an adult. Without hesitation, he said, "Conflict resolution. It's had such a big impact on me."

"How?" I asked.

"I learned to see things through other people's eyes. I learned how to walk in their shoes. It's totally ingrained in me to find a resolution and get past whatever the problem is. I do it with Tim (his brother) and with all of my friends."

He went on to relate an incident with a roommate that could have led to the end of their friendship, but by putting into practice the peacemaking skills and understandings he had grown up with, the relationship not only withstood the problem, it actually grew stronger.

John started hanging around with a group of people I didn't like.
They started getting together pretty often and they wouldn't include
me. John and I had always been really good friends, but at that point

we started drifting apart. I felt hurt and he felt guilty. Rather than letting things go on that way, I decided to talk to him. I used what I'd learned growing up.

I started by telling him what was on my mind and asked him to tell me what was on his. We listened to each other and showed respect for each other's point of view. By talking it out we were able to empathize with each other and we started to realize the problem wasn't as big as we'd thought it was. The resolution came as we began to understand each other's feelings. Then we were able to find ways of compromising. This is how I handle conflicts. I can't imagine doing it any other way.

Michael's willingness to talk things out and listen with an open mind inspired his roommate to follow suit. The conflict was resolved and the friendship salvaged. It pleased me no end to see what Michael learned as a child still has such a great impact on the way he lives his life.

People sometimes ask, "What if the other person doesn't know about peacemaking? How can the process work?"

I always reply that most times, **people will follow your lead when you are open, respectful, and willing to hear them out**. When you act in this manner, it often defuses their defensiveness and fear. If the element of confrontation is absent, you can move forward and begin seeking solutions. And surprisingly, this can happen even if only one person knows how to work out conflicts, as we saw in Michael's situation.

Exercise:

Is there anyone in your life with whom you have unresolved conflicts? What steps can you take to work things out?

Are there any unresolved conflicts your children have with each other? How can you help them resolve these conflicts? Write about this.

Concluding Thoughts

The words we choose, the ideas we express have enormous power. Words can keep us stuck in the old paradigm of "I win, you lose," or they can move us into a new paradigm where we seek solutions to common problems: **a win/win paradigm.** When we come from this perspective, we stop making each other the enemy and we start seeking common ground. We move from thinking "it's us against each other" toward knowing "it's us against the problem."

The words we choose have the power to shape the world, and the influence we have as parents is manifested in the words we speak. Never doubt for a moment the profound impact you make.

Recap

Peaceful Parenting Key #13:
***I resolve conflicts peacefully
and teach my children
to do the same.***

~

By taking steps to make our home a peaceful one, we are laying the groundwork for the prevention and resolution of conflicts.

People, especially children, can resolve conflicts without fighting.

In order for conflict resolution strategies to be effective, you must first create the willingness to compromise.

Before mediating any conflicts, introduce the following rules:

Rules for Win/Win

We agree to do the following:

1. Tell the truth.
2. Treat each other with respect.
3. Attack the problem, not the person.
4. Wait for our turn to speak. No interrupting.
5. Be willing to compromise.

Use the following six-step strategy for resolving conflicts:

The Win/Win Guidelines

1. Take time to cool off.

2. Take turns stating the problem as you see it, using "I messages." No put-downs, blaming or name-calling.

3. Take turns stating the problem as the other person sees it, reflecting back what you have heard.

4. Take responsibility for your role in the problem.

5. Brainstorm solutions together, and choose a solution that satisfies both people, a win/win solution.

6. Affirm, forgive, or thank each other.

Help your child move away from thinking, "It's us against each other," and toward understanding, "It's us against the problem."

Teach your kids to say no to fighting. Show them how to stand tall, look the person in the eye, and assertively say, "This isn't worth fighting over."

Resolving conflicts peacefully can become a lifelong strategy if it's practiced at home when children are young.

**Note: Parents, post these charts
in your home for easy use:**

Abbreviated Win/Win

1. Cool off.

2. Talk it out using "I messages."

3. Say back what you heard.

4. Take responsibility.

5. Brainstorm solutions.

6. Affirm, forgive, or thank.

Rules for Win/Win

We agree to do the following in order to resolve our conflicts fairly and peacefully:

1. Tell the truth.

2. Treat each other with respect.

3. Attack the problem, not the person.

4. Wait for our turn to speak. No interrupting.

5. Be willing to compromise.

RESOURCES FOR PARENTS

Faber, Adele and Mazlish, Elaine. *Siblings Without Rivalry: How to Help Your Children Live Together so You Can Live Too.* New York: Avon, 1988. How to resolve conflicts among siblings; anecdotes, personal stories, and strategies.

Fisher, Roger and Ury, William. *Getting to Yes.* New York: Penguin, 1981. The definitive guide to negotiating using conflict resolution strategies personally, locally, and globally.

Fried, S., & Fried, P. *Bullies and Victims: Helping Your Child through the Schoolyard Battle-field.* New York: M. Evans & Co., 1996. Bully-proofing strategies for your children.

Levine, Stewart. *Getting to Resolution: Turning Conflict into Collaboration.* Berrett-Koehler Publishers, 1998. Offers tools that get to the core of every conflict; provides accessible guidelines that take the reader step-by-step through the process of resolving conflicts.

McCoy, Elin. *What to Do When Kids Are Mean to Your Child.* Pleasantville, NY: Reader's Digest Press, 1997. Techniques for helping your child deal with teasing, bullying, and other aggressive behaviors.

Paley, Vivian Gussin. *You Can't Say You Can't Play.* Cambridge, MA: Harvard University Press, 1992. Renowned teacher and MacArthur Fellow tells us how we can create inclusive environments for young children.

Ury, William L. *Getting to Peace: Transforming Conflict at Home, at Work, and in The World.* New York: Viking, 1999. From one of the world's leading negotiation specialists, a treatise on achieving peace at home, at work, in the community, and in the world so we can live together peacefully.

Website

Gun Free Kids—www.gunfreekids.com—"Coming together to keep guns away from kids."

RESOURCES FOR CHILDREN

Adams, Lisa K. *Dealing With Teasing.* Rosen Group, 1998. Explains the difference between playful teasing and teasing that hurts. Talks about why children tease and how to deal with it. This book is part of The Conflict Resolution Library. Other titles are: *Dealing With Arguments, Dealing With Hurt Feelings, Dealing With Lying, Dealing With Someone Who Won't Listen,* (Grades K–4)

Bates, Betty. *Tough Beans.* New York: Dial Books for Young Readers, 1992. With the help of his best friend, Nat comes to terms with having diabetes and being plagued by a bully. (Grades 3–6)

Berenstain, Stan & Jan. *The Berenstain Bears Get in a Fight.* New York: Random House, 1995. When Brother and Sister Bear get into a major fight, Mama Bear helps them work it out. (Grades K–2)

Byars, Betsy. *The Cybil War*. New York: Viking, 1981. A conflict between two long-term friends arises from misinformation. (Grades 3–6)

Ferguson, Alane. *Cricket and the Crackerjack Kid*. New York: Avon, 1990. The teacher sets up a jury to resolve a disagreement between two students. (Grades 2–5)

Fitzhugh, Louise. *Bang, Bang, You're Dead*. New York: Harper Collins, 1969. Two children fight for control of a hill, then work out their conflict. (Grades K–3)

Fox, Mem. *Feathers and Fools*. New York: Harcourt Brace, 1996. Swans and peacocks get into battle and self-destruct. In the ruins, they leave behind two eggs which hatch and form an alliance for peace and reconciliation. (Grades K–3)

Gilson, Jamie. *Sticks and Stones and Skeleton Bones*. New York: Lothrop, 1991. Best friends have a conflict that goes from bad to worse. (Grades K–2)

Greene, Constance Clark. *Your Old Pal, Al*. New York: Viking, 1979. Perceptive story about how words can hurt and forgiveness can heal. (Grades 3–6)

Jones, Rebecca C. *Matthew and Tilly*. New York: Puffin Books, 1995. Matthew and Tilly find out how to solve their problems after having a fight. (Grades K–2)

Kasza, Keiko. *The Rat and the Tiger*. New York: G. P. Putnam's Sons, 1993. Tiger bullies Rat because Rat is smaller. One day Rat stands up to Tiger. (Grades K–3)

Lionni, Leo. *Six Crows*. New York: Alfred A. Knopf, 1988. A farmer and six crows are at odds about who has the rights to the wheat crop. A wise owl helps them solve their problem. (Grades K–2)

Lucas, Eileen. *Peace on the Playground*. New York: Franklin Watts, 1991. Shows kids why it's important to work out conflicts and how to do so. (Grades K–6)

Mauser, Pat Rhodes. *A Bundle of Sticks*. New York: Atheneum, 1992. A boy who is bullied learns how to handle conflicts. (Grades 2–6)

Millman, Dan. *The Secret of the Peaceful Warrior*. Tiburon, CA: H.J. Kramer, 1991. Wonderful story of a young boy's courage and humanity in the face of a bully. (Grades 1–6)

Romain, T. *Bullies Are a Pain in the Brain*. Minneapolis, MN: Free Spirit, 1997. Gives children insight into dealing with bullies. (Grades K–6)

Seuss, Dr. *The Butter Battle Book*. New York: Random House, 1984. Dr. Seuss shows how perceived differences can escalate to fighting and ultimately to war. (Grades K–4)

Spinelli, Jerry. *Maniac McGee*. Boston: Little Brown, 1990. Conflicting groups are brought together through the work of one child. (Grades 3–6)

Surat, Michele Maria. *Angel Child, Dragon Child*. New York: Scholastic, Inc., 1990. A little Vietnamese girl turns around the actions of the class bully and makes him her friend. (Grades K–2)

Webster-Doyle, T. *Why Is Everybody Always Picking on Me: A Guide to Handling Bullies*. Middlebury, VT: Atrium Publishing, 1991. What to do so you won't be a victim of bullies. (Grades K–6)

Zolotow, Charlotte. *The Hating Book*. New York: Harper Collins, 1989. Two friends eventually work out a misunderstanding and learn there are two sides to every conflict. (Grades K–2)

CHAPTER 9

Building Your Child's Emotional Intelligence and Self-Esteem

Feelings of self-esteem in particular, and happiness in general, develop as side-effects of mastering challenges, working successfully, overcoming frustration and boredom, and winning. The feeling of self-esteem is a by-product of doing well.

—Dr. Martin Seligman

Peaceful Parenting Key #14:
I find ways to help my children succeed.
~

What do we most want for our children? That they be happy, confident, successful and feel excited about life. Yet many of us are not quite sure how to make this happen. Did you know there are specific things we can do to foster success and confidence in our children? That's right, what we do in our homes can help our children develop all the wonderful potential they are born with. In this chapter, you will learn a variety of strategies for building self-esteem and emotional intelligence—keys to your child's success in life.

Building Self-Esteem

The University of Pennsylvania's Dr. Martin Seligman, our nation's top expert in developing children's self-esteem and optimism, tells us we can build self-esteem in our children by providing them with opportunities to succeed and teaching them the steps needed to reach their goals. According to Dr. Seligman, the secret of self-esteem is: ". . . Mastery, persistence, overcoming frustration and boredom, and meeting the challenge." We can provide the building blocks for self-esteem by giving our children opportunities to master new skills, encouraging them to persevere, and by helping them find ways to spend their time productively. Throughout this chapter, you will discover ways you can do each of these right in your own home.

Another factor crucial to our child's self-esteem, according to Dr. Seligman, is the way he *interprets* the good and bad things that happen to him in life. Take a look at the following examples of how different children interpret the same event:

Last week, Mrs. Jackson gave a pop geography quiz to her fifth grade class. Both Joy and Dana failed the test. Joy attributed her failure to a lack of studying, saying, "I feel bad about failing the quiz. I guess I should have kept up with my studying all along instead of waiting till the last minute and then planning to study all at once. If Mrs. Jackson is going to keep giving us pop quizzes, I'd better start doing a little studying each night so I do better next time."

Dana, on the other hand, saw herself as the problem, saying, "I'm not good at tests. I know it was just a pop quiz, but most of the kids in the class got at least a C. Maybe I'm just not as smart as they are. I've always felt kind of dumb. I guess I really am. I'll never do well in school."

Joy, who was raised to have an optimistic outlook, took responsibility for the failed quiz and realized what she has to do to prevent this from happening in the future. Dana, who is clearly pessimistic, personalized the explanation for her failure, saying that she's dumb and doesn't do well on tests. In giving these as the reasons for her poor performance, Dana shows she believes this is a permanent condition that will cause her to do poorly throughout her years in school.

If children believe failure is *personal* and *permanent*, they will see their failures as indicators of inevitable patterns in their lives. Seligman tells us that when this happens, children become vulnerable to developing low self-esteem for the long term. Conversely, self-esteem grows when a child understands there are specific causes of failure, but that these causes are not signs of her own personal deficiencies. A child who sees failure this way will take responsibility without feeling personally diminished.

An optimistic child who does poorly on a test says, "I didn't study hard enough," seeing the problem as separate from her inherent value as a person. The pessimistic child will say, "I'm stupid," seeing *herself* as the problem.

This is why, as parents, we need to be very careful about how we express criticism. "I'm unhappy about the condition your room is in," addresses the problem without personalizing it. "You're a slob," makes the child, not his room, the problem. One of our first lessons in building self-esteem is this: *Teach your child to take responsibility for problems through action, not by personalizing them.*

Children absorb the voices of their parents, learning to talk to themselves in the same way their parents have spoken to them. A friend of mine, an intelligent, well-educated person, forgot to pick up something she needed at the supermarket and said, "I can't believe what an idiot I am. I can't get anything right."

"Why do you talk to yourself in such a mean way?" I asked her.

"My mother's voice is still in my head," she responded.

Through the words we choose, we can help our children adopt either negative or positive outlooks.

Now for the good part: Here are seven proven things you can do at home to nurture your child's optimism and self-esteem.

Focus on your child's successes.

Describe to your child what you observe him succeeding in, and be specific. "You hit a home run, Keith! You've practiced very hard, you concentrated and kept your eye on the ball, and you had a strong, even swing. I'm so proud of all you did to make this happen!" Each time your child succeeds at something, no matter how small, verbalize it for him in this manner.

By the same token, avoid descriptions of success that are vague, personal, and permanent like this one. "Keith, you're the best baseball player in the world. You'll probably be hitting home runs forever." Responses like this one can actually lower a child's self-esteem by assigning to him unrealistic goals and giving the message that he has to live up to inflated expectations. If during his next game he doesn't hit a home run, then his self-image is diminished.

In contrast, in the first scenario Keith is guided to see that he achieved his home run by things he did: practicing, concentrating, keeping his eye on the ball, and swinging strongly.

Provide your child with opportunities to succeed.

Help your child find activities within the range of her own interests and encourage her to pursue them. Melissa, age 8, feels bad because her older sister is a star soccer player, but she herself feels like a total klutz when it comes to soccer or any other sport.

However, Melissa loves to draw and paint. In her athletic family this seems a little out of place, with mom and dad always on the tennis court and little brother Brad dribbling a basketball at age 6.

Melissa's mother is wise, though. She decides that rather than pushing Melissa into sports, she will encourage her to focus on her artwork and help her find opportunities to develop her artistic talent even more.

She has Melissa sign up for a course in watercolors, and each time Melissa brings something home she has created, her mother displays it and praises it sincerely and specifically. Melissa has started valuing herself for her unique talent instead of berating herself for not being more like her athletic family.

Display evidences of your child's successes.

When Melissa came home with her first completed watercolor, her mom framed it and hung it in the living room. Not only did Melissa feel proud, but her painting was now available to her waiting eyes as evidence of her success.

When relatives and friends came to the house, mom always made sure to show them Melissa's painting, pointing out how hard she had worked to create artwork with such color and vibrance. Each time this happened, Melissa's positive feelings about herself as an artist increased.

All her new paintings were displayed somewhere in the house. At the end of the course, Melissa chose one to be custom-framed. Now when her sister is out in the backyard practicing soccer, instead of feeling she can't measure up, Melissa will go to the self-styled studio she and her mother set up, and she'll paint or draw.

Exercise:

What are your child's areas of strength? How can you help her develop them? Write about this.

Help your child set realistic goals.

Research has proven that when we set goals that are too difficult or goals that are beneath our capabilities, we set ourselves up for disappointment, but when we set goals that are a little beyond what we are capable of and we work toward reaching those goals, we set ourselves up for success.

Ten-year-old Larry has developed a growing passion for rocks. Every time the family went on a trip, Larry collected as many unusual and varied rocks as he could find and then set them up on a table in his room. He has spent many hours studying his rocks with a microscope and trying to match them to names in the family's encyclopedia.

Les, his father, took Larry shopping for a rock identifying kit at the Nature Store. Larry wanted the most complex one, a kit containing fancy tools and advanced reading materials designed for high school geology students. Les hesitated and pointed out another kit designed for kids going into middle school. This kit had tools and reading materials slightly above Larry's age range and had the potential for providing Larry with a realistic challenge and less frustration. Although Larry balked, Les went with the middle-school-level kit. Within a few days, he saw his choice paying off: Larry had begun spending hours identifying the names and geological origins of the rocks he had found. He was inspired and energized by his work.

Instinctively, Les understood that if he had gotten Larry a kit too far above his level, Larry would have eventually met with the frustration and boredom that arises when we try to set goals that are far beyond our reach. By providing his son with a challenge just above his level, he is helping him create a bridge to the *next* level, which, before long, Larry will be ready for.

Encourage your child to set and reach his/her own goals.

Jonathan has always loved music. Now that he's 9 and starting fourth grade, he can learn to play an instrument in school. His father, Roger, encouraged Jonathan to set a goal for himself by choosing any instrument he was interested in learning to play. Jonathan decided on the trumpet.

"What goal do you want to set for yourself with the trumpet?" Roger asked.

Jonathan replied, "I want to become good enough to play in the spring concert."

"What do you think you'll need to do to reach your goal?" Roger asked.

"Well, Mr. Kirby says we have to practice at least three days a week after school, so if I want to be really good, maybe I'll practice every day," Jonathan answered enthusiastically.

"Is that realistic?" Roger asked. "What if you have other things to do on a particular day and you don't have time? Remember, you're taking gymnastics and you're in cub scouts, too."

"OK, 5 or 6 days a week—that's how much I'm going to practice," said Jonathan.

"What time do you think you'll practice each day?" asked Roger.

"What difference does it make?" Jonathan wondered.

"Well, if you know what time you're going to practice, then you'll be sure to schedule it in, instead of letting other things take over," answered Roger.

"How's 8:30 to 9:00 each night? Then I can get my homework done first," said Jonathan after thinking about it.

"Sounds good to me," said Roger. "Would you like to write that down somewhere to remind yourself?"

At that, Jonathan went into his room and made a sign that said "Trumpet Practice 8:30-9:00, Monday through Friday (and sometimes Saturday, too)." After that, Roger would check in with Jonathan several days a week to see if he was keeping to his schedule. He would compliment Jonathan when he stuck to the schedule and gently reminded him when he didn't, always mentioning the final goal he had set for himself of being good enough to be in the spring concert.

Along the way, Roger gave Jonathan a journal called "My Accomplishments." Every time Jonathan learned something new on his trumpet—or anywhere else, for that matter—he would record his accomplishments in the journal. The process of setting and reaching his goals and recording his steps along the way gave a tremendous boost to Jonathan's sense of competence, a key element of self-esteem.

Exercise:

Talk to your child about goals he would like to set. What specific steps can you help him take to achieve these goals?

Help your child build perseverance.

Five-year-old Sophie has a low frustration level. When she has trouble doing something, she cries, screams, and gives up quickly. Her mother, Esther, has been dreading teaching Sophie how to tie her shoes, but she knows she needs to do so before Sophie starts school. Esther decides to do some reading on helping kids deal with frustration, and she discovers several things she can do to help Sophie persevere through a difficult task, making it a challenge rather than a chore:

– *Create a positive mental set.* Esther tells Sophie she's going to learn how to do a "big girl job" and that it's going to be fun and easy, like playing a game. In fact, for this purpose, Esther has bought a used rag doll with a "lacing vest" that Sophie will be able to practice tying on. Immediately Sophie's anxiety level goes down and her enthusiasm is piqued.

– *Break the task into small, manageable increments and practice.* On the first day of learning how to tie, Esther just shows Sophie how to tie without a bow. Sophie practices on her new doll, on a dress she has in her closet, and on a string that she ties around the banister. Sophie enjoys doing this and looks forward to the next step. The next day, Esther teaches Sophie how to make a loop with the right side of the lace and wrap the left side around her thumb. This part is a little harder, so Esther encourages Sophie to take little breaks when she gets frustrated, all the while complementing her on any progress she makes. Again, she has Sophie practice on a variety of objects.

– *Compliment small steps along the way.* Each time Sophie succeeds at any step in the process, Esther gives her a sincere, specific compliment. "You're really sticking with this even when it's difficult for you. I'm so proud of you." Or, "I noticed how hard you're concentrating to get the shoelace around your thumb. Excellent!" And, "I'm impressed that even though this is hard, you're continuing to try and you're not giving up. That's a very grown-up way to handle this."

– *Model perseverance yourself,* particularly by not giving in to your frustration with your child's frustration. If your child starts to "lose it" somewhere along the way, avoid put-downs and stay positive. For example,when Sophie got to the part where she had to hold onto the loop with her right hand while making a loop with her left, she started to cry and say, "I can't do it. This is too hard!"

   In Esther's head, she heard herself say, "Darn it, Sophie, don't start with your whining now. Just shut up and tie the damned shoe!" Instead of voicing her own frustration, though, Esther repeated a positive goal statement in her head to get herself back on track: "I am patient and understanding with my daughter."

   She took a few deep breaths and reminded herself to focus on the positive. This was all she needed to keep herself from becoming negative. At this point she suggested they take a short break and try again later.

– **Celebrate the finished product.** When Sophie finally learned how to tie her shoes, Esther hugged and kissed her with unrestrained glee, all the while reiterating the specific ways she had reached her goal. Later, they drove over to Grandma's house so Sophie could demonstrate her newly achieved competency.

– *Show how achieving this goal will help with future successes.* "Sophie, now you know how to keep going even when something is hard for you. You saw that by practicing, sticking to it, and not giving in to frustration, you learned to tie your shoes. Next time something seems difficult, you'll find it will be easier than you thought, because now you know how to stick with things you start. What would you like to try next?" Esther even took a picture of Sophie wearing the sneakers she tied. Now Sophie has a visual reminder of her success.

Exercise:

   Are there any areas where your child needs to learn perseverance? What can you do to help him? Write about this.

Model optimistic thinking.

Research has indicated children learn optimism and pessimism in large part from their parents. Catch yourself in your own negative reactions, because you may be passing them on to your children.

If you find you express a lot of negativity, I would strongly suggest reading *Learned Optimism* and *The Optimistic Child*, both by Martin Seligman. Each will provide you with a plethora of wonderful ideas about nurturing optimism and relinquishing pessimism in yourself and your children. A positive outlook on life *can* be developed, regardless of age or past patterns. Read on to find out how.

Shifting From Pessimism to Optimism

When we have a sense of control over our lives and when we see things through positive eyes, our outlook is brightened and our self-esteem grows. Did you know that it is possible to move yourself (and your children) out of negative thinking and toward a more empowered perspective? Seligman and his colleagues have identified four major skills proven to help people gain freedom from pessimistic thinking, even people who are depressed. The effectiveness of these skills over time was documented in the University of Pennsylvania's Penn Prevention Program. Take a look at what they are:

Notice your negative thoughts.

When you can simply observe negative thoughts that pass through your head, even the small ones, you begin realizing that's just what they are—thoughts, not reality. Dr. Seligman says that sometimes quickly fleeting negative thoughts, "automatic" ones, can pull us down into a depressed or pessimistic place. By catching yourself getting caught in negative thinking and reminding yourself that you *can* let go of bad thoughts, you'll be taking the first crucial step to let go of pessimism. The same holds true for children.

Kevin, age 8, is a worrier. The other day he came home from a friend's house moody and irritable. When his mom, Gloria, asked him what the problem was, he said, "I knocked down Matt's Lego building by mistake and he yelled at me. After that I started getting a stomachache and I finally told him I was going home. I don't feel well."

Sensing that Kevin's bad mood and stomachache were connected to what had just transpired between him and Matt, Gloria encouraged Kevin to keep talking about what had happened and how he reacted. Before long it became clear to both Gloria and Kevin that the way he was feeling came from his belief that Matt might not want to be his friend anymore. Now that Gloria had helped Kevin identify the automatic thought that was making him so anxious, she could help him move on to the next step.

Assess the negative thought.

When we assess our negative automatic thoughts, we gain some distance from them and enable ourselves to see that these thoughts are often inaccurate and exaggerated. When Gloria helped Kevin explore his belief that Matt wouldn't want to be his friend anymore, Kevin started to see that maybe he was overreacting and that Matt may have just been angry at the moment, not for the long haul.

Gloria encouraged Kevin to start thinking about all the things Matt liked about him and the many experiences they'd shared during their years of friendship. At that point Kevin started relaxing a little more, realizing it would be out of character for Matt to suddenly not want to be his friend anymore over a broken Lego building.

Looking at the problem logically.

"Maybe Matt was just upset about the Lego building, but he still likes me," said Kevin. Now he was ready to find out if this was the case. With Gloria at his side, he picked up the phone and called Matt.

"Hi, Kevin, how are you feeling now?" asked Matt. "Are you still sick? If you're not, maybe your mom would let you come back over. I have some new Lego ideas I want to try out with you."

Before Kevin had even gotten the words out of his mouth, Matt had already confirmed he still wanted to be Kevin's friend.

When he hung up the phone and told Gloria what Matt had said, Gloria asked, "So what do you think about Matt's being angry with you now?"

Kevin answered, "I guess Matt was just angry for a minute and then it went away." He was right.

Stop looking at problems as calamities.

Now Gloria helped Kevin understand that his bad thoughts were exactly that—bad thoughts, and just because he had bad thoughts it didn't mean his thoughts would come true. Kevin was able to remember other times when his calamatizing had gotten him worked up into a state of complete agitation, and he saw that in each instance, his fears were worse than anything that actually materialized. Going through this process enabled Gloria to help Kevin let go of a lot of the anxieties that plagued him. In time, Kevin would learn to start doing this for himself.

Use this method for yourself if you have a tendency toward negative thinking. As your children watch you respond to the positive and negative events of your life they will follow suit. If we have the will to do so, we have the ability to change old patterns no matter how ingrained they seem to be.

Exercise:

Is there any particular thing your child expresses pessimism about? Reflect on how to apply the above strategy to help him shift from pessimism to optimism.

Peaceful Parenting Key #15:
All my actions are guided by love, compassion,
fairness, respect, and integrity.
I nurture these attributes in my children.

~

Nurturing Emotional Intelligence

Like self-esteem, emotional intelligence can help people succeed in the most important areas of life—work, relationships, love, and friendship. When we treat our children with love, compassion, fairness, respect, and integrity, we model the basic building blocks of emotional intelligence. This is the essence of peaceful parenting: living all of the attributes we strive to embody in our children.

And what are some of the key attributes of emotional intelligence? Take a look:

- the ability to communicate effectively
- the ability to listen to others
- the ability to resolve conflicts
- the ability to handle stress
- impulse control
- the ability to delay gratification
- self-confidence
- self-awareness
- understanding what behavior is acceptable and unacceptable
- identifying feelings and expressing them appropriately
- self-control
- cooperation
- the ability to make and keep friends
- empathy
- problem solving

As you use this book, each of these attributes will grow in you. To keep yourself on track, ask yourself this question every day: "Are all my actions guided by love, compassion, fairness, respect, and integrity?" If the answer is yes, you will likely see the signs of emotional intelligence unfolding in your children, too.

Most of the attributes on this list above have been addressed in previous chapters. Now let's take a look at the last three:

Making friends
Building empathy
Problem solving

Read on for practical, hands-on strategies to help your children blossom in each of these areas of emotional intelligence.

Making Friends

In their wonderful book, *Emotionally Intelligent Parenting*, Maurice Elias, Steven Tobias, and Brian Friedlander talk about ways you can build many emotional intelligence traits in your children. When a child is able to make and keep friends with ease, they say he is adept at "befriendability." Here are some suggestions they have found help children grow in this area:

Be open-minded.
Encourage your child to look beyond the usual boundaries of age, race, gender, and color. Guide your children toward friendships based on common values and interests. As your kids grow older, caution them not to buy into stereotypes of friendship, like "You have to be popular to be happy," or "It's better to hang around with the cool kids."

Here's where the issue of integrity comes in—being true to oneself and not just going with the values of the crowd. Children who are open-minded have more options in their choice of friends, too.

Create new opportunities.
Build on your children's unique interests and guide them toward related activities where they can meet like-minded kids. For example, if your child loves music, take her to children's performances, enroll her in music lessons, and help her build a collection of favorite music. Along the way, encourage her to reach out to the children she meets. Sometimes limiting socializing to school and your neighborhood robs your child of the opportunity to have more enriching friendships.

Be the kind of person others want to be friends with.
Sit down with your child and have her look at things she does that either help or hinder friendships. Some things that hinder friendships are: not sharing, not listening, breaking promises, bragging, using put-downs, embarrassing others, not caring about other people's feelings.

The authors of *Emotionally Intelligent Parenting* recommend that you help your child identify any of the traits she has that hinder her "befriendability" and help her work on them. Set goals with your child as to which traits to work on, praise her when she does better, and remind her when she falls short. Don't criticize. Instead, say things like, "Remember your goal of improving your listening. When you interrupt like that, you're forgetting to work on that goal." And, of course, when she works at not interrupting, praise her.

More excellent suggestions for helping your children make friends come from Michele Borba in *Parents Do Make a Difference*. Here are four of my favorites:

Teach your kids how to give praise and encouragement to others.

Research bears this out: children who praise and encourage others have more friends. Borba advises parents to make a list of encouraging statements like, "You're really good at that," "Wow, that was terrific!" "Nice try," and "Great idea." Post the list and support your child in using it at home and with friends. Let your child know that praising siblings is a great way to strengthen this habit and improve relationships at home while preparing for the outside world.

Encourage cooperation.

Being conscious of the needs of others rather than putting one's own needs first is the beginning of cooperation. Encourage this at home as often as you can. At family meetings, talk about what it means to cooperate. Share the following list with your children or have them come up with one of their own:

Cooperation Is

– Noticing how other people feel and what they need.
– Showing your care for others by the way you act.
– Listening to what others have to say.
– Respecting, sharing, and compromising.
– Working together in a kind way.

Affirm your kids every time you notice them cooperating. Remind them that they're helping themselves become more "befriendable" every time they cooperate.

Teach your children how to start conversations.

Many children miss out on friendships simply because they don't know how to begin talking to someone they don't already know. Borba advises sitting down with your child and making a list of easy conversation starters for your child to practice. Role play scenarios with your child where she can strike up conversations in new situations. Here's an example:

> **Dad:** *Let's pretend we're at the park and you see a little girl your age you'd like to meet playing in the sandbox. I'll be the other girl and you come up and talk to me.*
>
> **Jamie (age 7):** *I'm too shy. I'd be scared to do that.*
>
> **Dad:** *Sometimes it is scary to make new friends. Practicing first makes it easier. Let's think of some things you could say.*
>
> **Jamie:** *How about, "Wanna play?"*
>
> **Dad:** *That's perfect. You could also try, "Wanna build a sand castle together?" or "Hi, my name is Jamie. What's yours?"*
>
> *(Jamie and Dad continue discussing openers, and then Dad hangs the list on Jamie's wall.)*
>
> **Dad:** *Now I'll pretend I'm in the sandbox, and you come over to me.*
>
> *(Jamie looks nervous and doesn't say anything.)*
>
> **Dad:** *Why don't you take some deep breaths first to calm yourself, and say something in your head like "I can do it!" Come on, we'll practice together.*
>
> *(Dad and Jamie take some nice deep breaths and say out loud, "I can do it!")*
>
> **Jamie:** *OK, I'm ready now. (She pretends she's approaching the sandbox.) Excuse me, wanna play together?*
>
> **Dad:** *Sure. What do you want to do?*
>
> **Jamie:** *We could build a sand castle.*
>
> **Dad:** *OK, here's a shovel.*
>
> *(Jamie beams, proud of herself for taking this step, even though it was pretend.)*
>
> **Dad:** *That was great, Jamie! Now that you were able to do this once, you'll be able to do it again. Let's go to the park tomorrow and try it out.*

Provide your child with opportunities for practicing this new skill, and give her lots of support and encouragement. Praise every step she takes.

Teach your child how to deal with rejection.

All people are rejected from time to time. Sometimes when children experience rejection, they take it as a sign that they're not popular or likable. What's worse is when kids regard these early rejections in a way Martin

Seligman cautions us to be aware of: they may interpret the rejection as personal and permanent. You can help safeguard your child against this by using the following suggestions:

- Share this research fact with your child: Everyone, even the most popular kids, experience rejection from time to time. Let your child know that it's very important not to take rejection personally because it happens to all of us.
- Prepare your child ahead of time that other kids might say no when asked to play. Explain that this doesn't necessarily mean the other child doesn't like her. Maybe next time the same child will say yes.
- Help your child think of alternatives if other kids say no. Caution against begging, whining, or crying, which will only turn off other children.
- If your child is dealing with repeated rejection, help him determine if he is doing something "unbefriendable" to make this happen. If he is, go back to the last section and help him work on whatever the turnoff behavior is.

Exercise:

How is your child at making friends? Do you see any "turnoff" traits? What are they? How do you plan to help her overcome them? Write about this.

Building Empathy

Empathetic children have more friends and do better in life. Empathy, the ability to read, understand, and care about another person's feelings, is one of the most important aspects of emotional intelligence. Listen to what Daniel Goleman says about empathy: "In tests with 1,011 children, those who showed an aptitude for reading feelings nonverbally were among the most popular in their schools, the most emotionally stable."

Goleman also tells us that empathy starts developing in infancy, when we give our babies eye contact, listen to their sounds, respond to their needs, and mirror their actions. This is called attunement. Parents who are highly attuned to their infants build emotional connectedness.

As our children grow, we nurture empathy by continuing to be responsive to them and by modeling empathetic behaviors. "By imitating what they see," says Goleman, "children develop a repertoire of empathic response, especially in helping other people who are distressed."

Aside from modeling, what else can we do to build empathy in our children? Believe it or not, you have already learned most of the strategies for building empathy in the previous chapters of this book: reflective listening, making eye contact, validating your child's feelings, expressing how you feel and encouraging your child to do the same, and building an awareness of the feelings of others. What else can you do to strengthen empathy?

Teach your child to put himself in the other person's place.

Do this through role plays. You can start with this one:

> *Ian and Jim are at the beach. Jim is sitting on the blanket eating a peach and Ian is playing Frisbee. All of a sudden Ian slides into the sand to catch the Frisbee and knocks sand into Jim's face.*
> *Jim calls out, "You klutz! Look what you just did!"*
> *Ian retorts curtly, "How did I know the sand would go in your face? I was looking the other way!"*

First, have your children assume one of the roles and act out the scenario focusing on his own point of view. Then have them switch roles and replay the scenario in a more empathic way. Ask them how it felt to be the other person. Ask them what insights they gained when they switched roles.

Here are some more role plays you can try this technique with:

> *Andrea and Karen are playing together. Lee knocks on the door and asks Andrea to come over to her house and bake cookies.*
> *Andrea turns to Karen and says, "I guess you'll have to leave now. I'm going to Lee's house."*

> *Jason gets a new map. He's going to hang it up after school. When he gets home, the map is folded in a jumbled up way, causing new creases. Jason asks his big brother Sal if he knows what happened to the map.*
> *Sal says, "Yeah, I needed to look something up. You can still use your map. It's no big deal."*

> *Shelly is supposed to clean up the kitchen after dinner while her mom is at the PTA meeting. Three of Shelly's girlfriends call in a row, and before she realizes it, her mother has returned home and the kitchen is still a mess. Mom explodes.*

> *Troy is on the Internet. There's only one phone line in the house,*
> *so whenever the Internet is in use, no one can get through by phone.*
> *At 10:00 P.M. Dad comes home, and he's livid.*
> *He says, "I tried to call five times to let everybody know I was held*
> *up. You can't keep hogging the Internet like that, Troy!"*

Try having your children switch roles to act out conflicts they've had. Ask them to put themselves in the other person's shoes and try to imagine how they must have felt. Encourage them to talk over what they discover when they switch roles. By the way, try this with your spouse—it can be very enlightening.

Encourage your children to identify the feelings of others.

You can do this with people they know, people they see, and characters in movies and on TV. Talk about the expressions on their faces, their body language, tone of voice, and other emotional cues. Have your children also look at the circumstances each person is involved in and ask them to imagine how the people might feel. For example, your son's friend Richie has a pet fish. Imagine Richie's fish is looking pale and listless. Ask your child, "How must Richie feel right now? What might he be thinking?"

Repeat this activity often to build sensitivity toward the emotions of others. Ask your children how they might feel if they were the other person. This is a variation of putting yourself in someone else's shoes. The next time your child comes home and expresses upset about something a friend did, ask her to tell you what happened, and then ask the question, "How would you feel if you were in her place?"

Exercise:

Is your child empathetic? Are there ways you'd like to help her grow in this area? How?

Problem Solving

Peaceful parenting requires that we help children become problem solvers in life, not just with conflicts. How many times have we seen our children burst into tears or lash out at a sibling because they're frustrated over a problem? As with all of the emotional intelligence skills we've read about, problem solving can be taught. Here's how:

Identify the problem.

Help your child learn how to do this by zeroing in on specifics and looking underneath feelings of upset. Here's an example:

> *Jen arrives home from school in a really bad mood. Mom knows something is up. She decides to take action right away.*
> **Mom:** *Jen, you look unhappy. Is something on your mind?*
> **Jen:** *I had a bad day.*
> **Mom:** *Want to talk about it?*
> **Jen:** *The gym teacher yelled at me. She said if I forgot my sneakers one more time she'd have me sit out on the side while the other kids get to play the game.*
> **Mom:** *So the problem is you forgot your sneakers again. How did that happen?*
> **Jen:** *I keep my sneakers in my locker so I don't have to lug them around in my bookbag, and then I forget to take them out before gym.*

Now that Jen's mother has helped her identify the problem, she's ready to go on to step two.

Explore solutions and consider their feasibility.

Let's see how the above conversation continues:

> **Mom:** *What can you do so you won't forget your sneakers again?*
> **Jen:** *I guess I can ask Trisha if she'll remind me to get my sneakers out of the locker at lunchtime. We always eat lunch together.*
> **Mom:** *Of course, Trisha could forget to remind you. Then you'd be stuck. What else can you come up with?*
> **Jen:** *I could write myself a note on a Post-It and put it on my assignment pad.*
> **Mom:** *And do you think that would work?*
> **Jen:** *Only if the Post-It doesn't fall off in my bookbag.*
> **Mom:** *Any other ideas?*
> **Jen:** *I guess I could wear my sneakers to school on the days we have gym. That's what Trisha does.*
> **Mom:** *How come you haven't done that before?*
> **Jen:** *Because sometimes I want to wear outfits that don't look good with sneakers.*
> **Mom:** *Maybe you could wear those outfits on the days you don't have gym.*

Jen: Sometimes I forget which days I have gym.
Mom: *What can you do about that?*
Jen: I guess I could write down my schedule and hang it in my room.
Mom: *Sounds like a good plan.*

Now that Jen has explored a few solutions, she's ready for the next step of problem solving:

Decide on a solution and an action plan to make it work.

Mom: *So which solution do you want to go with?*
Jen: Wearing my sneakers to school would probably be the best.
Mom: *What are you going to do to make sure your solution will work?*
Jen: I'm going to call Trisha. She has a copy of the schedule at home. I'm going to write down my gym days on a big piece of paper and hang it in my room.
Mom: *Where can you hang it so you'll see it each day?*
Jen: How about on my mirror? I always look there.

Jen is almost finished with her problem solving plan. Now there's only one more step:

Look at possible outcomes.

Mom: *Is there any way this plan might not work?*
Jen: If the sign falls down or if I get tired of wearing sneakers.
Mom: *What can you do to prevent the sign from falling down?*
Jen: I can use a lot of extra sticky tape.
Mom: *Sounds good. Now how about the other part, getting tired of wearing the same old sneakers?*
Jen: Maybe I could use some of my birthday money and buy some new sneakers. That way I could switch off.
Mom: *That sounds reasonable. Would you like to go shopping on Saturday?*
Jen: Saturday sounds great.
Mom: *Then it's a date. By the way, I want to compliment you on how well you solved this problem. You thought things through clearly and you came up with a good action plan. How about if we try the same thing the next time a problem comes up, OK?*
Jen: Sounds good, Mom.

Exercise:

Does your child have a particular problem he needs to solve now? Share the problem solving strategy in this chapter with him and write down the steps he decides to take to solve the problem.

Concluding Words

Peaceful parenting opens up a world of growth to ourselves and our children. We are fortunate that so much excellent research now exists to help us guide our children toward a future where they can feel good about themselves, express care toward others, and succeed in life.

Recap

Peaceful Parenting Key #14:
I find ways to help my children succeed.
~

Peaceful Parenting Key #15:
All my actions are guided by love, compassion, fairness, respect, and integrity.
I nurture these attributes in my children.
~

Help build your child's self-esteem by building on his successes.

Self-esteem flourishes when we show our children how to interpret failures without personalizing them or seeing them as permanent indicators of future failures.

Focus on your child's successes, provide her with opportunities to succeed, and display evidences of her successes.

Help your child set realistic goals and encourage her to reach them.

Help your child build perseverance by:

– Creating a positive mental set.
– Breaking the task into small, manageable increments and practicing.
– Modeling perseverance yourself.
– Complimenting small steps along the way.
– Celebrating the finished product.
– Showing how achieving this goal will help with future successes.

Model optimistic thinking.
Shift from pessimism to optimism by doing the following:

Notice your negative thoughts.
Assess the negative thoughts.
Look at the problem logically.
Stop seeing the problem as a calamity.

You can help your child make friends by encouraging him to:

- *Be open-minded* and look beyond the usual boundaries of age, race, gender, and color
- *Create new opportunities* using related activities where they can meet like-minded kids.
- *Be the kind of person others want to be friends with*; have her look at things she does that either help or hinder friendships.
- *Give praise and encouragement to others*; look for things to compliment in others.
- *Cooperate* and be conscious of the needs of others rather than putting your needs first.

Build empathy in your child by teaching her to put herself in the other person's place. Encourage her to identify the feelings of others.

Strengthen your child's problem-solving ability by helping her do the following:

- Identify the problem.
- Explore solutions and consider their feasibility.
- Decide on a solution and an action plan to make it work.
- Look at possible outcomes.

RESOURCES FOR PARENTS

Borba, Michelle. *Parents Do Make a Difference*. San Francisco: Jossey-Bass, 1999.
Practical, hands-on activities and advice on building confidence, competence, and character in children.

Briggs, Dorothy Corkille. *Your Child's Self-Esteem*. New York: Doubleday, 1970.
An absolute must-read. A classic and still the best book written on what parents can do to build self-esteem in children.

Coles, Robert. *The Moral Intelligence of Children*. New York: Random House, 1997. Helps us understand how to raise "good people." Focuses on ways to foster character, morality, and decent values.

Elias, Maurice J., Tobias, Steven, and Friedlander, Brian. *Emotionally Intelligent Parenting*. New York: Harmony, 1999. Practical, easy-to-use, thoroughly field-tested strategies and advice for helping kids get along in the family and in the world.

Frankel, Fred. *Good Friends Are Hard to Find*. Pasadena, CA: Perspective Pub., 1996. How to help your child make friends, resolve problems with friends, and deal with teasing and aggressiveness.

Goleman, Daniel. *Emotional Intelligence*. New York: Bantam, 1995. Groundbreaking book that explains how the emotional and social sides of people can lead to success or failure in life.

Isaacs, Susan and Ritchey, Wendy. *I Think I Can, I Know I Can*. New York: St. Martin's Press, 1989. Changing children's negative voices into positive voices. Contains a five-step plan.

Likona, Thomas. *Educating for Character*. New York: Bantam, 1991. Building character and fostering good decision making in children.

Seligman, Dr. Martin E.P. *The Optimistic Child*. New York: Houghton Mifflin, 1995. A must-read. Contains a wealth of information on building self-esteem and a positive attitude in children.

RESOURCES FOR CHILDREN

Aliki. *Feelings*. New York: Greenwillow Books, 1986. The emotions people experience are depicted through pictures, poems, and stories. (Grades K–3)

———. *We Are Best Friends*. New York: Greenwillow Books, 1987. Robert experiences a range of feelings when his best friend Peter moves away. He learns about making new friends. (Grades K–3)

Aylesworth, Jim. *Teddy Bear Tears*. New York: Simon & Schuster Children's Publishing Division, 1997. A little boy deals with fears through a discussion with his teddy bears. (Grades K–2)

Baker, Betty. *Digby and Kate*. New York: Puffin Books, 1993. Children learn about empathy, fairness, accepting differences, and how to solve problems with a friend. (Grades K–2)

Baker, Keith. *The Magic Fan*. New York: Harcourt Brace, 1989. Yoshi is laughed at by people in his village. He uses his creativity to solve the problem. A good book for helping children with self-esteem and peer pressure. (Grades K–4)

Barrett, Joyce Durham. *Willie's Not the Hugging Kind*. New York: Harper Collins Children's Books, 1991. A little boy who thinks he doesn't need hugs finds out just the opposite. (Grades K–2)

Brown, Marc; illustrated by Stephen Kronsky. *Perfect Pigs: An Introduction to Manners*. Boston: Little, Brown & Company, 1983. Children learn about using manners in a variety of settings. (Grades K–2)

Carlson, Nancy. *Arnie and the New Kid*. New York: Puffin Books, 1992. Arnie gains a deeper understanding about a child who is confined to a wheelchair. (Grades K–2)

Carlson, Nancy. *Harriet's Halloween Candy*. Lerner Publishing Group, 1994. Harriet finds out that you feel better when you share. (Grades K–2)

Carlson, Nancy. *How to Lose All Your Friends*. New York: Puffin Books, 1997. Children learn the importance of friendship. Humorous. (Grades K–3)

Cohen, Miriam; illustrated by Lillian Hoban. *So What?* New York: Bantam Doubleday Dell, 1998. A little boy learns self-acceptance. (Grades K–2)

Cohen, Miriam. *Will I Have a Friend?* New York: Macmillan Publishing Co., Inc., 1989. A little boy makes a friend by finding something he and another child are both interested in. (Grades K–2)

Cullen, Lynn. *Regina Calhoun Eats Dog Food*. New York: Avon Books, 1997. Regina's best friend gets friendly with another girl, so Regina tries everything to win back her friend's attention. (Grades 3–6)

de Paola, Tomie. *Oliver Button Is a Sissy*. New York: Harcourt Brace, 1979. Even though Oliver gets teased at school, it doesn't stop him from doing what he likes to do. (Grades K–2)

Giff, Patricia Reilly. *Ronald Morgan Goes to Bat*. New York: Puffin Books, 1990. Ronald loves baseball even though he's not good at it. Self-esteem, teasing, and overcoming problems are addressed in this story. (Grades 2–4)

Havill, Juanita. *Jamaica's Find*. Boston: Houghton Mifflin Company, 1996. The question of honesty comes up when Jamaica finds a stuffed animal and does not bring it to the lost and found. (Grades K–2)

Hurwitz, Johanna. *Aldo Applesauce*. New York: Viking Press, 1989. Aldo has difficulty finding friends when he moves to the suburbs. (Grades 3–6)

Kraus, Robert. *Leo the Late Bloomer*. New York: Harper Collins, 1998. Leo seems to have problems with everything. Over time, however, he blossoms. (Grades K–3)

Lionni, Leo. *It's Mine*. New York: Random House, 1996. Three greedy frogs argue over who owns the pond. They soon learn a vital lesson about sharing. (Grades K–2)

Marshall, James. *George and Martha Round and Round*. Boston: Houghton Mifflin Company, 1991. George and Martha are good friends who don't always agree on everything. (Grades K–2)

Martin, Ann. *Rachel Parker, Kindergarten Show-Off*. New York: Holiday House, 1993. Olivia's new neighbor is in her kindergarten class. They must overcome feelings of jealousy in order to be friends. (Grades K–2)

Paterson, Katherine. *Bridge to Terabithia*. New York: Harper Collins, 1996. Two children who are misfits develop a special friendship and create something special. (Grades 3–6)

Piper, Watty. *The Little Engine That Could.* New York: Scholastic, Inc., 1971. A children's classic showing how determination can help us succeed. Highly recommended. (Grades K–2)

Raschka, Chris. *The Blushful Hippopotamus.* New York: Orchard Press, 1996. Roosevelt has a negative older sister. He starts to feel better about himself when he listens to a friend instead. (Grades K–2)

Sachar, Louis. *Sixth Grade Secrets.* New York: Scholastic, Inc., 1992. Things begin to backfire after a girl starts a club with secret messages, secret codes, and something embarrassing from each member. (Grades 3–6)

———. *There's a Boy in the Girls' Bathroom.* New York: Random House, 1988. An 11-year-old misfit bully with a lovable side is helped by the school counselor, who teaches him to believe in himself. (Grades 3–6)

Winthrop, Elizabeth. *The Castle in the Attic.* New York: Bantam, 1986. A boy learns he has the power within him to fight any obstacle he encounters. (Grades 3–6)

———. *The Best Friends Club.* New York: Lothrop, 1989. Two children discover that it's not good to leave people out. (Grades 2–6)

Website

Heroes—www.myhero.com/home.asp
Kids can find out about real-life heroes and can also send in information on people they consider to be heroes, including their parents.

CHAPTER 10

How to Keep Peace When the Pressure's On

> *The hecticness, instability, and inconsistency of daily family life are rampant in all segments of our society, including the well-educated and well-to-do. What is at stake is nothing less than the next generation.*
>
> —Urie Bronfenbrenner

Peaceful Parenting Key #16:
I live my commitment to peaceful parenting; my commitment guides all my actions.
~

Alleviating Pressure

As we've learned, harmony in the home begins when we take care of ourselves and live congruently with our top priorities. The tenor of our family's rhythms can become dissonant if we're exhausted, stressed, or overscheduled, or if our kids are any of these. Because peace starts with us, we must do whatever we can to find peace and balance in our own lives. It is only then that we can best model what we need to for our children.

Sometimes it just takes stopping for a moment and listening to our inner voice to regain our balance. One busy mother learned this lesson on a snowy winter day:

> *"Hard as I try, some days just seem to get out of my grasp," said Charlotte, the mother of a 10-year-old boy, a 7-year-old girl, and 5-year-old twin boys. "I try to accomplish too much and I just lose my footing. On those days I start feeling tense and irritable, and find my-*

self snapping at the kids. Before I know it everyone in the house is tense and things start falling apart.

"Last week when the kids had a snow day, that's exactly what happened. I had a long list of things I needed to get done, and having all the kids around made it next to impossible to accomplish anything. I was trying to cook, do laundry, return some phone calls, and schedule a repairman for a leaky roof.

"The day started off OK, but before long the twins started whining that they were bored, and my two older ones started fighting. In the middle of all this, the phone rang, the dryer buzzer went off, and the roast I was making had to come out of the oven.

*"That's when I lost it. I started yelling, and that only made things worse. My kids' whining and shouting intensified, the twins' fight got worse, and before I knew it one pushed the other into a shelf and knocked over my favorite plant. That's when I knew that if I didn't send them to their rooms, I would do something I'd regret. I screamed at them to get into their rooms **this instant,** told them they were driving me crazy, and said they couldn't play video games for a week!*

"As soon as I said it, I knew I was overreacting. I felt like a real witch, and soon I found myself wishing I was single, childless, and living alone."

Sound familiar? As parents, we feel this kind of strain more often than we'd like to admit. We're all under pressure that's either self-imposed, placed upon us by external circumstances, or a combination of the two. When everyday tensions start to build and we have no outlet for them, we lose our grounding. That's when a chain reaction begins: We become overly reactive, our kids react to our reactions, then pandemonium sets in and everyone's miserable. But fear not: We have the ability to break this chain reaction. And the really good news is if you've been following the advice in this book thus far, you're already halfway there.

What follows are twelve pivotal steps you can take to break the cycle of tension-reaction-pandemonium, to deflect negative situations, and to restore balance when the pressure is on.

Stop, breathe, and tune in to your inner voice.

Charlotte knew she needed to retrieve her composure and regroup before dealing with her children. She decided to use the time her kids were in their rooms to take a short break; her list could wait.

So what if I don't fold the laundry or make phone calls right now? she thought to herself. As she began to calm down, she realized the pressure she'd been feeling had been self-imposed, and that insight freed her to make a new choice.

Charlotte's first choice was to make a nice hot cup of tea to calm her frazzled nerves. She decided to start a pot of hot chocolate for the kids while she was at it, knowing she'd want to smooth things over with them in a little while.

Next, she turned on the answering machine, turned off the dryer, took the roast out of the oven, and sat down at the table to drink her tea (instead of sipping it while she did a million other things, as she usually did). She took several slow deep breaths first, then slowly sipped her tea and let it warm her from the inside out.

Then Charlotte tuned in to her "peaceful place." (Remember doing this in Chapter 1?) Picturing herself on a beach in Acapulco with the warm sun on her face, Charlotte was able to recreate a sense of calmness and pleasure. With these good feelings restoring her sense of balance, Charlotte slowly savored the rest of her tea and sat back in her chair, feeling fully relaxed for the first time in days. In her calm state, she was able to see the solution to the problem this day had become.

Charlotte realized she really didn't want to finish her to-do list at all today. What she most wanted was to cuddle up on the couch with her kids, watch a funny video, and eat popcorn. Charlotte knew this was something the kids would love, too. It was something they had often asked her to do, but she'd always felt too busy to say yes.

What's the worst that could happen if I don't fold the laundry, make beef barley soup, and take care of the calls I had planned to make today? she asked herself, and quickly realized that the worst that could happen would be—she'd have to do these things tomorrow. *This is doable,* she said to herself, knowing that one of her highest priorities was to enjoy the time she had with her children, especially spontaneous moments of delight like the one she was about to create.

By the time Charlotte finished her tea, she felt reconnected to herself and was clear on what she needed to do next.

"Come on downstairs and have some hot chocolate, kids," she called to them. "Mommy wants to tell you about her special plan." Seeing the change in Charlotte's demeanor, the children immediately felt more relaxed.

First, Charlotte apologized for shouting and told them that a week of no videos was a little harsh. One night would be enough.

Then she said, "I've decided Mommy's taking the day off and

we're going to watch a video and eat popcorn together for the rest of the afternoon. What do you think of that?" The children gathered around her, gave her a big hug, and thanked her for thinking of such a great plan. Charlotte was touched to see how much her children wanted to spend time with her.

Before long, the five of them were sitting on the couch wrapped in cozy afghans as they shared a large bowl of buttered popcorn and watched a favorite video together. The kids were thrilled and Charlotte had a warm feeling inside knowing she had turned a day that was headed for disaster into one her children would be sure to remember fondly for a long, long time.

What's significant here is that by calming herself and listening to her inner voice, Charlotte was able to get very clear on her priorities. The underlying tension of the day surfaced in part because Charlotte was out of synch with herself. By stopping for a moment and listening to her inner voice, Charlotte reclaimed her grounding and created an opportunity to be with her children in a way that made them all happy. Knowing this made Charlotte feel more peaceful inside. That night when she went to bed, she told her husband how this had turned out to be one of the most special days she could remember having with the children.

By moving out of the realm of the "should," Charlotte empowered herself to choose what was really important to her. How often do we allow our obligations and responsibilities to become rigid taskmasters over the quality of our days? How often do we allow our to-do list dictate what we have to do, rather than looking to see what's most congruent with our highest priorities?

As one mom said, "When I die, if they write on my tombstone, 'Her laundry was always folded and her beds were always made,' will it really matter in the larger picture?"

If I could turn back the clock and change something I did while raising my boys, it would be to have abandoned my list a lot more often and to have created more moments like Charlotte did on that snowy afternoon.

Watch for signals that tension is building between your kids, and take steps to prevent eruptions before they happen.

Ariel and Erica are 8 and 9 and they have a classic love-hate relationship. As their mom, Lori, says, "Either they can't get enough of each other, or they can't be in the same room together. It's feast or famine."

*When asked if Lori noticed any patterns to their dissonant peri-
ods, she had to stop and think. After a while, she said, "Come to think
of it, I've noticed a certain tone of irritation in their voices before
their conflicts go into full swing, and it usually starts with Erica. Very
often she becomes short-tempered. Within moments, Ariel accuses
Erica of picking on her. Next thing I know, they're at each other's
throats. My husband, Mike, says the only solution is to let them live
in different houses, but I don't think that's going to happen."*

What can Lori and Mike do to prevent the frequent eruptions that go
on between their two girls? The answer for them lay in the signal Lori had
mentioned: changes in voice tone.

*The next time they held a family meeting, Lori brought this up,
saying, "We all agreed we want to become a more peaceful family and
that we'd do our best to reduce the bickering. Yet your dad and I
have noticed that fairly frequently when the two of you are playing
together, you start getting on each other's nerves. A tone of irritability comes into your voices, and then you end up getting into a fight."*

"Erica picks on me," Ariel jumped in.

"I do not," retorted Erica. "Ariel's just overly sensitive."

*"Hold on," said Mike. "Let's see if we can talk about this in a
peaceful manner. No blaming, no put-downs, no interrupting.
Agreed?" Both girls nodded their heads.*

*Mike went on. "Yesterday when you were playing Clue, you got
into a big argument and you both ended up in tears. Do you remember what happened?"*

*"Everything was going fine, and then Erica started talking to me
in that bossy voice of hers," answered Ariel.*

*"That's exactly what we're talking about," said Lori. "Sometimes
the two of you are getting along just fine, and then it starts to fall
apart. When we hear that sound in your voice, Erica, we usually
know the two of you are on your way to a fight."*

*"Ariel thinks I'm bossy when she makes a mistake and I try to tell
her the right thing to do," said Erica. "I'm not trying to be bossy, I'm
just trying to help."*

"But it feels bossy to me," said Ariel.

*Lori decided to do some reflective listening at this point, saying,
"So, Erica, you feel you're trying to help Ariel, but Ariel feels you're
getting bossy. What can you do to solve the problem?"*

Erica, getting a sudden insight, said, "It's hard to get along all the time. I mean, I really love Ariel, but sometimes she just gets on my nerves."

Ariel, surprised by her sister's honesty and kindness, said, "I guess I feel the same way. I love you, too, Erica, but sometimes you get on my nerves, too."

"Let's try something new," Mike offered. "How about the next time one of you feels like the other is getting on your nerves, stop and say break time. That means you'll both stop whatever you're doing together and choose something separate for a while. And if your mom or I notice the two of you starting to get that irritable tone in your voices, we might say break time, too. Would that work?" The girls looked at each other for a while and didn't say anything.

Lori chimed in saying, "Like the day you were playing Clue, we could have just put the board aside and the two of you could have gone to different areas of the house and played with your Beanie Babies, drawn, or read. Then you could have finished the game at a time when you felt like you really wanted to be together again."

"Do you really think this could work?" Erica asked.

Mike answered, "You know, what we just suggested is what Mom and I do when we feel like we're getting on each other's nerves. I'll go in the basement and putter around, and your mom might work in the garden or talk on the phone to a friend. It helps. People who love each other can still get on each other's nerves."

*The girls agreed to give it a try. Mike and Lori assured them that the words break time didn't signify a punishment. Far from it. They let the girls know that this was a way they could **prevent** negative situations from getting out of hand and gain some control over the outcome.*

By confronting this issue and offering a positive solution, Mike and Lori began teaching their girls to quell their irritability before it got the best of them. Eventually this would become an excellent self-management skill, one that would help the girls build an awareness of their feelings and prevent problems from getting out of hand.

Build calming activities into your day.

Deep breathing, envisioning, stopping what you're doing and taking a break when needed, finding ways to slow the pace of your day—all these calm the body and the mind, preventing the stress that leads to conflicts. Encourage yourself to turn down the volume on life and quell tension before it has the chance to overtake you.

When my boys were young, I built spaces of calmness into our daily routine with some simple habits. Just about every night of the week, I would make time for us to sit down, eat dinner together, and tell each other about our day. Dinners were usually relaxed, even playful. We would talk, tell jokes, laugh, and really enjoy each other's company. After dinner we would often go into the den and watch one TV show together before homework time. This was a shared activity, and we would often talk about whatever we watched. It relaxed us at the end of a busy day and made us feel warm and cozy together.

On the more hectic days when we didn't have time to sit down for a relaxed meal, we would often take some time together before going to sleep. The boys would come into my big bed where we would cuddle, talk, or read. I still remember those times with fondness, and so do my boys. And as I look back, I see a number of valuable outcomes:

– Our lives were brought into balance by the calm moments we spent together.
– The closeness between us was strengthened—and continues today.
– Both of my boys know how to relax now that they are grown. They've learned how to create calming moments for themselves no matter how hectic life gets.

Each time we build healthy, nurturing practices into our present lives, we teach our children how to do this for themselves.

Avoid rushing.

Even if you have to get up fifteen minutes earlier each day, take things slowly. Rushing causes pressure. Pressure causes stress. Stress leads to conflict.

As one busy dad of two children, ages 6 and 4, observed, "I rush all the time, trying to get the kids ready for the day and out of the house on time, getting to work, having appointments, making phone calls—all that stuff is constant. Then I started to realize something: rushing doesn't help you accomplish more, it just makes you tense. In fact, I think rushing makes me accomplish less, because when I get really tense I start forgetting things and making more mistakes. I'm actually defeating my own purpose by rushing too much."

It seems everyone lives hurried lives today. Maybe the place to begin changing this pattern is right in your own home.

Keep catching your children in the act of doing things right.

As we talked about in previous chapters, this simple act will guarantee your children's positive behaviors will occur with greater frequency, and will create a buffer for pressure-filled times.

Offering immediate praise and specifically describing the positive thing you observe your children doing allows them to see their best selves. Doing this can actually turn bad days around. I'm talking about those pressure-filled days when we're apt to feel short-tempered with our kids, spreading our bad moods to them. By looking for the good in our children's behavior, we can shift our focus and take the edge off some of the pressure we might be feeling.

When we redirect our minds to notice good things that are happening, we can usually find them, even if they are very small.

When Elaine started developing this awareness, she was able to observe herself getting grouchy and then shift her reaction. On a busy Saturday morning when she felt particularly edgy, Elaine encouraged herself to look for at least one good thing to affirm her children about.

Instead of yelling at the girls for being lazy and hanging around in their nightgowns (which is what she was about to do when she caught herself), she decided to quietly observe what they were doing for a moment. Elaine was shocked to notice not one, but three things she could compliment them on.

They were sharing Barbies, her oldest was showing her younger sister how to braid Barbie's hair, and they were being careful with the juice they were drinking so none of it spilled.

By stepping back for a moment, Elaine realized the girls weren't being lazy at all. They were engaged in productive, cooperative play.

By encouraging herself to look for something positive, Elaine was actually able to shift her own mood and gain a more positive perspective.

Live by the standards you have set.

Sometimes when we are under pressure, we let bad behaviors go that we shouldn't. We think maybe we should just overlook what's going on because we have too much on our plate. There may be times that's exactly what you should do to relieve some of your pressure, but be careful about what you choose to overlook. There's a catch-22 here, because if we let go of things that fly in the face of our standards, we can set ourselves up to have longer term problems. By addressing what we need to now, we can quell negative behaviors before they get firmly established.

For example, should Tommy be allowed to beat up his little brother because he thinks he has a good reason to and you're busy working on your taxes? Should Megan be excused from cruel acts toward her sister because you're on the phone? The answer to both of these questions is no. We need to give our children a clear sense of what *is* and *is not* acceptable under all circumstances.

Certainly there will be things we'll want to let go by, as long as they don't fly in the face of our standards. Stacy is hogging the remote control. You know it's not fair to her little brother, but you choose to ignore it this time. Matthew just ate his tenth graham cracker and it's going to spoil his lunch. Maybe you want to ignore that, too.

But when Amy pulls her sister's hair, that's a red flag. One of the family's standards is, "We don't hurt each other, ever." Amy's aggression shouldn't be ignored; if it is, we give the message that our standards have no backbone, or that when Mom or Dad is busy or stressed it's OK for kids to do things they aren't allowed.

Give *yourself* "time out" when you feel your pot ready to boil over.

The next time you feel on the verge of stress overload, try this: Stop whatever you're doing and choose one of the following things:

- Remind yourself to keep your cool even if you're boiling up inside. *Don't allow yourself to do or say something you will later regret.*
- Walk into another room, breathe deeply, repeat one of your positive goal statements, and picture it coming to life.
- Catch your bad thoughts and prevent them from making the moment worse. "These kids are driving me crazy; I'm not cut out to be a mother," can be turned into, "I'm just having a bad moment *right now*. It will pass."
- Look out the window and notice the sky, the trees, the sun, or the rain, whatever the case may be.
- Step outside for a moment and breathe in the fresh air.
- Splash cold water on your face.
- Make a hot cup of tea and sip it slowly.
- Eat something crunchy like a crisp carrot—this releases tension. (Be careful with this one; a box of Oreos wouldn't be a good idea!)

– Go into another room and do 30 jumping jacks.
– Keep your perspective and know that this moment will pass, as all moments do.
– Remind yourself that whatever is bothering you now probably won't matter in 10 years, and in the greater scheme of things, it's probably minor.

Sometimes life gets so tense that stopping for a moment can give us the kind of relief we might experience after hitting our thumb with a hammer, then removing it from the source of pain. Any of the above techniques can give you that kind of relief. Your job is to choose one and do it each time your pot is starting to simmer. Don't even wait until it gets to the boiling point.

Exercise:

What situations create the most pressure for you? What preventive measures can you take to alleviate the pressure before it starts to build? Write up an action plan.

Become a good observer. Be aware of the danger signals when your child is ready to "go off."

This step can save you from countless unnecessary catastrophes. Help your child cool off *before* he's out of control. Excessive whining, irritability, an angry look on the face, an agitated pitch to the voice, tense body language, aggressive talk, dark moodiness—all of these can be signals that your child might be ready to "pop."

Take a step back and notice when any of these things is beginning to happen, then go to the best resource you have—your child's cooling off list. Encourage your child to move to different physical surroundings, then look at the list together. Choose a cooling off strategy quickly and have your child do it until he feels calmer.

Don't forget about deep breathing, too. You can get at eye level with your child and breathe together—this really works.

Sometimes just changing the physical surroundings is enough to relieve pressure. Kate walks into her backyard and breathes in the fresh air when pressure and stress start to get the best of her. After a few minutes outside she feels better able to cope. Now her 5-year-old daughter Alicia asks to do the same when she feels upset. Both mother and child have learned a valuable coping strategy that helps them defuse the stress that leads to conflict.

Exercise:

What situations tend to set off your child? Write about what action steps you can take to ameliorate those situations.

Know how to handle tantrums.

Mary Sheedy Kurcinka, author of *Raising Your Spirited Child,* identifies two different types of tantrums: "manipulative" and "spill-over." A manipulative tantrum is one your child uses to get his way and gain control over you. A spill-over tantrum is not manipulative at all; rather, it happens when your child becomes overwhelmed by a flood of feelings, senses, and stimuli he can't control.

Children who are highly emotional, ultrasensitive, and easily overstimulated tend to have spill-over tantrums. Both types of tantrums can occur in children of any age.

Manipulative tantrums and spill-over tantrums need to be handled very differently, so your first step will be to determine which type of tantrum your child is having. If your child is yelling and screaming because you won't let him have ice cream, this is probably a manipulative tantrum. In that case, ignore it. Walk into another room and leave your child alone to yell without the benefit of an audience. Most importantly, don't give in to the tantrum. You'll just encourage your child to have one the next time he wants his way.

After the tantrum is over and your child is calm, explain, in no uncertain terms, that his behavior was *absolutely unacceptable,* and then give him a consequence like taking away his favorite toy for several days, or removing a special privilege. Firmly tell him that he is *not allowed to behave this way,* and if he ever does again, there will be an even stronger consequence, like taking away his favorite toy for a week, or losing two privileges.

Tell your child you expect better of him and that you were *extremely disappointed in his behavior.* During this whole discussion, use your firmest voice and demeanor and look him square in the eye.

Spill-over tantrums are an entirely different thing. If your child fits the earlier description, he may very well be caught in the syndrome of feeling flooded by his own emotions and losing control without wanting to. Imagine it's been a really stressful week and your child has had a long and overstimulating day. It's past his bedtime, and as he walks toward his bed he accidentally knocks over a block tower he just put together this morning. He starts wailing uncontrollably, gets louder and louder, and can't seem to calm down. Before long, he's flailing around completely out of control. This is a spill-over tantrum. Here are some of the many suggestions Mary Sheedy Kurcinka gives:

- *Do what you can to quell the flood of emotions.* In this case, helping him rebuild his block tower might work. Try to rectify the source of the problem if at all possible.
- *Stay close to your child if you can.* Let your presence be a calming influence while he's experiencing such intense emotions. Take deep breaths yourself to keep your own composure. If you can't, ask your partner to stay near him instead.
- *Give him space if he needs it, but don't leave him alone.* If you sense being too close is only making him react more intensely, move away but stay nearby. Kurcinka advises this because children who have spill-over tantrums are often soothed by our physical presence.
- *Touch your child gently if he allows it.* Try hugging or stroking to calm him down. Let him put his head in your lap or lean against you. Try to remain calm even if he keeps crying.
- *Use a firm but gentle voice and tell him to stop after about 10 to 15 minutes.* Have him take a series of slow, deep breaths to regain his composure. Breathe together if you can. This might be enough to calm him down.
- *Don't allow him to do anything destructive during his tantrum, no matter how upset he is.* Make sure he knows ahead of time what is acceptable and unacceptable. Hurting himself, others, or property are all unacceptable behaviors. After he calms down, give consequences if he has broken any rules.
- *Talk afterward and help your child identify the feelings that brought on his tantrum.* Help him devise a plan for next time, like letting you know when he's feeling overtired or in need of a break. Be on the lookout for situations that could trigger him, and do what you can to stop things before they get out of hand.

Exercise:

Does your child throw tantrums? Can you now identify which kind of tantrum it is? What steps can you take to alleviate your child's tantrums? Write about this.

Know when to seek professional help.

Many children go through phases when good behavior turns oppositional and they become hard to handle, but if a child is *consistently* oppositional and everything you've tried has failed, consider seeking the
assistance of a professional.

We went through a phase like this in my family around the time of my
divorce. My boys became moody, oppositional, and easily prone to conflict.
Nothing I tried seemed to work, and I knew I probably wasn't handling
things in the best way possible because I was going through a hard time of
my own. *Often when we want to see our children's behavior change, we
have to change our own behavior first.* I realized this, and I wanted to learn
what I needed to do differently myself.

Also, I didn't want my boys to form lifelong negative patterns rooted in
this difficult phase of their lives. I made the decision to seek family counseling, and it was one of the best decisions I ever made. The counselor
helped us all put things in perspective, and he enabled my boys to get off
their chest what they needed to. Before long, we were back on track. At
that point I made up my mind that I wouldn't hesitate to seek outside help
if it were needed again.

I view seeking outside help as a sign of strength, not weakness. It signi-
fies being open to change and being aware as a parent. In today's complex
world, we all encounter problems from time to time. The wise parent seeks
help in difficult times.

Children's negative behaviors can be triggered by a number of things:
events in the family like divorce, death of a relative, moving to a new home,
a parent's loss of a job, or the extended illness of a sibling, relative, or parent. Difficult behaviors can be rooted in other things like learning problems, Attention Deficit Disorder, substance abuse in the family, or
emotional problems of a child or parent. All of these things are surprisingly
common, and *you are not alone if you're dealing with any of them.* Better
to face the problem head-on and be proactive than to deny it and hope it
goes away. By intervening early, you will likely get your child and your family back on track.

Seek outside help if you see consistent problems in your child that
aren't alleviated by anything you try, or if you see sudden changes that include any of the following, especially in combination: *A child who becomes
overly withdrawn, easily set off, openly defiant, excessively agitated, prone
toward frequent crying or outbursts, overly aggressive, and/or preoccupied
with weapons and violence.*

Dr. Raymond B. Flannery of Harvard Medical School, the author of

Preventing Youth Violence, says one of the most important things parents can do to raise emotionally healthy children is to build resilience in them. We all go through difficult periods at one time or other. If we can help our children learn from the difficulties they face, we help build resilience. According to Dr. Flannery, other things that build resilience in children are:

– Having at least one caring, consistent adult in their lives.
– Acquiring a sense of mastery over their environment and themselves.
– Having a network of decent friends, even if it's a small one.
– Learning how to live a healthy lifestyle mentally, physically, and socially.
– Having concern for the welfare of others.

Let me reiterate: Seeking the support of a professional when you need to is a sign of strength and competence. Don't hesitate to take this very important step when you believe it could be necessary for the well-being of your child.

Plan ahead for pressured times.

Sometimes our children "go off" because of our poor planning. I remember recently sitting in a restaurant at nine o'clock in the evening, having a late dinner with my husband. Behind us, waiting for their dinner to be served, was a family with two young children, each whining and crying. My husband and I looked at each other and said at the same time, "Of course they're cranky. They're hungry and it's past their bedtime."

Children are often set off by fatigue, hunger, boredom, or lack of activities on their level. If you know you will be in a situation where your child might be subject to any of these, *prepare ahead of time.* Here are some lifesaving activities that will help in any pinch:

Mentally Prepare Your Child

Let her know you may be out late and talk about what she might need to help her cope—a snack, something to occupy herself with, a place to rest in between activities. Provide for adjustments and adaptations that will enable her to handle the situation ahead.

Surprise Box

Take a shoe box and have your child decorate it colorfully. Fill the box with paper, crayons, markers, small books, and other things of interest to your child. Take the surprise box along with you to places that lack appropriate activities for your child where there might be a long wait.

At home, keep the surprise box in a special place so it's a novelty when you take it out. You can change its contents from time to time to keep things interesting. A surprise box can be a lifesaver on long trips, overly scheduled days, or during appointments where your child has to sit and wait for long periods of time.

Goodie Bag

If you know you'll be out during a time when your child might get hungry or thirsty, you'll avoid needless aggravation by packing a goodie bag filled with healthy snacks and drinks. A water bottle on a hot day is also helpful.

Pick up some nonperishable snacks and boxed drinks your child enjoys. Put them in a Ziploc bag with a napkin or two, and you'll be ready for your next shopping excursion or errand run. Do yourself an added favor and throw in some individually packaged Handi-wipes, too.

Bookbag

Take a large Ziploc bag and pack away a few special books or magazines for your child. Save the book bag for times you're going to a place where she might need to be occupied. Alternate the books from time to time so they'll seem fresh and interesting. Include a journal, pencil, and small box of crayons in the bag in case your child wants to write or draw about what she read.

Walkman With Tapes

Now, with such a wide range of electronic media, there's so much more available for our children to occupy their minds with. Keep a few good listening tapes on hand for situations in which your child might otherwise be bored or restless. Bring the tapes and Walkman with you and surprise your child with something unexpected and interesting to do.

Soothing Accoutrements

In preparation for times when your child's anxiety may be high, such as going to the dentist or for a blood test, sit down ahead of time and plan together. Ask your child what she would like to bring along to soothe herself. A favorite stuffed animal or toy might be enough to take the edge off. Not only will you be helping your child alleviate a fearful situation, you'll also be teaching her the skill of self-soothing, something invaluable in terms of good mental health.

Revisit your Guidelines for a Peaceful Family.

Bring yourself and your family back to the commitments you made together. During pressured times we can lose our focus. Getting back in touch with the guidelines you created together will help you all keep your balance and stay on track no matter what kind of day you're having.

Relieving Another Kind of Pressure

"Mommy, I'm bored."
"There's nothing to do."
"I have no one to play with."

All these complaints can grow into pressure our children place upon us. In concert with our commitment toward peaceful parenting, we need to be aware of the more mundane pressures as well as the big ones. We can prevent so many problems by preparing ourselves ahead of time with preventive measures and effective remedies.

Problems like boredom and loneliness can be remedied in advance by helping your child discover and develop her unique strengths and talents. One of our most important jobs as parents is to guide our children to use the gifts they possess to enrich their lives.

In his book *A Call to Story*, psychologist and author Robert Coles says, "Each person's life has its own nature, spirit, meaning and rhyme." With our help and encouragement, our children can begin uncovering the meanings and rhymes of their lives. When this happens, you will both find a wonderful surprise—"nothing to do" will all but disappear!

Observe closely to see where your children's strengths and interests lie. Talk to their teachers, scout leaders, baby sitters, and friends to discover new strengths you may not have been aware of. By providing our children with time, opportunities, and materials relating to their unique strengths, we can help further develop the embryos of success they have within. Boredom becomes much less of a problem when we do this.

With our encouragement and acknowledgment of each step toward success, our children will learn to shine in their unique area of strength. The result? Our children will become better able to occupy themselves and find satisfaction in the activities they love. The stress of boredom and "alonetime" is alleviated when children can fall back on things they are drawn to. It is our job to help them find out what those things are.

Dr. Howard Gardner, expert on multiple intelligences, has identified seven distinct areas of optimal learning and areas of strength that live inside us all. He says that every person possesses one or more of the strengths listed below. Think about your children. In which of the following areas do you believe their strengths lie?

Musical

Have you ever met people who remember every tune they hear and always sing on key? As children they loved music, hummed, sang, and gravitated toward musical instruments. Musical people have natural talents in this area. They are happiest when listening to music, watching it being performed, or playing it themselves.

Bodily/kinesthetic

People who move with physical grace and ease fall into this category. They find motor activities easy to perform and might have a natural inclination toward sports, dance, or anything involving movement. Balance, agility, speed, and finesse with a ball or other equipment are possessed by people with body/kinesthetic strength.

Logical/mathematical

These people are drawn to computers, number games, and things that need to be figured out. With greater ease than the rest of us, they can do math problems in their heads, estimate accurately, and understand functions and relationships of numbers. People in this category also gravitate toward the sciences and enjoy experimentation.

Linguistic

People who are strong linguistically are articulate, have a fascination with words, and possess good vocabularies. They love to read and write and are drawn to things that are rich in words—poetry, plays, stories, books. Foreign languages come easily to people with linguistic strength.

Spatial

People possessing this strength draw well and are good at creating various forms of artwork. They may also be good at reading maps and following written directions. They can easily visualize things in their heads, read charts and graphs, and remember what they see. Spatial learners are also good at designing and constructing things.

Interpersonal

Friendly, gregarious, compassionate people who love to be around others comprise this category. They are adept at organizing groups, helping others resolve conflicts, making decisions, and understanding group dynamics. Leaders and people who have lots of friends are strong in interpersonal skills.

Intrapersonal

Self-direction and motivation are the hallmarks of this strength. People in this category have a strong sense of morality, are inner-directed, and like working alone. They can occupy themselves for long periods of time and don't depend on others for stimulation. They may demonstrate a long attention span and become easily absorbed in activities they are drawn to.

Exercise:

What are your child's unique strengths? Reflect on this question and talk about it with your child. Help him identify things he thinks he is good at or would like to become good at. What can you do to help him develop these areas further? Write about this.

Create an Idea Box with each of your children. Have them brainstorm at least 10 activities they would like to do in the area they are most drawn to, half "Things to Do at Home," and half "Things to Do Outside of the Home." Gather materials for your child relating to this special area of interest and put them in the Idea Box, along with the lists he has made. Include books, magazines, charts, and objects he can use whenever the need or desire arises. Hands-on things are best.

Kerry and Ed are encouraging their son Joshua's logical/mathematical abilities by providing him with as many opportunities as possible to explore and develop this strength, both inside and outside of the home. In his Idea Box, he has a variety of tools, along with old clocks and radios he can take apart. Jonathan literally can spend hours taking apart an object and then seeing if he can put it back together. He is learning the relationship between the parts and is beginning to see the logic of how each part works together. Rainy days cooped up inside can be a joy for him, because they afford him time to absorb himself in the treasures of his Idea Box.

By identifying, bolstering, and helping develop our children's strengths, we provide them with another way to win at life. Stress subsides and competency grows when children have things they can succeed at. In helping them find out what those things are, we remove the pressure of, "Mommy, there's nothing to do!"

Concluding Words

Sometimes we need to make a conscious effort to turn down the pressure of our lives and turn up our appreciation of each moment, especially during busy times with our kids. Sometimes the simplest things can make a huge difference: taking three minutes to look at the sky together before getting into the car and driving home after a busy workday, planning for five minutes of "hug time" before starting the next activity, or chucking the schedule for a while, climbing into bed, and reading books together.

The poet Molly Peacock wrote recently, "Being inside frenetic activity is like being, rhythmically, in the staccato grip of fear. Each syllable of your life seems stressed." Isn't it great to know we have the power to release ourselves from the grip of stress and to teach our children how to do this for themselves?

Recap

Peaceful Parenting Key #16:
I live my commitment to peaceful parenting; my commitment guides all my actions.
~

Alleviate pressure by doing the following things:

Stop, breathe, and tune in to your inner voice.
Watch for signals that tension is building between your kids, and take steps to prevent eruptions before they happen.
Practice calming techniques every day.
Avoid rushing.
Keep catching your children in the act of "doing it right."
Live by the standards you have set.
Give yourself time out when you feel your pot ready to boil over.

Become a good observer. Be aware of the danger signals that signal your
   child is ready to "go off."
Know what to do if your child throws a tantrum.
Know when to seek professional help.
Plan ahead for pressured times.
Revisit your Guidelines for a Peaceful Family.

Identify your child's unique strengths and help him develop them. This
relieves the stress of boredom and builds inner-directedness within your
child.

RESOURCES FOR PARENTS

Flannery, Jr., Raymond, B. *Preventing Youth Violence*. New York: Continuum,
   1999. Danger signals to watch for and preventive steps you can take.
Garber, Stephen. et. al. *Good Behavior: Over 1200 Sensible Solutions to Your
   Child's Problems from Birth to Age Twelve*. New York: Villard Books, 1987.
   Practical solutions to problems so many parents face.
Kurcinka, Mary Sheedy. *Raising Your Spirited Child*. New York: Harper Peren-
   nial, 1991. Excellent resource for parents of difficult children. Gives practical
   ways to handle tantrums, aggression, and acting out.
St. James, Elaine and Cole, Vera. *Simplify Your Life with Kids: 100 Ways to Make
   Family Life Easier and More Fun*. Andrews & McMeel, 1997. Practical advice
   on finding solutions for harried households.
Turecki, Stanley and Tonner, Leslie. *The Difficult Child*. New York: Bantam, 1989.
   Widely read book for parents on handling children who are a "handful."
Weinhaus, Evonne and Friedman, Karen. *Stop Struggling With Your Child*. New
   York: Harper Perennial, 1991. How to avoid power struggles.
Windell, James. *Children Who Say No When You Want Them to Say Yes*. New
   York: Macmillan, 1996. A highly usable guide for parents of stubborn, opposi-
   tional children through adolescence.

RESOURCES FOR CHILDREN

Blume, Judy. *The One in the Middle is the Green Kangaroo*. New York: Bantam
   Doubleday Dell, 1992. Freddy is a middle child. He finds out what's good
   about this when he gets a part in the school play. (Grades K–3)
———. *Tales of a Fourth Grade Nothing*. New York: Bantam Doubleday Dell

Books for Young Readers, 1983. Peter has to find ways of dealing with his 2-year-old brother Fudge, who constantly annoys him. (Grades 2–6)

———. *Superfudge.* New York: Bantam Doubleday Dell, 1994. Peter deals with the pressure of living with his mischievous younger brother. (Grades 2–6)

Bunting, Eve. *The In-Between Days.* New York: Harper Collins, 1994. George's father has a girlfriend George does not want in his life. (Grades 3–6)

Cleary, Beverly. *Ramona Quimby, Age 8.* New York: William Morrow, 1981. Ramona has to deal with being misunderstood wherever she goes. (Grades 1–3)

Gretz, Susanna. *Frog in the Middle.* New York: Macmillan Publishing Co., 1991. Jealousy does not hinder the friendship in a threesome. (Grades K–2)

Hurwitz, Johanna. *DeDe Takes Charge!* New York: William Morrow, 1984. DeDe helps her mom deal with the life after divorce. (Grades 3–6)

Kehret, Peg. *Cages.* New York: Simon & Schuster, 1993. Kit is so upset about problems, she steals a gold bracelet and gets caught. She is sentenced to volunteer at the humane society and finds solutions to her problems. (Grades 3–6)

Martin, Jr., Bill and Archambault, John. *White Dynamite and Curly Kidd.* New York: Holt, Rinehart & Winston, 1995. A little girl uses the power of her mind to feel better when she is afraid. (Grades K–2)

Page, Michael. *The Great Bullocky Race.* New York: Dodd, 1988. Teams realize they must work cooperatively to overcome difficulties and eventually win. (Grades 2–5)

Raschka, Chris. *Elizabeth Imagined an Iceberg.* New York: Orchard Books, 1994. Elizabeth finds inner strength and assertiveness when she is intimidated by another person. (Grades 2–4)

Springer, Nancy. *The Great Pony Hassle.* New York: Dial, 1997. Nine-year-old Elliott competes for the attention of his best friend when an overachieving girl moves in. (Grades 3–6)

Thomson, Pat. *One of Those Days.* New York: Bantam Doubleday, 1987. A little girl complains about her bad day at school, and her mother shares about her own bad day. (Grades K–2)

Van Leeuwen, Jean. *Dear Mom, You're Ruining My Life.* New York: Puffin Books, 1990. Sam is 11 and too tall. Her disastrous year is made worse by her total embarassment over everything her mother does. (Grades 3–6)

Viorst, Judith. *Alexander and the Terrible, Horrible, No Good, Very Bad Day.* New York: Learning Links, 1992. Alexander learns that we all have bad days. (Grades K–3)

CHAPTER 11

Raising Humane, Caring Children

We are members of one another. Yes, there are differences between us. Yes, there are all kinds of divisions. But peace is not won by those who fiercely guard their differences but by those who with open minds and hearts seek out connections.
—Katherine Patterson

In a real sense all life is interrelated. All [people] are caught in an inescapable network of mutuality, tied by a single garment of destiny.
—Martin Luther King, Jr.

Love and compassion are necessities, not luxuries. Without them, humanity cannot survive.
—The Dalai Lama

Peaceful Parenting Key #17:
*I remember daily that we each
have an impact on the world around us
and I teach this to my children.*
~

Did you know that one of our children's greatest concerns is about the world around them? Dr. Georgia Witkin conducted a survey of 800 youngsters between the ages of 9 and 12 for her book *Kidstress*, and one of the most surprising pieces of data to surface was that "inequality, injustice, and human cruelty" made kids angrier than anything else.

In fact, these issues raised the ire of children even more than bad behavior from siblings, hurtful friends, or bossy parents. Pretty amazing, isn't it, to think that our children already have such a deep concern about conditions in our world?

This fact speaks to the importance of providing our children with avenues for making a contribution to the world around them. As Witkin says, "Remind your children that feeling helpless about the things that make us angry is more destructive and stressful than just feeling angry. *Help them help others and you'll be helping children help themselves.*"

We can also let our children know that by living the skills of peacemaking at home, at school, and in their neighborhoods, they'll be taking a huge first step toward making our world a more caring and humane place. Remind your children that peace on every level starts with individuals just like us.

The Hierarchy of Peacemaking

The best way I can describe the link between individual acts and the larger whole is through a concept I developed for my first book called the Hierarchy of Peacemaking. Its message is that peace starts with each and every one of us, and that our actions and attitudes make a difference on all levels of human interrelatedness. Take a look at the heirarchy, then read on to find out how individuals make an impact at every level, right up to the global.

Notice how we, as individuals, are holding up the entire ladder. If we let go, it collapses. So it is with all relationships. The individual is at the base of each, be it family, small group, community, national, or global. No law was ever passed, war ever fought, nor peace treaty forged without the involvement of individuals. The attitudes, actions, and choices of each individual are critical to all areas of human interaction, be they large or small, personal or global.

Think about this: Every future leader of the world is somebody's child right now. The person who may find a cure for cancer or a remedy to world hunger is somebody's child right now. Our children will be tomorrow's teachers, doctors, poets, laborers, and CEOs. The lessons we teach at home today will affect the future of our planet and the lives of every person on it, one way or another.

THE LADDER OF PEACEMAKING
World Peace

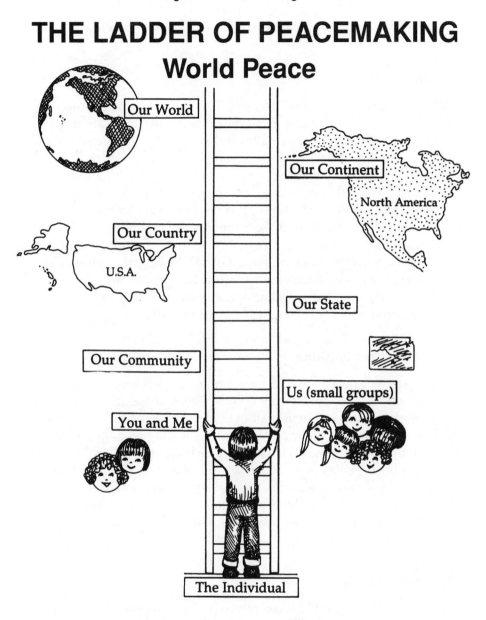

Our World

Our Continent

North America

Our Country

U.S.A.

Our State

Our Community

Us (small groups)

You and Me

The Individual

The Levels of the Hierarchy—A Quick Overview

The Individual

Take a look at the first level, the self. This is our first relationship and our most crucial. How we feel about ourselves permeates every relationship we have. When we feel cared for and nurtured, we can care for and nurture others. When we're stressed, overloaded, or depleted, it becomes difficult to give or even relate to others in a positive way. If we are unaware of our own power and magnificence, we are unable to grasp the impact we have. We might believe, erroneously, that our lives don't matter. Yet by the sheer virtue of being born, we make an impact on other people and on the world around us.

As parents, we make the most impact of all. We have the ability to create, nurture, and guide another human being, passing ourselves on through our children. We have the awesome opportunity to leave a legacy of love, peace, and compassion, all emerging from who we are.

One-to-One Relationships

We relate to so many people on a one-to-one level: our spouse, our child, our best friend, our neighbor, our child's teacher, the clerk at the pharmacy, the person in line in front of us at the grocery store, the person who cuts us off on the highway. We have countless one-to-one relationships, and the way we respond to each creates the texture of our lives. Our one-to-one relationships thrive when we function from a base of respect for ourselves and others, when we are empathetic, and when we are both willing and able to resolve the conflicts that inevitably arise between us. Peace starts with each of us; we need to be role models, remembering that people learn from each other.

Group Relationships

The choices we make and the actions we take affect any group we are a part of. Think about small groups you belong to: your church or synagogue, PTA, civic organizations, social groups, and more. Think about your children's groups: sports, scouting, religious groups, and school groups. How your children behave within these groups, the choices they make, and the attitudes they hold will affect the overall tenor of their group.

Our interactions, beliefs, biases, and attitudes have an impact on the groups we are in and the communities these groups are a part of. Think about groups that are based on shared biases, the Ku Klux Klan, Neo-Nazis and others. In contrast, think of groups that make a positive difference such as Greenpeace, The Anti-Defamation League, Habitat for Humanity, and Save the Children.

Who we are as individuals affects the groups we belong to, and groups, in turn, affect the larger world for better or for worse.

Community

Our choices and actions as individuals affect the communities we live in *positively*, through acts of compassion, care, and responsibility, or *negatively*, through apathy, hatred, and cynicism. Sometimes in our sense of isolation, we forget how much each individual can affect entire communities: vandalism, robbery, and murder are all acts of single individuals. Conversely, we must remember how much good we can do through acts of giving, care, and concern. Peace at the community level is linked solely to choices made by individual people.

State, Nation, World

People often wonder if individuals make a difference at these levels. Yet think about this: One man, a single individual living in Kosovo, decides to cleanse his country of those considered to be "the other," and countless people die.

Fifty years ago, another man made a similar decision, and millions upon millions were put to death.

But think about this, too: one man, jailed for 20 years and then released, becomes the first black president of South Africa and helps set up the first democratic government in his country's history, one single person leading others to freedom and hope. Or a young Jewish girl, hidden away in an attic, writes in a diary before an unjust death wrenches her from the hands of life. Her words eventually inspire millions with their courage and grace—one single girl whose memory still inspires hope and compassion.

Don't think, for even a moment, it has ever been otherwise: Individual people, acting out of their beliefs, have always affected the greater good of the world around them.

The Heirarchy of Peacemaking in Action

This is what the Heirarchy of Peacemaking represents: the power of individuals to affect the world we live in. Through the commitment of people like us, we can create a more humane world. Historian Howard Zinn writes: "We don't need to engage in grand, heroic actions to participate in the process of change. Small acts, when multiplied by millions of people, can transform the world."

Know that each act of compassion we model for our children creates the fabric of positive change. What actions can we take on each level of the hierarchy to contribute to the world we live in? Read on to discover concrete activities you and your family can participate in to make a difference.

Individual Acts

There are so many acts we can perform as individuals that express care for our world and the people in it. They may be something as simple as recycling and picking up litter or as personal as including people in need in our prayers. Anita's 8-year-old son, Gabriel, expressed his care for the world through a simple but profound daily act:

> One day Gabe and I were listening to author Marianne Williamson speaking about the impact individuals can make on the world. It was during the war in Kosovo, and Marianne asked everyone who was listening to stop what they were doing each day at 3:00 P.M. and send prayers and love to the people of Kosovo. She said that if people all over the world did this at the exact same moment every day, our individual prayers would join together to be received by the people who were suffering. Gabriel, though only 8, was moved. He decided on that day to be one of the many people who send prayers and love to Kosovo. To insure that he wouldn't forget, he set the alarm on his watch to go off at precisely 3:00 P.M.
>
> Each day after that, without fail, Gabriel sent his prayers and love to the people of Kosovo. This was easy at first, because he was being home-schooled, but in September of that year he entered the public schools. How could he continue his ritual, he wondered. Unsure if his moment of meditation and prayer would fit into the school's schedule, Gabriel decided to ask the principal when they met for the first time if he could stop what he was doing each day at 3:00 to continue sending his prayers to Kosovo. Trying to be understanding, but not wanting to interfere with the regular schedule, the principal suggested that Gabriel continue his ritual, but that he change the time.

Gabriel thought about this and realized that although changing the time would be more convenient, it wouldn't work—he wanted his prayers to join with those of others all over the world at precisely 3:00 each day. So Gabriel decided to approach his new teacher and ask if this would be OK.

Later that day, when Gabriel came home, he excitedly ran up to his mother announcing his news, "I think it's gonna work, Mom. My teacher's pretty cool. She's the kind of person who will let me keep on sending prayers to Kosovo at 3:00 each day."

So, from that day on, Gabriel continued his ritual. And even as I write these words, he still does.

What I love about this story is that Gabriel cared so much. How many 8-year-old children take the pains to create a reliable ritual for the sake of others? Also, Gabriel's instinct was actually in line with some current research. In his book *Meaning and Medicine*, Dr. Larry Dossey documents the power of prayer in the healing process, citing a double-blind study of almost 400 patients who'd had heart attacks.

The patients were divided into two groups, each given the conventional treatment. One group, however, was being prayed for by a number of prayer groups throughout the country. The other was not. At the end of the study, the prayed for group did remarkably better, so much so that national interest was aroused. Dr. Dossey concluded that "prayer exerts a powerful effect that can be readily measured."

So who knows? If prayer can help heal the sick, maybe it can also help heal the broken spirits of the people of Kosovo. Gabriel had translated his care into action—action that may have helped in some small way. He was committed to helping, even when he had to put himself on the line.

What daily rituals will allow your children to express care for others? Some easy ones are picking up litter, planting seeds, performing random acts of kindness for people in the neighborhood, visiting a nursing home, and many more. Be creative. Sit down with your child and do some brainstorming. Then think about how your child can translate his concerns into concrete action.

One-to-One Acts

There's a wonderful book called *Spiritual Literacy* that helps people see the connection between everyday acts and developing a higher sense of purpose. In his foreword to the book, author/philosopher Thomas Moore talks about the need for ". . . transcending a materialistic view of culture and finding values and visions in the ordinary . . ." The way we choose to contribute to people in our lives, even in the simplest ways, can create value in ordinary moments. Here's an example from *Spiritual Literacy* by Alan Epstein:

> *Thank someone for something. Go out of your way today to acknowledge the generosity of a person you know. It doesn't matter if you have known this man or woman your entire life, or have just met him or her and don't know if you will ever see the person again. Thanking him for a service rendered, or a favor given, or for help of some kind will enlarge your personal community to include yet another person.*

Now let's take a look at some acts of service other families have performed. A single mom named Ruth wanted to help her 8-year-old daughter, Natalie, become more aware of ecology and each person's responsibility in propagating the earth's bounties. So she gave Natalie a small plot of land in which to plant her very own garden.

Natalie separated her plot into two smaller ones: one where she would grow things for her mother, and the other for her dad, who lived in a different town. Each day, mother and child would go out to their gardens, sowing, planting, weeding, and watering. They watched tiny seeds grow into lush plants, and as the vegetables grew, they picked them and brought them inside to make delicious meals. Natalie always made sure to put aside the vegetables that she had grown for her dad, and when she went on her visits, she'd bring them to him.

What better way to teach a child reverence for the earth, appreciation of its bounty, and generosity of spirit? Natalie's bond with the earth was forged and strengthened through this activity, and her relationship with her father was touched in a special way.

One-to-one acts of service can be many and varied. A busy working mom named Sharon didn't have much free time, but wanted to find a family activity that would make a difference even in a small way. With a little thinking, she came up with the perfect activity: dog walking.

Sharon had come across a flier from the local animal shelter asking for volunteers to walk "orphaned" dogs. "Perfect!" she thought, realizing this activity would fill a special need in her children, who had always wanted to own a pet but couldn't because of Sharon's allergies. Dog walking would enable her children to be around pets on a regular basis, and would also be of service to the animal shelter. So Sharon and her children walked dogs for an hour every week, and experienced the mutually gratifying feeling of giving love to pets who would otherwise have had none.

Think about simple activities like this that you and your family can do. If contributing time once a week is too much, then think about doing something once a month or biweekly. Whatever service you choose to perform will help your children form the habit of translating concerns into action and making a positive difference.

Small Group

When we're open to giving, there are so many ways to express it. One mother of three decided to involve her children in helping out at their school. Joanne had begun volunteering for the PTO, and she started running the school store. After school, her daughters would pitch in by helping to stock the store and organize the items. This gave them a clear sense of contributing and making a difference in their own school.

Judy, another mom, decided to pitch in so the school's playground could be cleaned up. She asked to speak to her son's class prior to Earth Day, and had the children imagine what the playground would look like if it were cleared of all the random debris that had been carelessly scattered around it.

Judy provided each child with a trash bag and gloves. She and the teacher took the children out to the playground to clean it up. The children ended up collecting 11 bags of trash.

Judy says the results were wonderful. "The kids were so excited. So many of them said, 'Wow, look at what we did!' What a sense of pride they experienced knowing they had made a difference in the place they go to every day."

The children also gained a deeper understanding of how people affect the environment they live in, realizing that if they throw their straw wrapper on the ground, and someone else drops a juice box, and another person lets a gum wrapper blow away, a huge accumulation of garbage can result, something no one wants on their playground—or anywhere else, for that matter.

Community Acts

Judy also decided to engage her entire family in cleaning up the grassy fields along the edge of the highway they passed every day. By now, the family had developed a growing concern about littering, so Judy once again got trash bags and gloves from the local recycling center and took her family out to the field along the highway, far enough from the road that no one would be in danger.

They all proceeded to pick up as much garbage as they could find. Judy says, "After that, each time we passed that part of the highway we would look at how clean it was and say, 'We did that.'" Judy's family benefited from this activity, and so did her community.

One of my favorite stories of community service came from a 15-year-old girl named Erin. When she was 7, she started contributing to her community through Girl Scouts. One of the first activities she remembers was going to a local home for the aged during the holidays with songs and handmade gifts. She was moved by the reactions of the people she came in contact with, and felt a sense of pride in bringing a smile to the faces of seniors who had no one else visiting them.

After that, Erin continued with a variety of service activities, recently creating a project that has earned her a national award. It's called "Welcome Bags."

Erin had learned that the majority of moms and children who came to her town's battered women's shelter had little else but the clothes on their backs. Erin decided to start collecting supplies that every woman and child needed when they arrived: a T-shirt to sleep in, a toothbrush and toothpaste, toiletries and other personal items, and a teddy bear for the children.

At the start of the project, she had no idea where to get all the supplies that were needed. Undeterred, Erin started asking people she knew to donate. Before long her dentist came up with toothbrushes and toothpaste, her swimming coaches came up with T-shirts, and local businesses she contacted came up with the rest. In time, Erin had amassed more supplies than she'd ever thought possible.

How to assemble all of the supplies into Welcome Bags was the next challenge. Once again, Erin reached out to everyone she knew. "I started grabbing every friend that came into my house and getting them involved, and my family, too. We set up the dining room table with all the supplies and formed a kind of assembly line to get everything into the bags. By now we've donated about 600 Welcome Bags to the shelter."

When I asked Erin if she plans to continue this huge task along with the growing demands of school, swim team, scouting, and many other activities she's involved in, without hesitation she said, "Yes." The reason: "Because the people still need help."

Erin has learned that in giving to her community, she gets back so much: a sense of pride, the knowledge that she makes a difference, and the respect and recognition of those who know her.

State, National, or Global Acts

When my boys were young, we "adopted" a child from Save the Children. For $15 a month, we were able to help this child be fed and clothed. My boys contributed from their allowance, and each month we'd send money to a little girl from an impoverished Mexican village. We received a picture of her which we displayed in the living room along with other family pictures. We would read the letters she sent us, amazed that such a small amount of money could make a difference in her life. Our contribution didn't take tremendous effort or resources on our part, but it was significant in her world. From this and other acts of care and charity, my sons learned that we need to express our care toward others, even people in need we may never meet.

Barbara Lerman Golomb, social action director of a large synagogue, has involved her children and others in countless service activities for as long as she can remember. Below is a special calendar she and her children put together that you can use to get your children involved in a wide range of social action activities.

A Good Deeds Calendar

Hi, I'm Joie Golomb and I'm 11 years old; I'm Sophie Golomb and I'm 7. Each month our family gets involved in a different project to help kids and adults in our community and around the world. All the projects we do are ones you and your family can do, too, through your church, synagogue, school, scouting group, or even on your own. Take a look:

September:

We had a canned food drive. We helped hand out bags to families in our congregation. We kept a paper bag in our kitchen and filled it up, then returned it to the synagogue a week later. The food was given to a local food pantry. Find out if your town has a place that collects canned food and then collect food for them.

October:

We collected Halloween candy from the kids at our religious school and regular school. We delivered it to our local hospital for children who wouldn't be trick or treating this year. Find out if your local hospital has a children's ward, and try this next Halloween. It's fun getting kids to donate Halloween candy. We all have so much and other kids have so little.

November:

We got together with other churches and synagogues for an interfaith Thanksgiving service. Many choirs sang, including the children's choir we're in. We collected winter coats for homeless families, too. Find out if groups from different backgrounds in your area gather to celebrate Thanksgiving. It's a great way to learn more about each other. Also, see if there's a place where you can donate warm clothing for those who don't have it. Make your next Thanksgiving one of *thanks* and *giving*.

December:

We helped collect and wrap hundreds of holiday gifts for our "Children-to-Children" project. Then we helped deliver them to several places that take care of homeless families and others who need help in our community. Find out if your town collects "Toys for Tots" during the holidays. If not, you can get a project like this started. It will really make you feel good!

January:

We got together with other houses of worship and had an interfaith service in honor of Dr. Martin Luther King. Dr. King is one of the most important peacemakers who ever lived. He once made a speech called "I Have a Dream," in which he shared his vision of a world where people of different colors and religions would all get along. Do you have a celebration in your town for Dr. King? If not, get one started, even if it's just in your school. *We need kids like you to make Dr. King's dream come true.*

February:

Did you know that countless trees are cut down unnecessarily throughout this country? Trees purify the air and provide homes for many animals. We found out about a company in California that's cutting down ancient redwood trees, so we wrote letters to many government leaders about the problem, and all the kids in our classes signed it. We also collected money to plant more trees. Find out if there's an environmental cause in your community that you can help out with. Plan to plant some trees this spring. You'll be helping the environment with that simple act.

March:

We made gifts with other kids in our Sunday school for people living in our local senior citizen's home. We delivered them with our parents and visited the people there. We also collected small gifts for the people to use as prizes at their weekly bingo games. Find out if there's a local senior citizen's home where you can visit or volunteer your time. Seniors really appreciate this. Some of the people we met have no families of their own. You can be like substitute family members.

April:

In honor of Earth Day (April 22) we collected pennies from friends, family, and classmates to contribute to the World Wildlife Fund's "Pennies for the Planet" project. The money went directly to programs that protect rain forests and other animal habitats with endangered species. Find out if there's a way you can help protect endangered animals and plants. It's fun, easy, and it makes you feel so good to help. (Check out the websites at the end of this chapter.)

May:

We collected "gently used" sporting equipment for needy kids going to camps and summer programs. Find out if there are any local recreation facilities that can't afford sports equipment. Get your friends, neighbors, classmates, and school to contribute sports equipment for them. They'll really appreciate it.

June:

We collected backpacks and school supplies for homeless kids who go to local schools so they can start school in September with new things just like everyone else. See if there are homeless children in your community who need school supplies. Find out what you can do to organize donations for them.

July:

We kept on collecting school supplies, but this time we gave them to children living in Ethiopia, a very, very poor country. Did you know that some children don't even have pencils, crayons, and paper? Some schools in poor countries don't even have books! Get together with people in your school, church, synagogue, or scouting group to collect books, markers, notebooks, erasers, pencils, crayons, paste, and other school supplies, and send them to one of the organizations listed at the end of this chapter. Think how much your efforts will be appreciated by those who have so little.

August:

We turned a back-to-school haircut into a good deed. When Sophie said she wanted her long hair cut short, our mom suggested she cut off a 10-inch braid and send it to Locks of Love, a charitable organization that uses hair that is at least 10 inches long to make wigs for children who've lost their hair due to illness or injury. (Find out more about Locks of Love by looking in the resource section at the end of this chapter.)

Giving to others gives you a warm feeling in your heart. Make this a part of your life, and you'll see how much you can make a difference!

Exercise:

What "make-a-difference" activities can your family participate in? Have a family meeting to discuss this. Come up with an action plan and follow through on it as soon as possible. Make "making a difference" a high priority.

Dealing With Differences

One of the most profoundly important understandings we can pass on to our children is that we are all the same inside even if we look different on the outside. All people have a need for love, respect, acceptance, and dignity, and sometimes those most in need of acceptance are marginalized and made the brunt of cruel jokes and taunts.

We must sensitize our children to the crucial need for all people to be treated with dignity and respect.

Handicaps

Bring out the issue of differences and begin talking about it. Use books, videos, and personal experiences to sensitize your children to different kinds of handicaps. See if your school has a handicap awareness program. If they don't, request one.

Sometimes simple discussions can make a world of difference. Take a look at the following story from a fourth grade teacher to see what I mean.

> *Ben, one of Mrs. Weiss's most difficult students, seemed like the last person anyone would expect to accept differences. But because of lessons taught when he was in second grade, Ben had actually become sensitized to the issue of handicaps.*
>
> *Mrs. Weiss discovered this the day she showed her class a video about children with mental retardation. Mrs. Weiss asked her students how they would react if they were to meet these children. As muted snickers started to surface, Ben's hand shot up, and with compassion in his voice he said, "I would see those kids as human beings, just like me. When I was in second grade, my teacher taught us that we're all the same inside, even if we look different on the outside. Those kids are more like us than we realize, and we shouldn't make fun of them."*
>
> *Mrs. Weiss was floored. Little had she imagined a child like Ben could not only absorb such an important lesson, but would have the courage to share it with the entire class.*

Have an open discussion with your children about handicaps. There are some wonderful books available now on the subject. Check the resource section at the end of this chapter for a wide variety of titles.

Talk about the fact that even if people seem to be different on the outside, we're indeed the same on the inside. We have hearts, and minds, and feelings. Gestures of kindness under all circumstances are so necessary. Gestures of exclusion can wound deeply and can stay with a person for years, even for life.

Discuss this with your children and let them know how important kindness and tolerance are in the face of handicaps or any other perceived differences.

Combating Racism and Intolerance

In his wonderful and touching book, *Tuesdays with Morrie*, Mitch Albom shares the lessons he learned from his old professor, Morrie Schwartz, during the last year of his life. Here's one of my favorites:

> *The problem, Mitch, is that we don't believe we are as much alike as we are. Whites and blacks, Catholics and Protestants, men and women. If we saw each other as more alike, we might be very eager to join in one big human family in this world, and to care about that family the way we care about our own.*

Morrie's words remind me of another quote I heard: "We are all part of the same race—*the human race.*"

Even though this is true, more blood has been shed and wars fought over perceived differences than anything else. Our differences in religion, race, skin color, sexual orientation, and ethnicity have been like splinters in the fabric of human interrelatedness. People have been driven to kill, maim, exterminate, and exclude others strictly based on these factors.

And now, in a country defiled by the "easy-as-going-to-Kmart" availability of handguns and "protected" by stockpiles of nuclear weapons, it is absolutely imperative that we find ways to live together. We must begin focusing on our likenesses rather than our differences, for it is truly a stain on the human soul that we have done such harm to one another. Change must begin with each of us and the lessons we teach at home.

Start by creating an atmosphere of acceptance. Help your children learn about people who have another way of life, come from other cultures, have different color skin, speak another language, or practice different religions. When they are old enough, help them have compassion for those who have a different sexual orientation.

Matthew Sheppard, the gay teenager who was beaten to death by a group of his peers, was sombody's child. Empathy toward people who are different helps prevent intolerance and acts of senseless violence.

In her book *Teaching Peace*, educator Jan Arnow says, "It is critical that we learn to build meaningful relationships with our neighbors despite . . . differences. It is time to stretch our cultural comfort zone, adapt to the change that is around us, and learn to benefit from the richness of our diversity for the sake of our children . . ."

A wonderful example of teaching tolerance came to me from the African-American director of the senior citizen center in my own community, Helen Holmes. Helen told me how her father, a wonderful man

named Harold Vereen, Sr., taught her and her 7 siblings about racial tolerance and self-acceptance in a way none of them will ever forget. Here is
her story:

> *My father was a great man. Although he worked as a laborer all
> his life and never finished high school, he was a person of dignity and
> wisdom. I remember the day I came home from school upset because
> someone had made a remark about the color of my skin. My father
> sat me down and said, "Don't be sad, Helen. The color of your skin is
> just as beautiful as anyone else's." Then he opened a box of crayons
> and said, "Take a look inside. Do you see all the different color
> crayons laying side by side? Each is beautiful in its own way. No
> color is better than the other. All the crayons are here together, and
> each one is special and equal in its beauty, just like us."*

Helen has passed this story on to her children and grandchildren, and
now she is passing it on to you to share with yours. This story has guided
Helen throughout her life and has helped her be aware of her own self-
worth, as well as the inherent worth of others.

Tell your children Helen's story. Have a frank conversation about race
and the ways people allow differences to come between them. Help your
children see that we are all special and unique in our own way, just like
crayons of many different colors. Think how boring a box of crayons would
be if every color were the same. This holds true for people, too.

Now take a look at more ways you can combat intolerance right in your
own home:

Never allow slurs of any kind to be spoken in your home. Make
this a hard and fast rule. This applies to all races, colors, religions, and sexual orientations. It's easy to pass on the habit of intolerance to children.
However, the reverse is true as well. If you raise your children in an atmosphere where prejudice of any kind is regarded as totally unacceptable, then
you'll pass on your openmindedness instead. Present intolerance as something that's as immoral as lying, stealing, or maiming another person.

Be aware of your own biases. We all have biases of one kind or another.
Sometimes just having the awareness of prejudices under the surface can
help us let them go—but sometimes not. If this is the case, refer to some of
the books in the resource section at the end of this chapter. Opening our
hearts and minds to letting go of biases is a very important first step.

Be aware of your facial expressions and the subtle looks that can pass from
one adult to another when a particular racial, ethnic, gender-orientation, or

religious group is mentioned. In fact, be vigilant. Don't let your children learn intolerance from unspoken messages. They are just as powerful as our words.

Don't tolerate ethnic or homophobic jokes. It's hard not to be "one of the guys" when a whole table full of people is laughing at the same joke. But too often jokes are made at other people's expense in this "Howard Stern" kind of culture. When that happens, make your sentiments known; otherwise your silence may indicate you are in agreement. A simple "I message" can help, like, "I'm not comfortable with that joke," or, "This kind of conversation makes me uncomfortable."

Expose your children to other cultures and ethnic groups. This can be done by taking your children to festivals, parades, cultural events, and restaurants. Treat your children to ethnic foods they've never experienced. Talk to people when you participate in multicultural events so you can all learn more. We live in a country rich with different cultures; let's celebrate this and make connections with one another.

Take your children to other communities where they can meet people who are different than they are. Try visiting new places of worship, or attending community events in another town. Jacqueline G. Wexler, former president of the National Conference of Christians and Jews, said, "Prejudice is forged and fueled in faceless crowds. Healthy human relations are born and nurtured in personal encounters." Open your child's eyes so she can begin to see the world in a broader sense, gaining understanding of others through personal encounters. Help her learn at an early age that the world we live in includes people who look, live, and act different from us. That's what makes it such an interesting and multifaceted place.

Introduce your child to multicultural literature. There are so many wonderful books available for children about different countries and different people. Encourage your child's teacher and school librarian to introduce multicultural literature, posters, and activities.

Encourage your child's school to have an ethnic heritage festival. With the rich cultural heritage present in our country, schools can create events celebrating the diversity of their students. Some schools create whole teaching units around this theme, having children study and report on their ethnic backgrounds. The unit can culminate in a multicultural feast where parents and other relatives bring in ethnic foods, music, and costumes for the whole school to enjoy. This provides a wonderful learning experience for children and will open their minds to different cultures.

Talk openly about racism. Hard as we may work to build humane values in our families, our children are often exposed to racism in one form or other as they go through life. Here are some disturbing facts: The Intelligence Project of the Southern Poverty Law Center identified 462 white supremacist hate groups throughout our country. This does not include racist and anti-Semitic militia groups. An estimated 150,000 people purchase hate literature and take part in racist activities; an additional 450,000 people read this literature. There are at least 250 "hate sites" on the Internet.

Talk to your children. Encourage them to let you know if they encounter racism and intolerance. You'll find a number of excellent books recommended at the end of this chapter to help you broaden your understanding of racism and intolerance and take steps to combat them.

Exercise:

What will you do to help your children grow up bias-free? Write about this.

Concluding Words

In his book *The Moral Intelligence of Children*, Robert Coles urges us to turn nouns such as "generosity, thoughtfulness, sensitivity, and compassion into verbs—words of action." Caring is not enough; we must translate our concerns into viable actions, and we must teach our children to do the same. Imagine the changes that could take place in our world if every individual did just *one* thing to make it a better place. Just one thing. Imagine the infinite possibilities of such an accumulation of gestures.

And as we reflect upon how we might contribute, let's not forget the countless children who are withering in the oppressive heat of neglect. Their needs have been forgotten by too many. Children of the poor, homeless children, those who live in neighborhoods blighted by drugs and violence—they, too, are our children. We must keep them in our hearts and minds, because they, too, are our future.

I implore all of you to see yourselves as advocates for all children, not just those who are lucky enough to live with you. Surely a special place will be reserved in heaven for all who reach out to other people's children as well as their own.

In this vein, consider the following anecdote from *Spiritual Literacy*, contributed by David Wolpe. His words beautifully exemplify what I've been talking about:

"There is a marvelous story of a man who once stood before God, his heart breaking from the pain and injustice in the world. 'Dear God,' he cried out, 'look at all the suffering, the anguish and distress in your world. Why don't you send help?' God responded, 'I did send help. I sent you'."

Recap

Peaceful Parenting Key #17:
I remember daily that we each have an impact on the world around us and I teach this to my children.
~

Find ways that your family can make a difference in your community or the larger world. Use the "Good Deeds Calendar" to discover activities your child can do each month of the year.

Talk to your child about differences: racial, religious, gender, handicaps, etc. Encourage acceptance of all people.

Combat racism by doing the following things:

– Never allow slurs of any kind to be spoken in your home.
– Be aware of your own biases.
– Don't tolerate ethnic or homophobic jokes.
– Expose your children to other cultures and ethnic groups.
– Take your children to communities where they can meet people who are different than they are.
– Introduce your child to multicultural literature.
– Contact your child's school and present the idea of doing an ethnic heritage festival.
– Talk openly about intolerance.

Exercise:

Look through the following resource section. Choose a service organization to contact and several books to read—some for you, some for your children. Tell your friends about the books and organizations you become familiar with. Encourage them to get involved.

Service Organizations for the Whole Family

Christmas in April USA. A leading volunteer organization that works with communities to rehabilitate homes of low-income people, particularly the elderly and disabled. Christmas in April culminates in a National Rebuilding Day in April. Volunteers from all ages and walks of life come together to help their neighbors. Contact: Patty Johnson, President, Christmas in April USA, 1536 Sixteenth Street NW, Washington, DC 20036-1402. Phone: (202) 483-9083; fax: (202) 483-9081; web address: www.pdi.com/cina-usa/index.html

Global Volunteers. Helps build a foundation of peace through mutual understanding. Volunteers live and work in communities in Africa, Asia, the Caribbean, the Americas, and Europe. No age limit; minors must be with an adult family member or guardian. Contact: Global Volunteers, 375 E. Little Canada Road, St. Paul, MN 55117. Phone: (612) 482-1074 or (800) 487-1074; e-mail: email@globalvlntrs.org; web address: www. globalvlntrs.org

Habitat for Humanity International. Invites people from all walks of life to work building houses with and for needy families in more than 50 countries. Contact: Habitat for Humanity International, 121 Habitat Street, Americus, GA 31709. Phone: (912) 924-6935 or (800) HABITAT; fax: (912) 924-6541; e-mail: public_info@habitat.org; web address: www. habitat.org

ImpactOnLine—Volunteer America. Provides a matching service for volunteers and nonprofits, Virtual Volunteering, a research project on volunteer activities, and information and resources on volunteerism. The idea is to make it easier for people to volunteer, particularly if they cannot commit to a fixed schedule. Contact: Volunteer America. Phone: (415) 327-1389; e-mail: info@impactonline.org; web address: www.impactonline. org/volunteer

Locks of Love. This organization provides quality hair for children in chemotherapy. You can contact them for their hair donation guidelines at 1640 Congress Ave., suite 104, Palm Springs, Florida. Fax: (561) 963-9914. Their toll-free number is (800)435-4357; web address: www.locksoflove. org/hair

Mobility International. Promotes equal opportunities for people with disabilities. "No age limitations for participation in internship and volunteer programs." Contact: Mobility International USA, P.O. Box 10767, Eugene, OR 97440. Phone: (541) 343-1284; fax: (541) 343-6812; e-mail: info@miusa.org; web address: www.miusa.org

Raventalk. Provides information, resources, and volunteer activities for taking care of the earth. You can reach them at P.O. Box 50, San Jose, NM 87565. Phone: (800) 255-9979; web address: www.raventalk.com

Save The Children. Helps children in need through sponsorship or contribution. You can reach them by writing: Save the Children, Att: Donor Services, 54 Wilton Road, Westport, CT 06880. Phone: (800) 243-5075; web address: www.savethechildren.com

The Giraffe Project. This organization recognizes people who "stick their necks out" to help others. Help is provided for anyone who works with kids and wants to build care and responsibility in them. They have an excellent curriculum for schools. Their web address is www.giraffe.org/giraffe

VISIONS, International, Inc. A nonsectarian summer program offering cross-cultural community service experiences for students 11–18; a blend of service work, outdoor adventure, and intercultural opportunities in the United States and the Caribbean. Contact: Joanne Pinaire, Director of Summer Programs, VISIONS, 110 North Second Street, P.O. Box 220, Newport, PA 17074-0220. Phone: (717) 567-7313 or (800) 813-9283; fax: (717) 567-7853; e-mail: visions@pa.net; web address: www.visions-adventure.org

Youth Service America, SERVEnet. An alliance of organizations committed to community and national service. "Our mission is to build healthy towns and cities, and foster citizenship, knowledge, and personal development through a powerful network of service opportunities for young Americans." To make it easier for people to volunteer, Youth Service America has developed **SERVEnet**, an on-line matching service for volunteers and nonprofits (www.servenet.org). Contact: Youth Service America, 1101 15th Street NW, Suite 200, Washington, DC 20005. Phone: (202) 296-2992; fax: (202) 296-4030; e-mail: info@ysa.org; web address: www.servenet.org

Websites:

Anti-Defamation League—www.adl.org—Provides resources for parents, classrooms and communities. Offers a free catalog of materials that teach communication and respect among diverse groups; assists in promoting diversity and strengthening tolerance in our society.
The American Red Cross—www.redcross.org
World Wildlife Fund—www.wwf.org—Provides opportunities to help endangered species and the environment.

If you want to donate supplies and other resources to people in need throughout the world, they will direct you to places where help is needed most through the International Red Cross.

RESOURCES FOR PARENTS

Arnow, Jan. *Teaching Peace*. New York: Perigee, 1995. Teaches parents and teachers how to raise children to live in harmony, free of violence or prejudice.

Ben Jelloun, Tahar. *Racism Explained to My Daughter*. New York: The New Press, 1999. In this book which won the United Nations Global Tolerance Award, the author shares insights about racism with his 10-year-old daughter.

Dalton, Harlon. *Racial Healing: Confronting the Fear Between Blacks and Whites*. New York: 1995. Insights on racial divisions written by a Yale Law School professor; a pleasure to read.

Ellis, Susan, et. al. *Children As Volunteers*. Energize, 1991. Tells how children under the age of 14 can be included in volunteer programs.

Jacobs, Bruce. *Race Manners: Navigating the Minefield Between Black and White Americans*. New York: 1999. Deals with the countless ways we confront the racism that occurs between blacks and whites on public transportation, on the street, at work.

Lewis, Barbara A., *The Kids Guide to Social Action*. Minneapolis, MN: Free Spirit, 1991. Activities you can guide your children to do to help their communities.

Miles, Betty. *Save the Earth*. New York: Knopf, 1991. Environmental activities you can do with your children.

Teaching Tolerance. *Starting Small*. Montgomery, AL: The Southern Poverty Law Center, 1997. Written by the people who put together *Teaching Tolerance Magazine*, this book tells teachers and parents how to teach tolerance to young children.

Wallace, Aubrey. *Green Means: Living Gently on the Planet*, Bay Books, 1994. "Eco-heroes" are the focus of this nonfiction book which highlights people who have worked hard to help the environment against big odds. "Ordinary people with extraordinary commitment can make sweeping change for the long-term benefit of the earth and its residents."

RESOURCES FOR CHILDREN

Adoff, Arnold. *Black is Brown is Tan*. Montclair, NJ: Great Owl Books, 1991. This sensitive book is the story of an interracial family. (Grades K–2)

Anno, Mitsumasa et. al. *All in a Day*. New York: Philomel Books, 1986. Ten internationally known artists depict a day in the lives of children in countries around the world. Our common humanity is revealed through words and pictures. (Grades 3–6)

Birdseye, Debbie Holsclaw and Birdseye, Tom. *Under Our Skin*. New York: Holiday House, 1997. Six children of different racial backgrounds talk about the issue of race and their own experiences with prejudice. (Grades 3–6)

Blume, Judy. *Iggie's House*. New York: Bradbury Press, 1970. A young girl learns about prejudice and tolerance when a black family moves into her all-white neighborhood. (Grades 4–6)

Bruchac, Joseph. *Eagle Song*. New York: Puffin, 1999. Fourth-grader Danny Bigtree moves from a Mohawk reservation to Brooklyn and must find ways to deal with stereotypes about his Native-American heritage. (Grades 3–6)

Bunting, Eve. *A Day's Work*. Boston: Houghton Mifflin, 1994. A Mexican-American boy learns important lessons from his Spanish-speaking grandfather. (Grades 3–6)

Carlstrom, Nancy White. *Light: Stories of A Small Kindness*. New York: Little, Brown, 1990. Stories about children from different parts of the world who overcome obstacles. (Grades 3–6)

Cohen, B. *Molly's Pilgrim*. Lothrop, Lee & Shepard, 1978. Beautiful, moving story of a Jewish immigrant child and her desire for acceptance amid anti-Semitism. Molly triumphs. (Grades 1–4)

Coles, Robert. *The Story of Ruby Bridges*. New York: Scholastic, Inc., 1995. The true story of the little girl who was the first black student in her segregated school. (Grades K–3)

Dodds, Bill. *My Sister Annie*. Honesdale, PA: Boyds Mill Press, 1997. Charlie has a sister with Down's syndrome. He must deal with teasing and various emotions. (Grades 2–4)

Estes, Eleanor. *The Hundred Dresses*. San Diego: Harcourt Brace, 1972. Shy Wanda comes from Poland. The children who tease her eventually come to understand the effects of what they have done. (Grades 3–6)

Frank, Anne. *Anne Frank: The Diary of A Young Girl*. New York: Pocket Books, 1958. In Anne Frank's actual diary, she tells her story of attempting to survive the Nazis for two years. It is a story of tolerance as well as anti-Semitism. (Grades 4–6)

Hahn, Mary Downing. *December Stillness*. New York: Harper, 1991. A 13-year-old girl befriends a homeless Vietnam veteran and learns a lot about the meaning of compassion. (Grades 4–6)

Hamanaka, Sheila. *All the Colors of the Earth*. Fairfield, NJ: Morrow Junior Books, 1994. Through beautiful oil paintings and lyrical words, children see that people of different colors are as beautiful and unique as the elements of nature. (Grades K–2)

Hoberman, Mary Ann. *Fathers, Mothers, Sisters, Brothers: A Collection of Family Poems*. New York: Little, Brown, 1993. Poems about all different kinds of families. Includes multicultural illustrations. (Grades K–2)

Houston, Jeanne W. and Houston, James D. *Farewell to Manzanar*. New York: Bantam, 1983. A young girl's memoir of growing up in a Japanese internment camp during World War II. (Grades 4–6)

Kidd, Diana. *Onion Tears*. New York: William Morrow, 1993. A young girl from Vietnam grieves over the loss of her family, deals with teasing, and must make new friends in America. (Grades 2–4)

Knight, Margy Burns. *Welcoming Babies*. Gardiner, ME: Tilbury House, 1998. Shows how families around the world celebrate the birth of their babies. (Grades K–2)

Lewis, Barbara A. *What Do You Stand For?* Free Spirit Press, 1997. Real children challenge the reader to build traits such as empathy, citizenship, leadership and respect. Focuses on volunteering. (Grades 3–6)

————. *The Kid's Guide to Service Projects*. Free Spirit Publishing, 1995. Helps older children develop service actvities and carry them out. (Grades 5–6)

Lowry, Lois. *Number the Stars*. New York: Houghton Mifflin, 1989. The must-read story of a Jewish family's survival during the Holocaust as they are protected by their Danish neighbors. (Grades 3–6)

McKissack, Patricia. *Martin Luther King, Jr. A Man to Remember*. Chicago: Children's Press, 1984. King's story of leading the fight against racism and his efforts to bring tolerance, dignity, and understanding to this fight. (Grades 4–6)

Merrill, Jean. *The Girl Who Loved Caterpillars*. New York: Putnam & Grossett, 1992. Izumi is a free-spirited girl who discovers she does not need to be confined by her role as a female. (Grades K–3)

Morris, Ann. *Bread, Bread, Bread*. Fairfield, NJ: Mulberry Books, 1993. This is one book in a series by this author, each showing how people around the world meet their basic needs for food, clothing, shelter, and love. Other books in this series include *Shoes, Shoes, Shoes; Houses and Homes;* and *Loving*. (Grades K–3)

Nikola-Lisa, W. *Bein' With You this Way*. Emeryville, CA: Lee and Low Books, 1995. Children of many different backgrounds share fun and friendship in Central Park, buoyed by all the things that make them the same. (Grades K–3)

Osborn, Kevin. *Tolerance*. New York: Rosen Publishing Group, 1990. This book of nonfiction helps children understand the meaning of tolerance and shows them how to be tolerant of people in a world filled with too much intolerance. (Grades 3–6)

Polacco, Patricia. *Chicken Sunday*. New York: Philomel, 1992. The story of a group of children of different races who are friends and the wonderful woman who influences their lives. (Grades K–3)

————. *Pink and Say*. New York: Philomel, 1994. Incredibly moving story of two young boys, one black and one white, who fought in the Civil War. Shows the outcome of intolerance and the power of love. (Grades 2–6)

Schmidt, Jeremy. *Two Lands, One Heart*. New York: Walker and Co., 1995. The true story of TJ, a boy who journeyed from Colorado to Vietnam to see where his family was born. (Grades 2–5)

Seuss, Dr. *The Sneetches and Other Stories*. New York: Random House, 1961. The issues of tolerance and discrimination are adressed through humorous illustrations. (Grades K–4))

Simon, Norma. *Why Am I Different?* Chicago: Albert Whitman & Company, 1976. Children who see themselves as being different in a variety of ways, yet realize that being different is fine. (Grades K–3)

Tate, Eleanora E. *Thank You, Dr. Martin Luther King, Jr.!* New York: Bantam Doubleday Dell, 1999. Mary Eloise is African American. Her attitude about her heritage improves when two wonderful storytellers come to her school. (Grades 3–6)

Uchida, Yoshiko. *A Jar of Dreams.* New York: Simon & Schuster, 1985. Eleven-year-old Rinko wants to be like everyone else, but is ridiculed because she is Japanese. She eventually learns the value of her own strength and uniqueness. (Grades 3–6)

Vigna, Judith. *Black Like Kyra, White Like Me.* Albert Whitman, 1996. A story of friendship between two young girls and the prejudice of the adults in their lives. (Grades K–4)

Wood, Douglas. *Old Turtle.* Pfeifer-Hamilton Publishers, 1991. Book of the Year award winner uses the voices of animals to look at our place in the world and the responsibility we have for taking care of it. (Grades K–2)

Yashima, Taro. *Crow Boy.* New York: Viking Press, 1976. The issue of accepting differences is addressed as a little boy goes to school for 6 years in a village in Japan. (Grades K–3)

CHAPTER 12

Peaceful Parenting: A Step-by-Step Plan

We are your future, America. So pay attention to our needs. We need an example to follow.
—Jennifer Clark, fourth grader

Congratulations! You have come to the end of one journey and the beginning of the next. The road you traveled as a parent before reading this book has come to an exciting intersection, one where the path of peaceful parenting rises before you. This path isn't linear; it curves and winds along the terrains of time, marked by bumps and detours, magnificent in its imperfection. The quality of your journey will be defined by the decisions you make and the actions you take moment to moment, day by day.

Pause to reflect upon all the new possibilities available to you now. Having read this book, you now know how to lower the volume on stress, use positive discipline techniques, manage anger, resolve conflicts, communicate more effectively, and, most importantly, you've learned how to teach all this to your children. If you're like so many parents, you're probably wondering how you can make all this knowledge usable and not forget about it when you finish this last chapter and close the book.

For this reason I've put together an easy-to-use 14-day action plan that will help you practice what you've learned. Each step has been carefully designed to help you and your children keep peacemaking alive in your home and in your daily lives.

Here's how the system works: For each day, you will find a page for you and a page for your children devoted to one or more of the Seventeen Keys to Peaceful Parenting. Each page contains affirmations and action steps related to the key or keys at the top.

Start by copying all of the pages of the action plan for both you and your children. Have a family meeting and talk about the action plan. Set goals together about how you plan to use each daily page.

You might want to start by planning to meet again at the end of the first week to discuss how you did with the action steps for that week. Children 5 and up should be able to do the daily pages, although the youngest in this group may need some simplification.

Plan some kind of reward or celebration, too. For example, you and your children might set a goal of doing three of the recommended action steps each day for the keys you are following. If you all reach your goal (or come pretty close), then plan something special—ice cream sundaes, a dinner out, a favorite video that the family can watch together, or any other special event you can think of.

Avoid promising material rewards like new toys if your child reaches his goal. When we use material rewards, we run the risk of having our children work toward earning a "thing" rather than working toward achieving the goal. The underlying purpose in rewarding positive behaviors or the achievement of goals is to build self-motivation. Remember, intrinsic self-discipline and altruism are the ultimate aims.

The night before you begin, go over the key you will be posting the next day. Then hang your key and your child's key in a place where you will each see it as soon as you get up. Have your keys be the first thing you focus your attention on in the morning. Say the affirmation as soon as you get up, then read the prescribed action steps.

At the end of the day, read the affirmations one more time and review the page. Acknowledge yourself for the action steps you took, then take that page down and post the page for Key #2. Have your child follow the same procedure. Encourage him to talk about how he did with his action steps. Compliment your child for whatever he accomplished.

By the end of day 14, both you and your children will have covered every key in this book. Talk about what you learned and acknowledge each other for any changes you've made, even the smallest ones. Then be sure to celebrate your accomplishments in some special way.

On day 15, go back to Key #1 and begin again. By continuously following this routine, over time your lives will begin to change. The texture of your relationships will improve, and you will probably have more to celebrate each time you complete the cycle.

If you need to take a break every so often, do so, but keep up with your family meetings and be sure to follow the precepts of peaceful parenting. A break from the keys doesn't mean a break from peaceful parenting. If you take a break from the keys, *be careful not to allow yourself or your child to lapse into old negative patterns.*

Research shows it takes 30 days of repeating a new action to turn it into a habit. For example, if you exercise for 30 days in a row, you will develop the habit of exercising; if you give up coffee for 30 days, you will develop the habit of not drinking it.

The same holds true for strategies in this book. By practicing them for the first 30 days, you will begin developing the habit of peaceful parenting. And by continuously rotating through the prescribed cycle, you will likely internalize peaceful parenting as long-term habit.

Will all your problems disappear then? Will your children never act up again? Let me say this unequivocally: nothing is a panacea. As long as we are human, we will have our ups and downs, and so will our children. How boring life would be if every moment were even and predictable. That's not going to happen. But if a negative situation should arise, you now possess the tools to cope with it. Hopefully you'll have fewer challenges and more joys.

So sit back and read through the following pages. Photocopy each one (you might even laminate them, if you can). Then, on Day One and every day thereafter, you can begin living the keys for peaceful parents and peaceful kids. Enjoy the journey!

Note to parents: Before beginning the 14 day plan, copy the following note and give it to your child. It explains what the Keys to Becoming a Peaceful Kid are all about. Make sure your child understands all of the terminology ahead of time. Carefully go over each page before beginning. Let your children know that affirmations, like positive goal statements, help us manifest what we want to achieve. By saying them in the present tense, we program our minds to act on the words we are affirming.

Dear Boys and Girls,

Do you know you have the ability to help make your family a more peaceful one? That's right. You can actually help your family become more peaceful by the things you do. You can also help yourself become a more peaceful person, now and *for the rest of your life!*

How do I know this? Because I did it with my own children and with many children I've worked with over the years and I do it myself. That's why I know *you* can become a peaceful kid, too.

Did you know that peaceful kids have more friends, do better in school, and feel happier inside? Peaceful kids reap many benefits, and I want *you* to experience all the good things other peaceful kids experience.

I'll bet you're wondering what you need to do to become a more peaceful kid. Well, your mom and dad will be giving you 14 small posters to hang in your room, one for each day of the week over a two-week period of time. These posters contain the Keys to Becoming a Peaceful Kid. Read them over with your parents and ask them to answer any questions you have. Then start with Key #1. Say the affirmations and go over the action steps you'll be doing that day. Every day after that, follow this procedure with each new key. When you finish all 14, start again. By doing this, you will unleash the power you have inside of yourself to become a more peaceful person.

Here's the best part: Your parents have their own set of keys. They're learning how to become more peaceful, too. By working together, your whole family will get along better, resolve conflicts that come up in a more peaceful manner, and have a deeper sense of happiness and connection.

I'd love to hear from you after you've used the Keys to Becoming a Peaceful Kid for a while. Write me a letter in care of my publisher and let me know how you're doing. I look forward to hearing from you. Good luck!

In peace,

Naomi Drew, Author

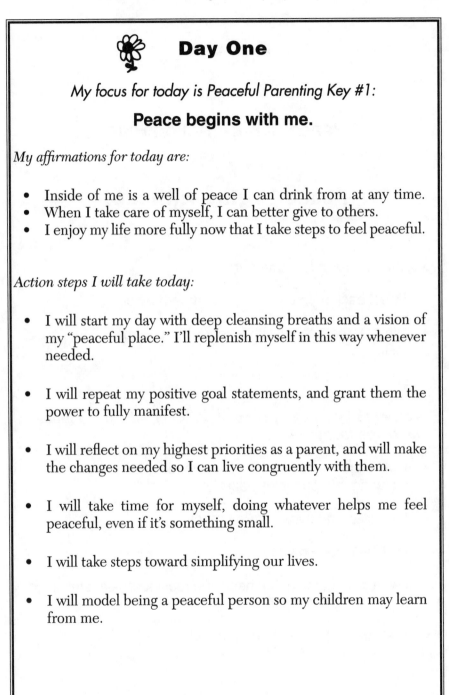

Day One

My focus for today is Peaceful Parenting Key #1:

Peace begins with me.

My affirmations for today are:

- Inside of me is a well of peace I can drink from at any time.
- When I take care of myself, I can better give to others.
- I enjoy my life more fully now that I take steps to feel peaceful.

Action steps I will take today:

- I will start my day with deep cleansing breaths and a vision of my "peaceful place." I'll replenish myself in this way whenever needed.

- I will repeat my positive goal statements, and grant them the power to fully manifest.

- I will reflect on my highest priorities as a parent, and will make the changes needed so I can live congruently with them.

- I will take time for myself, doing whatever helps me feel peaceful, even if it's something small.

- I will take steps toward simplifying our lives.

- I will model being a peaceful person so my children may learn from me.

Note: This coordinates with Chapter 1.

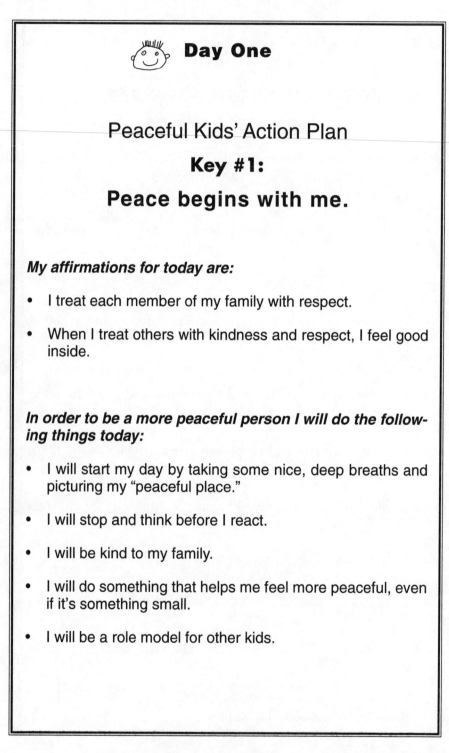

Day One

Peaceful Kids' Action Plan
Key #1:
Peace begins with me.

My affirmations for today are:

- I treat each member of my family with respect.

- When I treat others with kindness and respect, I feel good inside.

In order to be a more peaceful person I will do the following things today:

- I will start my day by taking some nice, deep breaths and picturing my "peaceful place."

- I will stop and think before I react.

- I will be kind to my family.

- I will do something that helps me feel more peaceful, even if it's something small.

- I will be a role model for other kids.

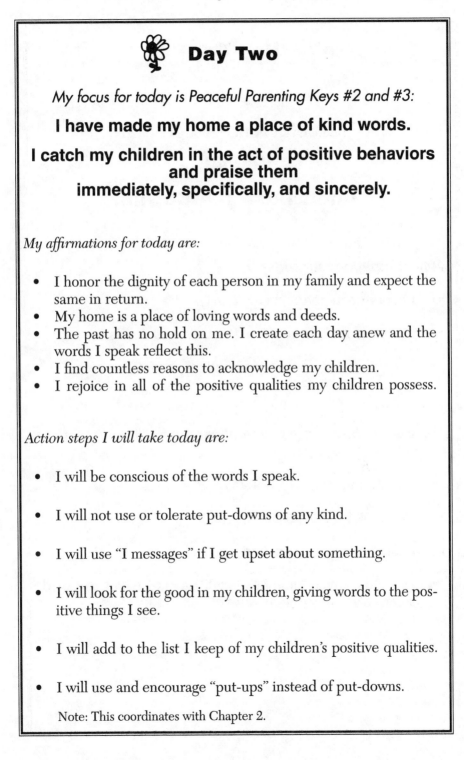

🌸 Day Two

My focus for today is Peaceful Parenting Keys #2 and #3:

I have made my home a place of kind words.

I catch my children in the act of positive behaviors and praise them immediately, specifically, and sincerely.

My affirmations for today are:

- I honor the dignity of each person in my family and expect the same in return.
- My home is a place of loving words and deeds.
- The past has no hold on me. I create each day anew and the words I speak reflect this.
- I find countless reasons to acknowledge my children.
- I rejoice in all of the positive qualities my children possess.

Action steps I will take today are:

- I will be conscious of the words I speak.

- I will not use or tolerate put-downs of any kind.

- I will use "I messages" if I get upset about something.

- I will look for the good in my children, giving words to the positive things I see.

- I will add to the list I keep of my children's positive qualities.

- I will use and encourage "put-ups" instead of put-downs.

  Note: This coordinates with Chapter 2.

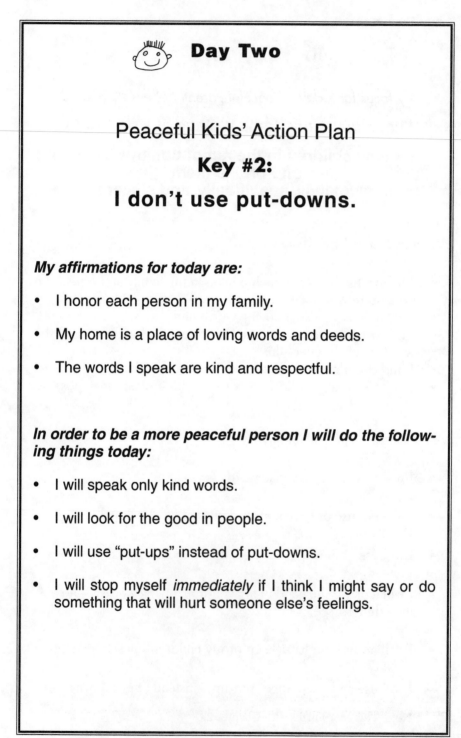

Day Two

Peaceful Kids' Action Plan
Key #2:
I don't use put-downs.

My affirmations for today are:

- I honor each person in my family.

- My home is a place of loving words and deeds.

- The words I speak are kind and respectful.

In order to be a more peaceful person I will do the following things today:

- I will speak only kind words.

- I will look for the good in people.

- I will use "put-ups" instead of put-downs.

- I will stop myself *immediately* if I think I might say or do something that will hurt someone else's feelings.

Day Three

My focus for today is Peaceful Parenting Key #4:

I spend at least 15 to 20 minutes a day with each child, listening, interacting, and giving my full attention.

My affirmations for today are:

- The time I spend with my children is a highlight of my day.
- I am nourished by the time we spend together.
- My children thrive on the time I give them.
- No matter how busy I get, I can find 15 to 20 focused minutes to spend with each child.

Action steps I will take today are:

- I will make sure my partner and I spend 15 to 20 relaxed, attentive minutes with each child.

- I will creatively examine my life and eliminate activities of less importance so I can consistently have 15 to 20 minutes a day for each child.

- I won't let unnecessary priorities take precedence.

- I will hug each of my children warmly and tell them how much I love them, no matter how busy I am.

- I will guard the 15 to 20 minutes I earmark for my child like the precious commodity it is, knowing I will never again have this day.

Note: This coordinates with Chapter 2.

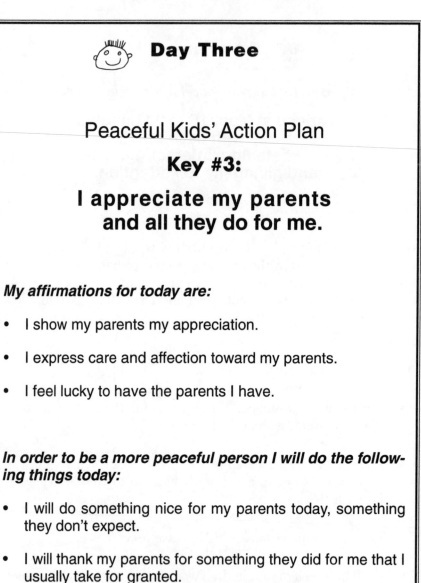

Day Three

Peaceful Kids' Action Plan

Key #3:

I appreciate my parents and all they do for me.

My affirmations for today are:

- I show my parents my appreciation.

- I express care and affection toward my parents.

- I feel lucky to have the parents I have.

In order to be a more peaceful person I will do the following things today:

- I will do something nice for my parents today, something they don't expect.

- I will thank my parents for something they did for me that I usually take for granted.

- I will tell my parents how much I love them.

- I will give my parents a big hug and kiss.

- I will ask my parents about their day.

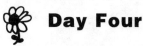 **Day Four**

My focus for today is Peaceful Parenting Key #5:

**I am clear on the standards of behavior
I expect of my children.
I honor those standards
and expect my children to do the same.**

My affirmations for today are:

- My standards reflect my highest values.
- I trust my own wisdom and good judgment.
- I am guided by what's highest within me.
- I believe in my children's ability to honor the standards I have set.
- My standards help my children become more peaceful, responsible, successful people.

Action steps I will take today are:

- I will make sure my children know what my standards are and why they are important to me.

- I will clearly define what behaviors are acceptable and unacceptable.

- I will honor my own standards.

- I will continuously expect my children to honor the standards that have been set.

- I won't forget about my standards even if I'm having a bad day.

- I'll be firm, fair, and compassionate in giving consequences if my children ignore my standards.

Note: This coordinates with Chapter 3.

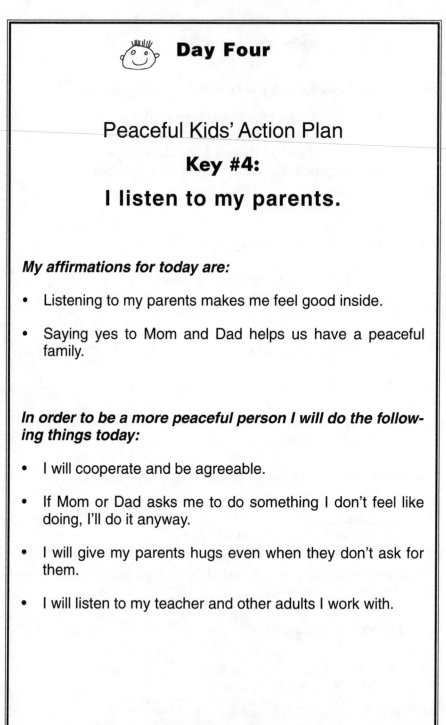

Day Four

Peaceful Kids' Action Plan

Key #4:

I listen to my parents.

My affirmations for today are:

- Listening to my parents makes me feel good inside.

- Saying yes to Mom and Dad helps us have a peaceful family.

In order to be a more peaceful person I will do the following things today:

- I will cooperate and be agreeable.

- If Mom or Dad asks me to do something I don't feel like doing, I'll do it anyway.

- I will give my parents hugs even when they don't ask for them.

- I will listen to my teacher and other adults I work with.

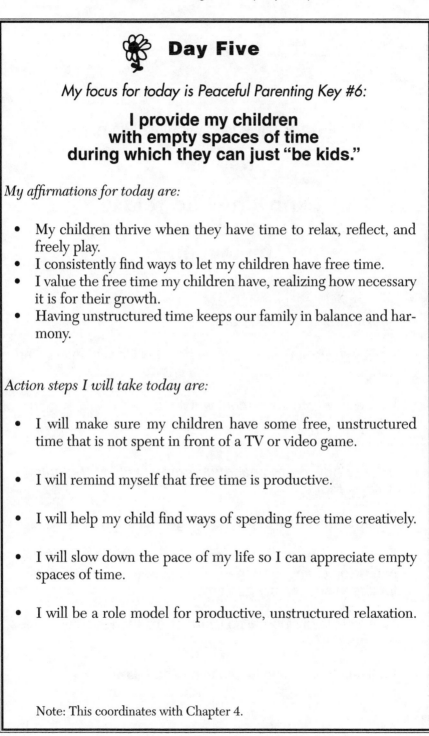

🌼 Day Five

My focus for today is Peaceful Parenting Key #6:

I provide my children with empty spaces of time during which they can just "be kids."

My affirmations for today are:

- My children thrive when they have time to relax, reflect, and freely play.
- I consistently find ways to let my children have free time.
- I value the free time my children have, realizing how necessary it is for their growth.
- Having unstructured time keeps our family in balance and harmony.

Action steps I will take today are:

- I will make sure my children have some free, unstructured time that is not spent in front of a TV or video game.

- I will remind myself that free time is productive.

- I will help my child find ways of spending free time creatively.

- I will slow down the pace of my life so I can appreciate empty spaces of time.

- I will be a role model for productive, unstructured relaxation.

Note: This coordinates with Chapter 4.

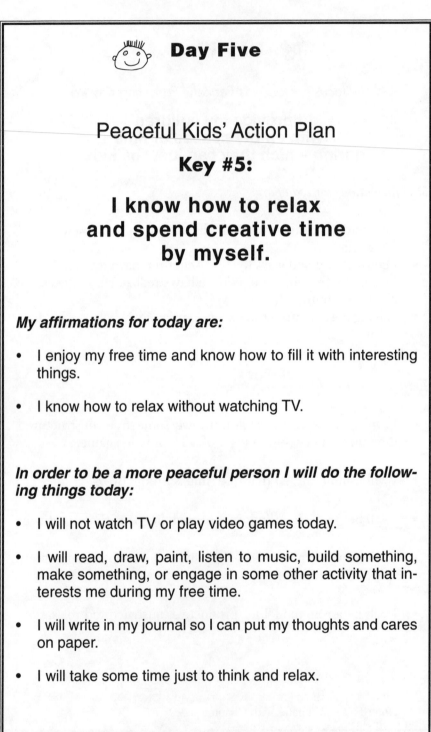

Day Five

Peaceful Kids' Action Plan

Key #5:

I know how to relax and spend creative time by myself.

My affirmations for today are:

- I enjoy my free time and know how to fill it with interesting things.

- I know how to relax without watching TV.

In order to be a more peaceful person I will do the following things today:

- I will not watch TV or play video games today.

- I will read, draw, paint, listen to music, build something, make something, or engage in some other activity that interests me during my free time.

- I will write in my journal so I can put my thoughts and cares on paper.

- I will take some time just to think and relax.

 **Day Six**

My focus for today is Peaceful Parenting Keys #7 and #8:

I hold regularly scheduled family meetings where my children have a voice in the workings of our family.

I have set a foundation for peacefulness in our home by creating with my children "Guidelines for a Peaceful Family."

My affirmations for today are:

- Our family is harmonious, peaceful, and cooperative.
- Working together is joyful and creative.
- Our shared decisions enrich our family.
- My children make a valuable contribution to the workings of our family.

Action steps I will take today are:

- I will check in with the people in my family to see if we are all living by the guidelines we have set, our "Guidelines for a Peaceful Family."

- I will try to schedule a family meeting for tonight, even if it's a short one.

- I will share my commitment to peacemaking and ask every member of my family to participate in our regularly scheduled family meetings.

- I will mark on my calendar the dates of family meetings for the next 2 months.

- I will think of ways to make our family meetings something we all look forward to, times of sharing and love.

Note: This coordinates with Chapter 4.

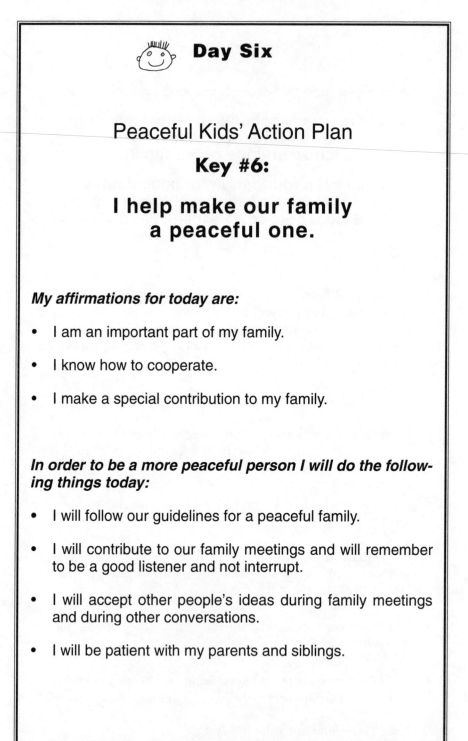

Day Six

Peaceful Kids' Action Plan

Key #6:

I help make our family a peaceful one.

My affirmations for today are:

- I am an important part of my family.

- I know how to cooperate.

- I make a special contribution to my family.

In order to be a more peaceful person I will do the following things today:

- I will follow our guidelines for a peaceful family.

- I will contribute to our family meetings and will remember to be a good listener and not interrupt.

- I will accept other people's ideas during family meetings and during other conversations.

- I will be patient with my parents and siblings.

Day Seven

My focus for today is Peaceful Parenting Keys #9 and #10:

**I always remember
that I am the parent
and I deserve to be listened to.**

**I have fair, reasonable consequences
for negative behaviors
which I only use when necessary.**

My affirmations for today are:

- I discipline my children with dignity and respect.
- My children are respectful toward me; I model respect and expect it under all circumstances.
- I trust my own judgment, knowing when I need to set limits and when it's best to compromise.
- I am fair, loving, and compassionate.

Action steps I will take today are:

- I will calmly, firmly, and respectfully set limits for my children when I need to.

- I will keep my cool in the face of resistance and will not lose my patience.

- I will follow through on what I say I'm going to do.

- When I set limits, I will stand by what I say, knowing that my judgment as a parent is sound and valid.

- I will look for ways to compromise when I feel compromising is the best thing to do.

Note: This coordinates with Chapter 5.

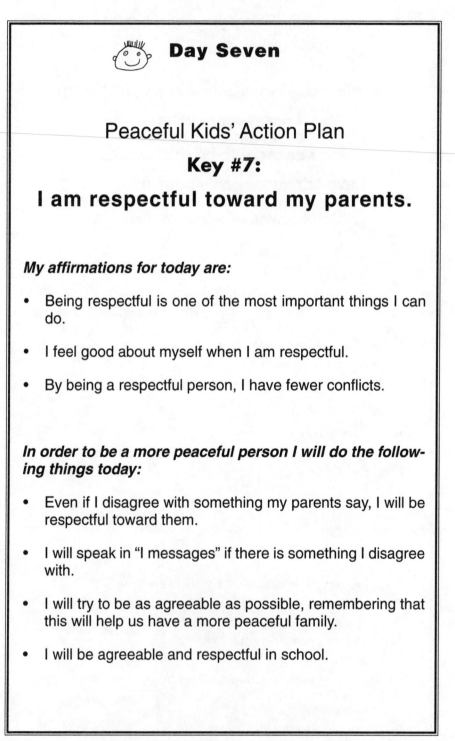

Day Seven

Peaceful Kids' Action Plan
Key #7:
I am respectful toward my parents.

My affirmations for today are:

- Being respectful is one of the most important things I can do.

- I feel good about myself when I am respectful.

- By being a respectful person, I have fewer conflicts.

In order to be a more peaceful person I will do the following things today:

- Even if I disagree with something my parents say, I will be respectful toward them.

- I will speak in "I messages" if there is something I disagree with.

- I will try to be as agreeable as possible, remembering that this will help us have a more peaceful family.

- I will be agreeable and respectful in school.

 **Day Eight**

My focus for today is Peaceful Parenting Key #11:

**I listen with all my heart
to what my children have to say,
and teach them to be good listeners
for others.**

My affirmations for today are:

- When I listen with all my heart, my children thrive.
- I grow closer to my children by listening to what they have to say.
- All my relationships flourish as the result of my good listening.
- My children become better listeners when I listen attentively to them.

Action steps I will take today are:

- I will practice good listening by giving my fullest attention without interrupting.

- I will encourage good listening in my children, asking them to look at me and listen when I speak.

- I will catch my children in the act of good listening and affirm them immediately, specifically, and sincerely.

- I will be careful to avoid the seven biggest blocks to communication: criticizing, opinion-giving, preaching, fixing, comparing, denial, and taking what my child says and making it about myself.

- I will try to learn something new about my child today through the simple act of listening.

Note: This coordinates with Chapter 6.

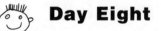 **Day Eight**

Peaceful Kids' Action Plan

Key #8:

I will work on being a good listener.

My affirmations for today are:

- I tune in when people speak to me.

- I stay focused on what the other person is saying.

- People like being around me because I am a good listener.

In order to be a more peaceful person I will do the following things today:

- I will concentrate on good listening all day long.

- I will listen without interrupting.

- When people talk to me, I will look at them and focus on what they are saying.

- I'll ask questions and take an interest when other people talk to me.

- I will listen well in school.

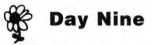 **Day Nine**

My focus for today is Peaceful Parenting Key #12:

I teach my children how to handle anger in nondestructive ways and I model this consistently.

My affirmations for today are:

- I make rational choices in the face of anger.
- I know how to cool off and calm down.
- I have the power to maintain my dignity in the face of anger.
- I safeguard the dignity of others no matter how angry I feel.
- I am a good role model for my children in handling anger.

Action steps I will take today are:

- If I get angry I will *stop*, *breathe*, and *chill* before doing anything else.

- If my child gets angry I will help her *stop*, *breathe*, and *chill* before doing anything else.

- I will review the anger management strategies from Chapter 7 and will choose one to practice today.

- I will have my children practice an anger management strategy from Chapter 7.

- I will practice forgiveness.

- I will make a promise to myself to always control my temper.

Note: This coordinates with Chapter 7.

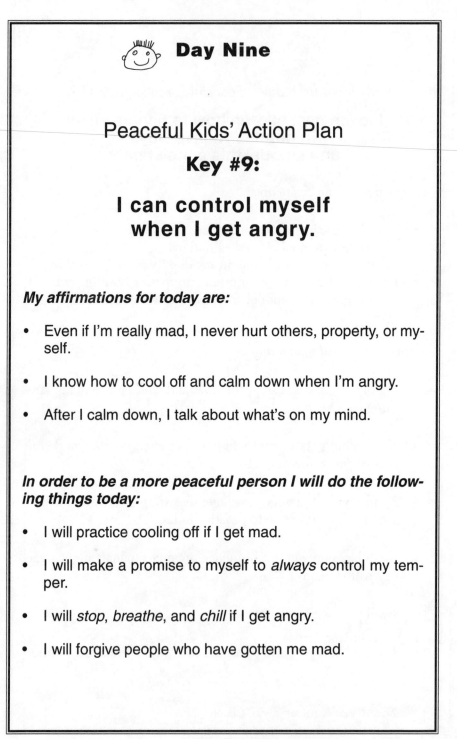

Day Nine

Peaceful Kids' Action Plan

Key #9:

I can control myself
when I get angry.

My affirmations for today are:

- Even if I'm really mad, I never hurt others, property, or myself.

- I know how to cool off and calm down when I'm angry.

- After I calm down, I talk about what's on my mind.

In order to be a more peaceful person I will do the following things today:

- I will practice cooling off if I get mad.

- I will make a promise to myself to *always* control my temper.

- I will *stop*, *breathe*, and *chill* if I get angry.

- I will forgive people who have gotten me mad.

 **Day Ten**

My focus for today is Peaceful Parenting Key #13:

I resolve conflicts peacefully and teach my children to do the same.

My affirmations for today are:

- Conflicts are an opportunity for growth; I learn from each one.
- I handle conflicts with dignity and respect.
- I am proud of the way I deal with conflict.
- I am a role model for my children in handling conflicts.

Action steps I will take today are:

- I will adopt an attitude of "willingness" to resolve conflicts.

- I will be open to compromise.

- I will let go of the "win/lose" way of thinking.

- I will review the Win/Win Guidelines and the Rules for Win/Win; I'll go over them with my children.

- I will use the Win/Win Guidelines if I have a conflict.

- I will mediate conflicts my children have by using the Win/Win Guidelines.

Note: This coordinates with Chapter 8.

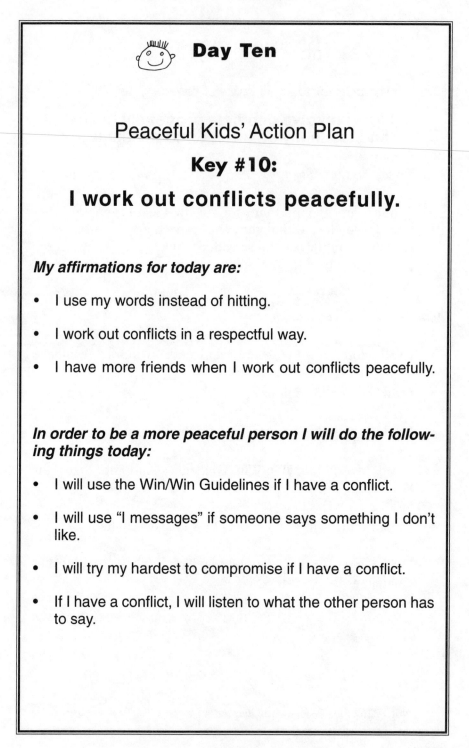

Day Ten

Peaceful Kids' Action Plan

Key #10:

I work out conflicts peacefully.

My affirmations for today are:

- I use my words instead of hitting.

- I work out conflicts in a respectful way.

- I have more friends when I work out conflicts peacefully.

In order to be a more peaceful person I will do the following things today:

- I will use the Win/Win Guidelines if I have a conflict.

- I will use "I messages" if someone says something I don't like.

- I will try my hardest to compromise if I have a conflict.

- If I have a conflict, I will listen to what the other person has to say.

 **Day Eleven**

My focus for today is Peaceful Parenting Key #14:

I find ways to help my children succeed.

My affirmations for today are:

- I can build my child's self-esteem by focusing on his strengths.
- I believe in my child's ability to do whatever he sets out to do.
- I am a role model for perseverance, creativity, and success.
- I trust the process of life and believe that good things happen for me and my family.

Action steps I will take today are:

- I will look for my child's areas of strength and will provide him with opportunities to build on them.

- I will focus on my child's successes and help her find ways to continue succeeding.

- I will praise my child's successes and display evidence of them.

- I will help my child set realistic goals and will encourage her to reach them.

- I will encourage my child to persevere in the face of difficulties, and I will model this for her.

- I will give up pessimistic thinking by following the steps outlined in Chapter 9 and will help my child do the same.

Note: This coordinates with Chapter 9.

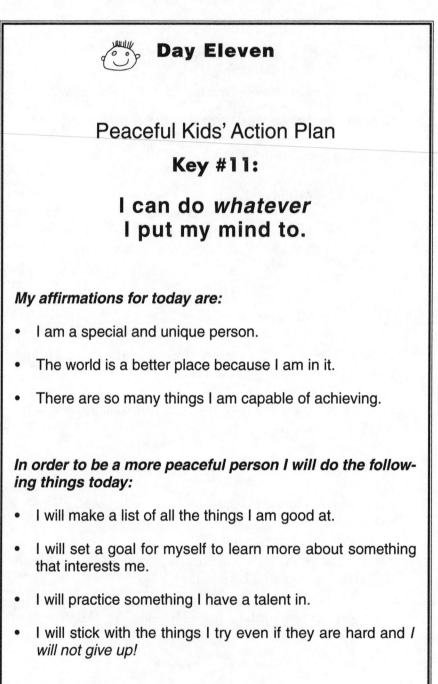

Day Eleven

Peaceful Kids' Action Plan

Key #11:

I can do *whatever* I put my mind to.

My affirmations for today are:

• I am a special and unique person.

• The world is a better place because I am in it.

• There are so many things I am capable of achieving.

In order to be a more peaceful person I will do the following things today:

• I will make a list of all the things I am good at.

• I will set a goal for myself to learn more about something that interests me.

• I will practice something I have a talent in.

• I will stick with the things I try even if they are hard and *I will not give up!*

Day Twelve

My focus for today is Peaceful Parenting Key #15:

All my actions are guided by love, compassion, fairness, respect, and integrity. I nurture these attributes in my children.

My affirmations for today are:

- I am tuned in to the feelings of others.
- I continuously model compassion, empathy, and cooperation.
- I creatively and fairly solve whatever problems I face.
- I radiate integrity and pass this on to my child.

Action steps I will take today are:

- I will tune in to the feelings of others and will encourage my children to do the same.

- I will help my child be "befriendable" by encouraging empathy, cooperation, acknowledgment, and fairness.

- I will use the problem solving strategy outlined in Chapter 9 to solve any problems I face today.

- I will help my child creatively solve problems.

- I will plan at least one cooperative activity my family can do together.

Note: This coordinates with Chapter 9.

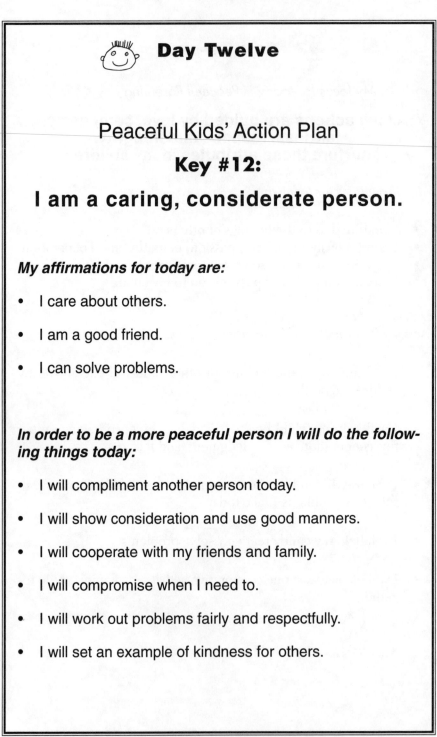

Day Twelve

Peaceful Kids' Action Plan
Key #12:
I am a caring, considerate person.

My affirmations for today are:

- I care about others.

- I am a good friend.

- I can solve problems.

In order to be a more peaceful person I will do the following things today:

- I will compliment another person today.

- I will show consideration and use good manners.

- I will cooperate with my friends and family.

- I will compromise when I need to.

- I will work out problems fairly and respectfully.

- I will set an example of kindness for others.

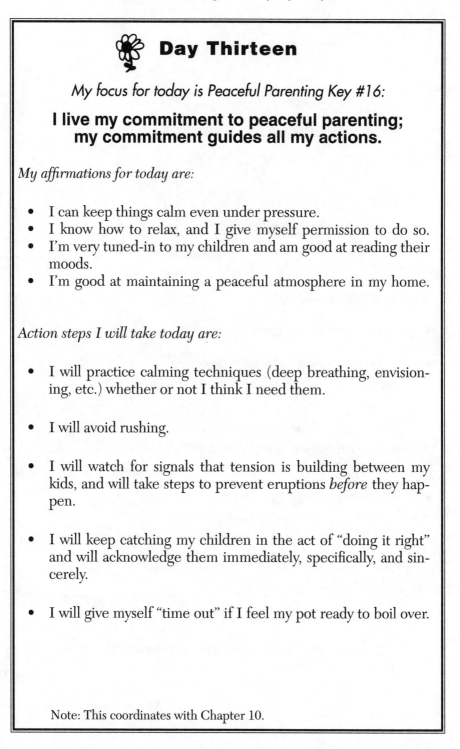

🌸 Day Thirteen

My focus for today is Peaceful Parenting Key #16:

I live my commitment to peaceful parenting; my commitment guides all my actions.

My affirmations for today are:

- I can keep things calm even under pressure.
- I know how to relax, and I give myself permission to do so.
- I'm very tuned-in to my children and am good at reading their moods.
- I'm good at maintaining a peaceful atmosphere in my home.

Action steps I will take today are:

- I will practice calming techniques (deep breathing, envisioning, etc.) whether or not I think I need them.

- I will avoid rushing.

- I will watch for signals that tension is building between my kids, and will take steps to prevent eruptions *before* they happen.

- I will keep catching my children in the act of "doing it right" and will acknowledge them immediately, specifically, and sincerely.

- I will give myself "time out" if I feel my pot ready to boil over.

Note: This coordinates with Chapter 10.

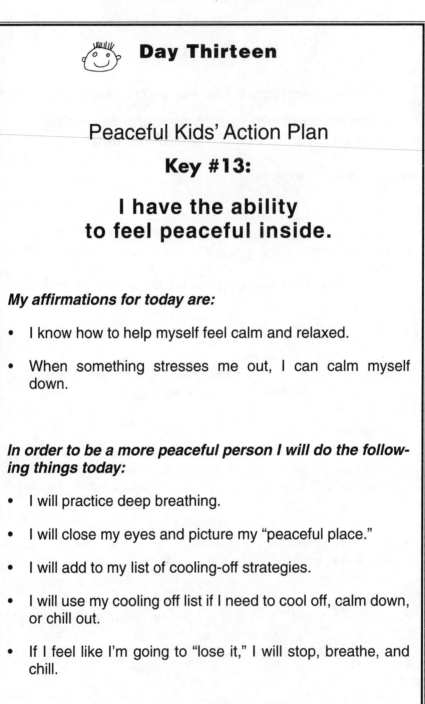

Day Thirteen

Peaceful Kids' Action Plan

Key #13:

I have the ability to feel peaceful inside.

My affirmations for today are:

- I know how to help myself feel calm and relaxed.

- When something stresses me out, I can calm myself down.

In order to be a more peaceful person I will do the following things today:

- I will practice deep breathing.

- I will close my eyes and picture my "peaceful place."

- I will add to my list of cooling-off strategies.

- I will use my cooling off list if I need to cool off, calm down, or chill out.

- If I feel like I'm going to "lose it," I will stop, breathe, and chill.

 # Day Fourteen

My focus for today is Peaceful Parenting Key #17:

I remember daily that we each have an impact on the world around us and I teach this to my children.

My affirmations for today are:

- I am a member of the human family. My actions make a difference.
- What I teach my children at home touches the larger world.
- I set an example of humaneness and care for others and our world.

Action steps I will take today are:

- I will do something kind for another person.

- I will do something kind for the environment.

- I will make a promise never to do harm to another human being or to the earth itself.

- I will plan a volunteer or charitable activity to do with my family.

- I will think of new ways for my family to be of service to others.

Note: This coordinates with Chapter 11.

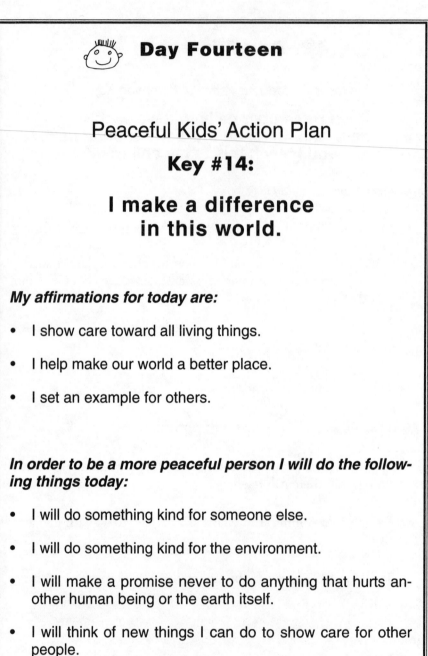

Day Fourteen

Peaceful Kids' Action Plan

Key #14:

I make a difference in this world.

My affirmations for today are:

- I show care toward all living things.

- I help make our world a better place.

- I set an example for others.

In order to be a more peaceful person I will do the following things today:

- I will do something kind for someone else.

- I will do something kind for the environment.

- I will make a promise never to do anything that hurts another human being or the earth itself.

- I will think of new things I can do to show care for other people.

- I will set an example for my friends about caring for others and our earth.

Forming a *Peaceful Parents, Peaceful Kids* Support Group

Making changes alone is difficult. Having support can make the difference between trying out some new ideas that you'll soon forget and actually transforming the way you parent. We need each other to get through the hard times, to commiserate with, to share our successes, to look for solutions, and to cheer each other on. We need someone there to hand us a tissue when the tears start to fall, to give us a hug when the day's been stressful, or to laugh with us about the funny, crazy, frustrating but gotta-love-them-anyway things our kids do.

Consider networking with other parents and asking them to join you on your journey to becoming a more peaceful parent. Walking the path with like souls will soften the hard times and make the good times better. Here are some suggestions to get you on your way:

Talk to other parents and share what you have learned in this book. Invite them to your home to talk about forming a group to help each other succeed in creating more peaceful families. Talk to parents in your neighborhood, in your child's school, at the soccer field, at PTA meetings, at the pediatrician's office, at the supermarket, at the gym, at work, at your church or synagogue, or wherever else you might meet them.

Try to keep your group small, no more than 6 or 7. If you've attracted more than that, split into two groups. Smaller groups allow for more intimacy and deeper sharing.

Plan to have the first meeting in your home, and then rotate to other members' homes. Whoever is hosting the meeting can lead the session for that evening. The leader helps get things going, keeps people on the topic, reminds members not to judge, criticize, or give unsolicited advice, and encourages everyone to share.

Meet once a week if you can. You can start each meeting by going around the circle and asking each person to share either a success or challenge. End each meeting with several spoken affirmations in unison. Use the affirmations included in this chapter.

Use this book as your guide. The easiest way to do this is to go chapter by chapter. Your first meeting can be for getting to know each other, setting goals, and going over the ground rules. After that, members of the group can read a chapter before every meeting and then talk about whatever related issues come up. You can discuss questions, problems, successes, challenges, or anything else that's relevant.

Set ground rules before you begin. This is very important. Make sure every member of the group agrees to follow these ground rules every time you are together:

1. Respect each other's confidentiality. Promise not to discuss what anyone says outside the room. This is vital to building and keeping trust.
2. Listen without judgment.
3. Don't interrupt, criticize, or give unsolicited advice. If a member wants feedback, she can ask for it. Otherwise, listen with an open mind and remember to treat others the way you want to be treated.
4. Each person gets a chance to speak. This should be a collaborative experience where every member of the group has an equal voice.
5. Be honest with one another and use "I messages" if someone says something that makes you feel uncomfortable or tries to dominate the group. Let the person know in a respectful, authentic way. Be gentle.
6. Encourage, affirm, and cheer each other on. Remember that you're travelers along the same path.
7. Make it warm and cozy—this is *very* important! Be comfortable, have fun, drink tea, eat snacks, and be sure to give lots of hugs and smiles. Most of all, enjoy yourselves and savor your camaraderie.

Concluding Thoughts

A beloved friend of mine recently passed away. Two years ago, she was diagnosed with a fatal illness. As she faced the harrowing months following her diagnosis, she made the decision to live out her days in the fullest grace and dignity possible.

Each time we spoke, my friend would say, "I've been given this path to walk, for whatever reason I'll never know, but what I do know is: this is the only path I have." And each time my friend spoke these words, she did so with incredible grace and courage. These words of acceptance guided my friend during the last year of her life, and she walked her path with stunning dignity and clarity of purpose.

You have been given a path of your own to walk—the path of peaceful parenting. The clarity and purpose you bring as you walk this path will determine the quality of your journey. You would not have been drawn to this book had this not been your path.

And as you face your own changes and challenges, I leave you with a simple prayer. It comes from "The Book of Remembrance," which is read on the high holy day of Yom Kippur:

Give me the gift of hope.
May I always believe
in the beauty of life,
the power of goodness,
the right to joy.

May you be blessed with an abundance of hope, beauty, goodness, and joy as you walk the path of peaceful parenting. Shalom.

BIBLIOGRAPHY

Brussat, Fredrick and Mary Ann. *Spiritual Literacy*. New York: Touchstone, 1996.

Chopra, Deepak. *The Seven Spiritual Laws of Success*. San Rafael, Calif.: New World Library, 1994.

Church, F. Forrester, et. al. *Resources for Study and Worship*. Boston: The Unitarian Universalist Denominational Grants Panel, 1987.

Coles, Robert. *The Call of Stories*. Boston: Houghton Mifflin, 1989.

Dossey, M.D., Larry. *Meaning & Medicine*. New York: Bantam, 1991.

Educators For Social Responsibility. *Perspectives*. Cambridge, Mass.: ESR, 1983.

Fisher, Roger and Ury, William. *Getting to Yes*. New York: Penguin, 1983.

Flannery, Jr., Raymond, B. *Preventing Youth Violence*. New York: Continuum, 1999.

Gardner, Howard. *Multiple Intelligences*. New York: Basic Books, 1993.

Johnson, D. & Johnson, R. *Teaching Students To Be Peacemakers*. Interaction Book Co., 1991.

Le Guinn, Ursula K. *Tao Te Ching*. Boston: Shambala, 1998.

Likona, Thomas. *Educating for Character*. New York: Bantam, 1991.

Patterson, Katherine. *A Sense of Wonder*. New York: Plume Books, 1989.

Peacock, Molly. *How to Read a Poem*. New York: Riverhead Books, 1999.

Prutzman, Priscilla, et. al. *The Friendly Classroom for a Small Planet*. Nyack, New York: Avery Publishing.

Roberts, Elizabeth and Amidon, Elias, ed. *Earth Prayers*. San Fancisco: Harper, 1991.

INDEX